I0142020

Trends in Classics – Supplementary Volumes

Edited by
Franco Montanari and Antonios Rengakos

Volume 146

Page and Stage

Intersections of Text and Performance
in Ancient Greek Drama

Edited by
S. Douglas Olson, Oliver Taplin and Piero Totaro

DE GRUYTER

ISBN 978-3-11-221537-1
e-ISBN (PDF) 978-3-11-124802-8
e-ISBN (EPUB) 978-3-11-124861-5
ISSN 1868-4785

Library of Congress Control Number: 2023937080

Bibliographic information published by the Deutsche Nationalbibliothek
The Deutsche Nationalbibliothek lists this publication in the Deutsche Nationalbibliografie;
detailed bibliographic data are available on the Internet at http://dnb.dnb.de.

© 2025 Walter de Gruyter GmbH, Berlin/Boston
This volume is text- and page-identical with the hardback published in 2023.
Editorial Office: Alessia Ferreccio and Katerina Zianna
Logo: Christopher Schneider, Laufen
Printing and binding: CPI books GmbH, Leck

www.degruyter.com

Acknowledgements

It is true: as Oliver recalls in his beautiful introduction to this volume, the idea was born on a cold and gloomy November evening in Basel, where we were both invited speakers at a conference on metatheatre co-organized by our dear friend Silvia Milanezi (who in turn actively participated in our project as well). In the elegant atmosphere of the "Au Violon", over a warm and tasty supper and inspired by an intensely fragrant red wine, Oliver and I made concrete our common desire to construct together a meeting (hopefully a series of meetings, to be spread over time) that, going through different case studies in concrete fieldwork experiences — *in corpore vivo* of Greek dramatic texts — would show by example the toil (sometimes frustrating) and challenge (always fascinating) of scholars (often starting from already problematic texts) in trying to understand, deduce or imagine the practice of stage performances: texts — it is always worth repeating this — conceived with the primary purpose of being represented in a theatre. "Page and Stage", precisely: the brilliant title Oliver immediately suggested, with the lightning spontaneity of a leading expert in this field of research. I discovered then, again thanks to Oliver, that the phrase had a tradition in Shakespearean studies, a fact that to my eyes and curiosity made what we were about to create even more stimulating, in the sense of not considering Greek drama a phenomenon in its own right, a closed, separate and distant monad in the ancient times in which it was produced, but an extraordinary theatrical civilization, capable of fostering other extraordinary experiences in the centuries up until our time.

My first thanks go to Oliver, as well as to Douglas, who was immediately enthusiastic about becoming involved in the project (and, among other things, through his revision of the non-native speakers' English in this volume). Both of them make me feel honoured for their friendship and for their love for the beautiful land of Apulia, in which I am happy to have been born.

Equally vigorous thanks go to another good friend of mine (and of my mentor, Peppino Mastromarco), with whom it is always a joy to share ideas and planning: Franco Montanari was with us in May 2019, when *Page&Stage* was held in Bari, in the role of Chair of the final session of the Conference as well as during the Final Remarks. Enthusiastic about the scientific level of the meeting, and generous with ideas as always, he proposed publishing the proceedings in the *Trends in Classics Supplementary Volumes* series. I owe him and Antonios Rengakos gratitude for accepting this book in their collection.

Along with Oliver and Douglas, I also thank the other friends whose contributions have given life to this volume: Eric Csapo, Giuseppe Mastromarco, Enrico

https://doi.org/10.1515/9783111248028-202

Medda, Fausto Montana, Christian Orth, Martin Revermann, Alan Sommerstein and Bernhard Zimmermann.

To my pupils, Pietro Berardi and Daniela Cagnazzo, who provided me with invaluable assistance in the material organization of the *Page&Stage* conference, as well as in the preparation of this volume, I offer a warm thank you for the patience they have shown (or have successfully feigned) in enduring on a number of occasions my nagging, anxious, boring pedantry.

To a *Page&Stage 2*, we hope! And without a painful pandemic in the meantime.

Piero Totaro

Contents

List of Figures

https://doi.org/10.1515/9783111248028-204

Oliver Taplin
Introduction to Page and Stage

It is (amazingly!) fifty years now since I was working on my doctoral thesis, which was in due course turned into *The Stagecraft of Aeschylus* (1977). I can see in retrospect how I was very fortunate in the confluence of three preoccupations that converged in my choice of topic. One: I was enthusiastic about theatre. I acted in student productions, and went to performances whenever I could, and was especially taken with those directed by Peter Brook, and — formatively — by the Greek National Theatre seasons at Epidaurus in 1962, 1964 and 1966. Secondly: I was soaked in Shakespeare, and intrigued by both scholarly and practical approaches to his dramaturgy through the significance of performance and theatricality. Third: I was a keen participant in the last six years of Eduard Fraenkel's celebrated seminars. Although they were structured around the textual criticism of disputed passages, Fraenkel also conveyed a searching awareness of larger cultural context; and he encouraged me in my interest in theatre and dramatic technique.

I was made particularly aware of the third element of this this formation — and made to feel rather like ancient history! — when I read Martin Revermann's shrewd assessment of my work within a longer perspective of classical scholarship in *Comic Business* (2006) 10–12. He locates it as having appealed to cautious scholars because it "somehow felt both traditional and innovative ... reassuringly grounded for being textual to an almost positivistic degree and seemingly less subjective than it often actually is [ouch!], yet at the same time seriously exciting...". "Performance criticism", he goes on, "opens up for further exploration fundamental issues about a host of areas: religious and socio-political frames; gender; dramatic technique; theatricality and ideology of costume, dance and music; the theatrical representation of class and ethnicity; and textual criticism...". That catalogue well incapsulates the varied subject-matters of this volume. Later (pp. 49ff.) Revermann justifiably picks some holes in my "rule of thumb" (less rigid than a "rule") that all significant action was indicated by the words of the tragedies themselves. At the same time, though, he sets out a more sophisticated version of the same methodology, and he extends it to comedy. He himself applies this approach to the area of "religious frame" in his ground-breaking chapter in this volume, "Divinity on the Classical Greek Stage: Proposing a New Model". This reaches towards large claims about the nature of the audience's religious experience through informed consideration of the gods in the performative actuality of theatre.

https://doi.org/10.1515/9783111248028-001

The anchoring of this methodology in the close reading of the dramatic texts (or, as I prefer the "playscripts") still has much to offer, and it forms the underlying foundation of this collection on "intersections of text and performance". Its enduring potential is outstandingly well exemplified by Enrico Medda's chapter "Dramatic Space and Theatrical Meaning. The Case of Sophocles' *Antigone*". He characterizes this kind of performance criticism as pursuing "the challenging objective of understanding ancient theatrical language through a laborious attempt to overcome the limitations imposed by the fact that only the verbal component of ancient performance survives...". By working in detail through the textually indicated delineations of physical space, both onstage and off-stage,[1] he persuasively reveals a key, and underappreciated, conceptual shaping of Sophocles' play around the borderline between life and death, between the world above and the world below, and dangerous contraventions of this frontier.

In his opening paragraph Medda also interestingly distinguishes this kind of approach to the "the overall interpretation of a play" from scholarship on the context of the performances and "the relationship between the organization of Dionysiac festivals and the political life of the polis". This approach, which might be termed "external" as opposed to "internal", is even now being given a completely re-evaluated and scrupulously documented basis in the three-volume undertaking, *A Social and Economic History of the Theatre to 300 BC*, by Eric Csapo and Peter Wilson.[2] In this collection Csapo gives a nice example of the social context surrounding victory celebrations after successful productions, relating these to references in some closing scenes of Aristophanes.

Four of the chapters are devoted to the "internal" playscript-based performance criticism of Aristophanic comedies. Douglas Olson rightly warns against the insinuation of anachronistic values and assumptions into such theatrical matters, taking examples of this from Dover's commentary on *Clouds*. The authors of all these chapters are all too circumspect and experienced to make such unjustified inferences, and rely on close textual attention rather than intuition or guesswork. Giuseppe Mastromarco shows how the sexualised female figures who appear in several comedies were not all represented as naked, as many (male) scholars have imagined. Piero Totaro concentrates on the (fake) Persians brought on in *Acharnians*, especially the exploitation of their various masks.

---

1 Following through approaches opened up in Di Benedetto and Medda *La tragedia sulla scena* (2002).

2 Volume II, "Theatre beyond Athens" was published in 2020. Volume I on Athens is nearing completion.

Bernhard Zimmermann demonstrates Aristophanes' exuberant deployment of props by bringing out the way that the Euripides scene in *Acharnians* "raids" and travesties the stage objects of his tragedies. Between them they throw new light on the multiple ways in which Aristophanes indicates and incorporates movements, material objects and accoutrements into his dramatic fabric. Christian Orth adds the point that even the smallest fragmentary bits and pieces can still offer clues to their theatrical as well as their verbal meaning, although even more caution is called for than with the complete plays. Old comedy was exuberant and inventive in its incorporation of portable objects (props), actions, gestures, body-language, outfits, masks … and more. There is still work to be undertaken to do justice to this wealth of performed meaning.[3]

The final two chapters rightly insist that the interactions of text and performance were and are not restricted to the original instantiation only. Alan Sommerstein shows how, while some of the *parepigraphai* preserved in texts are later inferences, some go back to Aeschylus. Fausto Montana uncovers through a meticulous study of the scholia on *Frogs* the interest of ancient commentators in theatrical performance; but also how with time this became a matter of verbal explanation rather than an evocation of experienced practicalities. In some ways much of the preceding volume has been attempting the reverse of this process.

This is an opportunity to thank the various contributors and to acknowledge the labours that have gone into compiling this volume. Pietro Berardi has given able assistance to the two hands-on editors, namely Douglas Olson, who has applied his usual chalcenteric editorial vigour, and Piero Totaro, who gathered together the occasion in Bari in May 2019, which lies behind this eventual publication. He and I hatched the idea for that conference over a pleasant supper in Basel, encouraged by Dionysus. Turning it into a reality was entirely thanks to his organisational skills and enthusiasm.

---

3 Alexa Piqueux, *The Comic Body in Ancient Greek Theatre and Art, 440-320 BCE* makes an important new contribution to this.

Enrico Medda
Dramatic Space and Theatrical Meaning: The Case of Sophocles' *Antigone*

Abstract: This paper aims to explore, by means of the significant example of Sophocles' *Antigone*, how much our perception of the construction and exploitation of dramatic space may contribute to the overall interpretation of an ancient tragedy. A detailed analysis of the indications Sophocles gives the spectator in order to orientate his perception of the off-stage space and of the space within the *skēnē* shows how the close intertwining between the construction of the characters and that of dramatic space offers a clear indication of Sophocles' primary dramatic idea for this play. The axis around which the poet has constructed the story is the subtle and dangerous boundary dividing the spheres of life and death, which informs the theatrical space and creates a perfect balance between the movement of the characters and their tragic experience. All the other themes of the play, such as conflicts between law and individual freedom, between State and family, between father and son or male and female, although they may seem the most relevant for modern interpreters, must be projected against the foil of this primary conception.

Keywords: Sophocles, Antigone, Creon, dramatic space, death and life

And the Red Death held illimitable dominion over all

The constantly growing attention to the theatrical dimension of ancient tragedy, which may be regarded as one of the most important achievements of scholarship in the field in the last fifty years, has generated a strong impulse to research in two directions. The first, mainly centered on the context of dramatic performances, has resulted in a remarkable deepening of our knowledge of the physical aspect of the Athenian theatre at different stages of its history, of the professional figure of the actor, of the recruiting and training of choruses, and of the relationship between the organization of Dionysiac festivals and the political life of the polis. The second, more focused on the plays, pursues the challenging objective of understanding ancient theatrical language through a laborious attempt to overcome the limitations imposed by the fact that only the verbal component of ancient performance survives, while the others (music, choreography, costumes, backdrops, movements of the actors) are either completely lost or very difficult to reconstruct.

https://doi.org/10.1515/9783111248028-002

What follows is an attempt to reflect on one aspect of this latter field of enquiry, exploring by means of a significant example how much our perception of so decisive a component of any theatrical creation as the construction and exploitation of dramatic space may contribute to the overall interpretation of a play. In dealing with this subject, we may benefit at least in part from the circumstance that much information about both the visible and the invisible aspects of every play was embedded by ancient authors in their texts. Matters are nonetheless not always clear, and decisive issues are sometimes obscured by thorny textual problems. Difficult though the research may be, it is nonetheless in any case worth pursuing, since only by putting the two components "Page" and "Stage" together again (as the lovely title of this conference exhorts us to do) can we hope to recover at least a portion of the powerful impact of ancient performances on their spectators.[1]

In my search for a tragedy that could offer an adequate subject for this occasion, three reasons rapidly led me to Sophocles' *Antigone*. The first is that Sophocles, as Oliver Taplin has shown in many illuminating papers, is particularly careful to construct for each play a 'scenic geography' deeply intertwined with dramatic action.[2] Second, the tension created in *Antigone* by the dramatist between the visible and the invisible parts of the dramatic space is so crucial, that the culminating point of the drama is represented by a movement of Creon, who leaves the stage at 1114 and comes back shortly thereafter (1257), completely overwhelmed by the events he has witnessed offstage. Finally, the range of interpretations proposed for this masterpiece of ancient theatre is so vast that I wonder whether scenic analysis can provide a *fil rouge*, as it were, bringing us closer to the dramatist's original idea.[3]

---

1 In this paper I build on a line of research I have been following for many years: see in particular Di Benedetto/Medda 2002 (to which readers are referred for a general treatment of the tragic conventions concerning retro-scenic and extra-scenic spaces) and the papers collected in Medda 2013. I shall not deal here with theoretical issues concerning the definition and meaning of 'space' in a theatrical rather than a literary dimension. (For a discussion of this in relation to ancient tragedy, see Rehm 2002, 1–34.)

2 See for example Taplin 1984, 13: "All of Sophocles' plays have a strong sense of locality, both of the precise setting of the play and of various important places off stage".

3 Interest in this great play goes far beyond the restricted circle of classicists and involves philosophers, lawyers, politicians and psychoanalysts looking to understand not only the ancient tragic conception of life, but also that of modern men and societies. *Antigone* has been read as a tragedy of rebellion against power and civil disobedience, or as a vindication of feminist issues; some critics have found in it the irresolvable conflict between family and State, while others have stressed the individual nature of Antigone as a member of a wretched and incestuous family, seeing her as a defender of the rights of all marginal persons characterized

The scenic cartography of *Antigone* is clearly inscribed in the text. The *skēnē* represents the royal palace of Thebes, visually symbolizing the power of the new king Creon, who exercises it in the public space before the house. One of the two *eisodoi* (which I shall by convention call *eisodos* A) leads to the rest of the city; it is from there that the chorus enters at 100,[4] as do Haimon at 631 and Teiresias at 988. The other (*eisodos* B) leads out of the walls of Thebes into the plain where the battle took place and Polynices' body lies unburied. Around the middle of the play, the spectators are informed that another relevant place, the rocky cave chosen by Creon as the prison of Antigone, is to be associated with the latter direction (as emerges clearly from the Messenger's narration at 1196ff.).[5]

From the very beginning of the drama, the space lying beyond *eisodos* B is characterized as disquieting and sinister. Antigone emphasizes at once its connection with death and, most of all, with the inappropriate and offensive refusal of burial for Polynices prescribed by Creon. The macabre image of the unburied corpse representing "a rich treasure house for birds as they look for food"[6] (ἄταφον, οἰωνοῖς γλυκὺν / θησαυρὸν εἰσορῶσι πρὸς χάριν βορᾶς, 29f.) provides the audience with a sort of bird's-eye view of this desolate extra-scenic place. It is not a matter of chance that Antigone's first scenic movement is in this direction. She comes out of the house together with Ismene in order to talk in secret,

by unique peculiarities. For a sample of approaches of the last forty years, see Winnington-Ingram 1980, 117–149; Di Benedetto 1983, 1–32; Oudemans/Lardinois 1987; Sourvinou-Inwood 1989; Cropp 1997; Griffith 1999 and 2001; Butler 2000; Montani 2001; Žižek 2001; Zagrebelsky 2002; Harris 2004; Paduano 2008; Carpanelli 2008; Burian 2010; Greco/Belardinelli 2010; Wilmer/Žukauskaite 2010; Irigaray 2010; Susanetti 2012; Carter 2012; Honig 2013; Liapis 2013; Cairns 2013 and 2016 (with a rich, up-to-date bibliography); Fisher 2014; Violante in Cartabia/Violante 2018, 93–121; Stuttard 2018, Goldhill 2022.

4 According to Griffith 1999, 139 the old men arrive "up one or both side-entrances", but it seems preferable that they come from the city as opposed to the other entrance. See Rehm 2002, 115.

5 Löwe 1987, 127 has rightly argued that Polynices and the cave are served by a single route offstage, since Creon visits both locales in succession without recrossing the stage. I take the opportunity here to rectify the view expressed in Di Benedetto/Medda 2002, 101, where we suggested that the cave and the body should be imagined as located in opposite directions. I would not go as far as Wiles 1997, 151 in associating the battlefield with the east (i.e. with the left *eisodos* of the Athenian theatre) and the city with the west (i.e. the right *eisodos*). He thinks that "the obvious staging calls for the chorus to enter from the city, west, and to address the east where the sun is supposedly rising after the pre-dawn prologue". But this is inconsistent with the fact that in real geography the river Dirce, near which the battle was fought, lies west of Thebes, not east. Both possibilities remain open.

6 All translations of Sophocles are from Lloyd-Jones 1994.

and after revealing her decision, announces her intent to exit through *eisodos* B and carry out the burial of Polynices: "I shall go to heap up a tomb for my dearest brother" (ἐγὼ δὲ δὴ τάφον / χώσουσ᾽ ἀδελφῷ φιλτάτῳ πορεύσομαι, 80f.). Her exit at 99 is then particularly meaningful, first because it enshrines her irretrievable breakup with Ismene and with what is left of their family, and second because her πορεύειν towards a place clearly associated with death expresses visually an essential feature of her temper.

Many clues in the text in fact reveal that, after the awful events that have struck the house of Laios, Antigone has developed a deeply rooted sense of estrangement from life and an extraordinary closeness to the netherworld. She affirms that it will be honourable for her to do her duty and die (κεῖνον δ᾽ ἐγὼ / θάψω· καλόν μοι τοῦτο ποιούσῃ θανεῖν, 71f.), and that she is utterly unafraid of death ("I shall suffer nothing so dire that my death will not be one of honour", πείσομαι γὰρ οὖν / τοσοῦτον οὐδὲν ὥστε μὴ οὐ καλῶς θανεῖν, 96f.). Antigone does not even take into account the possibility of saving herself, since what she really wants is to be reunited in death with her beloved Polynices ("I am his own and I shall lie with him who is my own", φίλη μετ᾽ αὐτοῦ κείσομαι, φίλου μέτα, 73). It is precisely the conviction that she has no future among the living that allows her to take on the burden of the burial, a pious action in her eyes, though criminal for others ("having committed a crime that is holy", ὅσια πανουργήσασα, 74). She feels bound to satisfy only the dead (τοῖς κάτω, 75), with whom she will spend a much longer time than with "those here" (τῶν ἐνθάδε, 75). When Ismene tries to divert her from this self-destructive plan, Antigone rules out any possibility of a change of mind, forcefully reasserting her estrangement from life: "Why, I know that I am giving pleasure to those I must please most!" (ἀλλ᾽ οἶδ᾽ ἀρέσκουσ᾽ οἷς μάλισθ᾽ ἀδεῖν με χρή, 89).

This unwavering determination to die is not free of disturbing implications, well perceived by Ismene, who attempts to dissuade her sister with an appeal to reason (φρόνησον εὖ, 49). Challenged by Antigone, who invites her to reveal to the world her plan of burying Polynices, Ismene significantly answers: "Your heart is fiery in a matter that is chilling" (θερμὴν ἐπὶ ψυχροῖσι καρδίαν ἔχεις, 88). Her words express the attitude of a normal human being, conscious of the need to outlive the violent death of the brothers and move on in spite of all adversity. Ismene cannot understand the behaviour of Antigone, whose flaming heart spends itself for those who lie in the netherworld.

We must therefore take into account the fact that Antigone *wishes* to die and feels that she already belongs to Hades. In the second episode, when Ismene, summoned by Creon, desperately tries to denounce herself ("I did the deed, if she agrees, and I take and bear my share of the blame", δέδρακα τοὔργον, εἴπερ ἥδ' ὁμορροθεῖ, / καὶ ξυμμετίσχω καὶ φέρω τῆς αἰτίας, 536f.), Antigone rejects her belated solidarity by referring to the testimony of the dead: "Hades and those below know to whom the deed belongs" (ὧν τοὔργον, Ἅιδης χοἰ κάτω ξυνίστορες, 542). Ismene insists ("Sister, do not dishonour me as not to let me die with you and grant the dead man the proper rites!", μήτοι, κασιγνήτη, μ' ἀτιμάσῃς τὸ μὴ οὐ / θανεῖν τε σὺν σοὶ τὸν θανόντα θ' ἁγνίσαι, 544f.), but in Antigone's eyes their different choices make them belong to incompatible dimensions, excluding any possibility of dying together: "Yes, you chose life, and I chose death" (σὺ μὲν γὰρ εἵλου ζῆν, ἐγὼ δὲ κατθανεῖν, 555). The offence (ἡ 'ξαμαρτία) cannot be "equal for us both" (ἴση νῷν), as Ismene says at 558; Antigone exhorts her to feel no responsibility, since she is alive, not dead: "Be comforted! You are alive, but my life has long been dead, so as to help the dead" (θάρσει· σὺ μὲν ζῇς, ἡ δ' ἐμὴ ψυχὴ πάλαι / τέθνηκεν, ὥστε τοῖς θανοῦσιν ὠφελεῖν, 559f.).[7] This desperate sense of belonging to Hades arises primarily from the fact that Antigone is a member of the wicked house of the Labdakids; her incestuous origin entails a powerful, albeit perverted bond with her dead relatives. This makes her choice so absolutely individual that it could not be transferred to any other living person (with the exception of Ismene, who is however excluded by her feminine weakness).[8] The members of the chorus are aware of her uniqueness, which results in an autonomous will to die, when they say: "Of your own will you alone of mortals, while yet alive, descend to Hades" (ἀλλ' αὐτόνομος ζῶσα μόνη δὴ / θνητῶν Ἅιδην καταβήσῃ, 821f.) and "You were destroyed by your self-willed passion" (σὲ δ' αὐτόγνωτος ὤλεσ' ὀργά, 875). For them, Antigone's origin is the ultimate cause of her transgression of justice: "You are paying for some crime of your fathers" (πατρῷον δ' ἐκτίνεις τιν' ἆθλον, 856).[9]

---

7 Battezzato 2019, 106 rightly argues that in interpreting Antigone's character we should resist the tendency to neglect this decisive aspect: "Antigone vuole morire. Rimpiange questa sorte, rimpiange la sua vita esclusa dalla comunità, dalle nozze, addirittura dai riti della sepoltura. Ma, dice lei stessa ad Ismene, è votata alla morte … La legge (*nomos*) che spinge Antigone a morire è fatta da lei. È la legge che lei si è scelta, come lei rivendica nei suoi due celebri discorsi. È la decisione che lei prende da sola, αὐτόγνωτος ὀργά. Antigone però ha buone ragioni, e le spiega. Siamo noi interpreti a non ascoltarle, perché non le vogliamo sentire. Preferiamo una Antigone martire, un'Antigone segno della disobbedienza civile, un'Antigone simbolo dell' opposizione al potere patriarcale o all'ingiustizia". On the morbid features of Antigone's character, see also Carter 2012, 125–127.
8 The absolute individuality of Antigone's choice is stressed in particular by Butler 2003. For the permanence in Antigone of the characteristics of the Labdacid family, see for example Liapis 2012, 93–95.
9 Cf. Cairns 2013, xxxvii: "The *Antigone* is a play that emphasizes the role of states of mind and character in choice and in the outcomes of choice, yet the choices that it dramatizes are also

Let us return now to Antigone's exit at the end of the prologue: the 'already dead' young woman moves towards the dimension to which she has belonged for a long time. The dramatic meaning of this stage movement is underscored by Ismene's final utterance, at 98f.: "Well, if you wish to, go! But know this much, that / in your going you are foolish, but truly devoted to your kin" (ἀλλ', εἰ δοκεῖ σοι, στεῖχε· τοῦτο δ' ἴσθ' ὅτι / ἄνους μὲν ἔρχῃ, τοῖς φίλοις δ' ὀρθῶς φίλη).[10] Two verbs of movement, στεῖχε and ἔρχῃ, are significantly included in a sentence interpreting Antigone's departure towards extra-scenic space as the clearest expression of her sincere love for the dead. At the same time, her movement visually embodies the isolation of a young woman who belongs to those lying 'out there' in the space of death.

I turn now to the conflict between Antigone and Creon, which is rooted in their opposite perception of death. First of all, Antigone can resist the dire threats of the king precisely because of her willingness to die (458–468):

> θανουμένη γὰρ ἐξῄδη, τί δ' οὔ;
> κεἰ μὴ σὺ προύκήρυξας. εἰ δὲ τοῦ χρόνου
> πρόσθεν θανοῦμαι, κέρδος αὔτ' ἐγὼ λέγω.
> ὅστις γὰρ ἐν πολλοῖσιν ὡς ἐγὼ κακοῖς
> ζῇ, πῶς ὅδ' οὐχὶ κατθανὼν κέρδος φέρει;
> οὕτως ἔμοιγε τοῦδε τοῦ μόρου τυχεῖν
> παρ' οὐδὲν ἄλγος· ἀλλ' ἄν, εἰ τὸν ἐξ ἐμῆς
> μητρὸς θανόντ' ἄθαπτον <ὄντ'> ἠνεσχόμην,
> κείνοις ἂν ἤλγουν· τοῖσδε δ' οὐκ ἀλγύνομαι.

---

presented as depending on factors that lie beyond the agent's control. For the Chorus, Antigone's own 'self-willed temper' (αὐτόγνωτος ... ὀργά, 875) has destroyed her; yet they also believe that she is paying for a debt incurred by her father (856, cf. 471–472) and that her actions instantiate a recurrent pattern of suffering in her family (594–598)". Cairns offers an illuminating discussion of the role assigned by Sophocles to archaic concepts like *atē*, *hybris*, Erinyes and *Blabai*, in order to present both Antigone's and Creon's suffering "as a universal experience with a variety of causes, from deliberate wrongdoing through culpable and non-culpable error to the working out of an ineluctable universal rhythm" (p. xxxviii).

10 I have slightly modified Lloyd-Jones' translation, since, with Campbell 1879, 466, I understand ὀρθῶς φίλη at 99 as active, "unfailing in kindness to your friends", i.e. "a faithful sister to thine own brother". Müller 1967 rightly observes that Ismene must express here a positive moral assessment of Antigone's behaviour (see also Kamerbeek 1978, 53 and Griffith 1999, 138). The alternative interpretation ("loved by those who love you") advocated by Schneidewin/ Nauck 1880, 43f. and Jebb 1900, 27 is not attractive, since the adverb ὀρθῶς highlights the legitimacy of Antigone's love (cf. Eur. *IT* 609f. ὦ λῆμ' ἄριστον, ὡς ἀπ' εὐγενοῦς τινος / ῥίζης πέφυκας τοῖς φίλοις τ' ὀρθῶς φίλος, "O brave spirit! How you were born from some noble stock, and are rightly a friend to your friends").

I knew that I would die, of course I knew, even if you had made no proclamation. But if I die before my time, I account that gain. For does not whoever lives among many troubles, as I do, gain by death? So it is in no way painful for me to meet with this death; if I had endured that the son of my own mother should die and remain unburied, that would have given me pain, but this gives me none.

Completely indifferent to human authority, Antigone considers dying before the natural end of life a κέρδος for anyone who lives among evils as she does.[11] For her, a failure to comply with the commitment imposed by familial ties would be a far worse grief than dying. This indifference to death allows her to refuse the political values advocated by her opponent. When Creon asserts that Eteocles, having fought in defence of Thebes, is a φίλος deserving honour, while the assailant Polynices is an ἐχθρός to whom the χάρις of burial should not be granted, Antigone counters him by challenging the viability of the distinction between φίλοι and ἐχθροί in the netherworld (519–521):

AN. ὅμως ὅ γ' Ἅιδης τοὺς νόμους τούτους ποθεῖ.
KP. ἀλλ' οὐχ ὁ χρηστὸς τῷ κακῷ λαχεῖν ἴσος.
AN. τίς οἶδεν εἰ κάτω 'στὶν εὐαγῆ τάδε;

AN. Nevertheless, Hades demands these laws.
CR. But the noble man has not equal claims to honour with the evil.
AN. Who knows if this action is free from blame in the world below?

Antigone' commitment to death extends to suicide, an extreme action conclusively delivering her to the world below and at the same time raising a supreme challenge to Creon's attempt to control her.[12]

Antigone's unceasing appeal to Hades is extremely disturbing for Creon, because he is unable to find any effective answer. He can only try to prevail on her by force, but this leads him to a new mistake even worse than the κήρυγμα forbidding the burial. The king believes that he can beat Antigone on her own ground by enforcing upon her an insulting and ferocious retaliation which tramples on the sacred distinction between life and death. His mocking utterance at 524f. contains a sarcastic debasement of Antigone's love for the dead: "Then go below and love those friends, if you must love them! But while I live, a woman shall not rule!" (κάτω νυν ἐλθοῦσ', εἰ φιλητέον, φίλει / κείνους· ἐμοῦ δὲ

---

11 In saying this, Antigone proposes a notion of profit that is precisely opposite to that of Creon. On the notion of κέρδος in *Antigone*, see Cairns 2013, xxxi ff.

12 For suicide as Antigone's supreme challenge, see Johnston 2006, 183f.

ζῶντος οὐκ ἄρξει γυνή).[13] Again, when Ismene reminds him of the marriage vows between Antigone and Haimon, asking if he really intends to rob his son of her, the king cruelly responds that Hades himself will put an end to the marriage (ΙΣ. ἦ γὰρ στερήσεις τῆσδε τὸν σαυτοῦ γόνον; / ΚΡ. Ἅιδης ὁ παύσων τούσδε τοὺς γάμους ἐμοί, 574f.)[14]. The unnatural overlapping of marriage and death implied by these words is full of ominous forebodings: Creon wrongly thinks he has Hades as an ally, but he will soon see his desire fulfilled in a way he cannot imagine. He makes recourse again to a mocking retaliation to put an end to the dialogue: "Yes, even those who are bold try to escape, when they see Hades already near their life" (φεύγουσι γάρ τοι χοἰ θρασεῖς, ὅταν πέλας / ἤδη τὸν Ἅιδην εἰσορῶσι τοῦ βίου, 580f.)[15].

Creon does not understand how dangerous the road he is on can be. While presenting himself as the champion of a correct vision of life and death against what he believes to be a foolish and unsound passion for the netherworld, he actually creates the conditions that will unleash death upon his family. He goes so far as to take an incredibly harsh stand even towards his son. When Haimon, accused of pleading only for Antigone, answers that he is speaking also on behalf "of you and of me, and of the infernal gods" (καὶ σοῦ γε κἀμοῦ, καὶ θεῶν τῶν νερτέρων, 749), Creon's reaction envisages another hideous contamination of life and death: "You shall never marry this woman while she is alive" (ταύτην ποτ' οὐκ ἔσθ' ὡς ἔτι ζῶσαν γαμεῖς, 750). In this case too he cannot foresee that his desire will be fulfilled by a terrible marriage in death, which will join the couple forever. His contempt for the feelings of his son is cruel to the point of triggering thoughts of suicide in him, scarcely disguised in the prophecy "Then she will die, and by her death she will destroy another" (ἥδ' οὖν θανεῖται καὶ θανοῦσ' ὀλεῖ τινα, 751). Fueled by a furious rage, the king threatens to kill An-

---

13 It is not by chance that the sarcasm involves the idea of 'going' to the netherworld; see the discussion below of Antigone's exit at 839–943.
14 The arrangement of speakers at 572–576 is disputed. 572 ὦ φίλταθ' Αἷμον, ὥς σ' ἀτιμάζει πατήρ is given to Antigone by the manuscripts, while the Aldine edition assigns it to Ismene; 574 is pronounced by Ismene in the manuscripts, but was allocated by Boeckh to the chorus; at 576 the tradition is divided (*Ismenae trib.* **KAUYTTz,** *choro* **LR**), while Boeckh gives the line to Antigone. As Griffith 1999, 217 observes, "both stichomythic economy and dramatic logic demand that Ismene should speak all three lines" (cf. Mastronarde 1979, 95f.). Raeburn 2017, 102 n. 12 prefers "Jebb's much more dramatic arrangement which allows Antigone suddenly to break in at 572 with the cry, 'Dearest Haemon, how your father slights you!'". But Antigone is devoted to death and never utters a word about Haimon; it would be incongruous to alter this characteristic by giving her here a single line mentioning him.
15 For a similar image, cf. Soph. *OC* 1439–1440 σ' ὡρμώμενον / ἐς προὖπτον Ἅιδην, "when you are hurrying off to a death foreseen".

tigone before the eyes of Haimon, who, in order to escape this monstrous sight, runs out through *eisodos* B toward the place outside the walls of the city where he will be found later by his father.

Let us now return to the treatment of dramatic space. After the prologue, Sophocles progressively reinforces the association between the extra-scenic space beyond *eisodos* B and the hideous contamination of life and death caused by Creon's κήρυγμα. In the first episode, the Chorus-leader invites the king to consider the possibility of interpreting the first mysterious burial as a manifestation of divine will ("King, my anxious thought has long been advising me that this action may have been prompted by the gods", ἄναξ, ἐμοί τοι μή τι καὶ θεή-λατον / τοὖργον τόδ' ἡ ξύννοια βουλεύει πάλαι, 278f.). The king angrily rebuts this suggestion by arguing that it would be foolish to believe that the gods can take any forethought (πρόνοιαν, 283) for the corpse of a traitor: "Did they conceal it so as to do him great honour as a benefactor, he who came to burn their colonnaded temples and their offerings and to destroy their country and its laws?" (πότερον ὑπερτιμῶντες ὡς εὐεργέτην / ἔκρυπτον αὐτόν, ὅστις ἀμφικίο-νας / ναοὺς πυρώσων ἦλθε κἀναθήματα /καὶ γῆν ἐκείνων καὶ νόμους διασκεδῶν;, 284–287). He has no doubt about the coincidence of his own will with the divine perspective (288 ἦ τοὺς κακοὺς τιμῶντας εἰσορᾷς θεούς; "Do you see the gods honouring evil men?").

Later, in the second episode, the Guard describes the miserable condition of the decaying corpse, which, after the removal of the thin layer of dust put on it by an unknown hand, is polluting the air with a terrible stench (409–412). Most of all, he relates the unexpected atmospheric phenomenon that immediately preceded the discovery of Antigone crying near Polynices' body (415–421). In the middle of a hot, sunny day, a terrible whirlwind rose up from the earth, kicking up dust and obscuring the sky; it filled the entire plain and shoke the treetops, clogging the upper air. All the guards were compelled to keep their eyes closed, trying to endure what the narrator calls "a god-sent affliction" (μύ-σαντες δ' εἴχομεν θείαν νόσον, 421). The Guard's entire narration is clearly intended to encourage the audience to associate what happened in that extra-scenic space with a dangerous and offensive overlap between life and death, to which the gods are beginning to react.

Within the framework of this strategy, a key passage is represented by Creon's choice of the penalty to be imposed on Antigone, which is again inspired by a perverted idea of retaliation (772–780). The culprit will be led to a track deserted by mortals, and immured in a hollow cave with a minimal amount of food, just enough to avoid pollution for the *polis*. The king cruelly mocks his victim by inviting her to pray to Hades (777–780):

κἀκεῖ τὸν Ἅιδην, ὃν μόνον σέβει θεῶν,
αἰτουμένη που τεύξεται τὸ μὴ θανεῖν,
ἢ γνώσεται γοῦν ἀλλὰ τηνικαῦθ' ὅτι
πόνος περισσός ἐστι τἀν Ἅιδου σέβειν.

And there she can pray to Hades, the only one among the gods whom she respects, and
perhaps be spared from death; or else she will learn, at that late stage, that it is wasted effort to show regard for things in Hades.

This culminating point of the improper commingling of life and death caused by
Creon completes the definition of the meaning of the extra-scenic space outside
the walls of Thebes. The cave, an intermediate spot between the upper and the
nether worlds, is collocated in a distant place, deserted of humans. As Rehm
has rightly observed, this feature creates an affinity between the prison and the
dusty plain where Polynices' corpse lies exposed on "dry, hard, unbroken
ground with no sign of human interference" (cf. 249–251).[16]

The importance attached by Sophocles to this extra-scenic place is clearly
shown by the variety of descriptions he offers of Antigone's prison. It is a rocky
underground cave (774 πετρώδει ... ἐν κατώρυχι, 1100 κατώρυχος στέγη) and a
dwelling place for the dead (818 κεῦθος νεκύων, 920 θανόντων κατασκαφάς,
1204 Ἅιδου κοῖλον, 848 ἔργμα τυμβόχωστον, and the more explicit τάφος, 849,
1069, 1215, τύμβος, 886, 891 and τυμβεύματι, 1215), but also a bridal chamber for
a γάμος with Hades (cf. 891 νυμφεῖον, 804, παγκοίτην ... θάλαμον, 1204 f. λιθό-
στρωτον ... / νυμφεῖον Ἅιδου κοῖλον). The cave is presented as a hybrid place, a
sort of fissure dangerously putting the underworld in communication with the
world of the living and confusing the two. Two passages in particular emphasize
its hideous nature. The first is Creon's order to immediately bring Antigone to
her prison (885–890):

οὐκ ἄξεθ' ὡς τάχιστα, καὶ κατηρεφεῖ
τύμβῳ περιπτύξαντες, ὡς εἴρηκ' ἐγώ,
ἄφετε μόνην ἔρημον, εἴτε χρῆ θανεῖν,
εἴτ' ἐν τοιαύτῃ ζῶσα τυμβεύειν στέγῃ.
ἡμεῖς γὰρ ἁγνοὶ τοὐπὶ τήνδε τὴν κόρην·
μετοικίας δ' οὖν τῆς ἄνω στερήσεται.

16 Rehm 2002, 115–116; see also p. 118 "Creon is now responsible for creating two unnaturally
desolated places within the city: the site where a corpse lies ringed with guards, preventing the
familial community that should gather at a proper grave; and the tomb that walls off a young
bride from the oikos she should create with her new husband".

Will you not lead her off as soon as possible, and when you have enclosed her in the en-compassing tomb, as I have ordered, leave her alone, isolated, whether she wishes to die or to be entombed living in such a dwelling? For we are guiltless where this girl is con-cerned; but she shall be deprived of residence with us here above the ground.

The king's insulting retaliation here reaches its peak: he condemns a living woman to inhabit a tomb, aiming to deprive Antigone of her μετοικία in the upper world.[17] The full horror of this decision is emphasized by the oxymoronic phrase τοιάυτη ζῶσα τυμβεύειν στέγη, which stretches the normal use of the verb τυμβεύειν by giving it an intransitive sense ('dwell in a tomb').[18]

The second passage is Antigone's final *rhēsis* (891–899 and 916–920):

ὦ τύμβος, ὦ νυμφεῖον, ὦ κατασκαφῆς
οἴκησις αἰείφρουρος, οἷ πορεύομαι
πρὸς τοὺς ἐμαυτῆς, ὧν ἀριθμὸν ἐν νεκροῖς
πλεῖστον δέδεκται Φερσέφασσ' ὀλωλότων,
ὧν λοισθία 'γὼ καὶ κάκιστα δὴ μακρῷ   895
κάτειμι, πρίν μοι μοῖραν ἐξήκειν βίου.
ἐλθοῦσα μέντοι κάρτ' ἐν ἐλπίσιν τρέφω
φίλη μὲν ἥξειν πατρί, προσφιλὴς δὲ σοί,
μῆτερ, φίλη δὲ σοί, κασίγνητον κάρα·
......
καὶ νῦν ἄγει με διὰ χερῶν οὕτω λαβὼν
ἄλεκτρον, ἀνυμέναιον, οὔτε του γάμου
μέρος λαχοῦσαν οὔτε παιδείου τροφῆς,
ἀλλ' ὧδ' ἐρῆμος πρὸς φίλων ἡ δύσμορος
ζῶσ' εἰς θανόντων ἔρχομαι κατασκαφάς.   920

O tomb, O bridal chamber, O deep-dug home, to be guarded forever, where I go to join those who are my own, of whom Persephassa has already received a great number, dead, among the shades! Of these I am the last, and my descent will be the saddest of all, before the term of my life has come. But when I come there, I am confident that I shall come dear to my father, dear to you, my mother, and dear to you, my own brother.

...

---

17 The description of Antigone as a μέτοικος in the world above corresponds to her "in-between status, not truly 'resident' among the dead yet disenfranchised from the upper world" (Griffith 1999, 272).

18 Elsewhere τυμβεύειν is always transitive and means 'to bury' or 'to dispose in a tomb'. Jebb 1900, 162 compares the oscillation between transitive and intransitive meaning of the verb σαλεύειν ('to put other on a σάλος' but also 'to be on a σάλος'); he also compares θαλασσεύω, 'to be on the sea'. The alternative, sarcastic interpretation proposed by Björk 1956, 55 f. ('to continue her burials') is far less attractive, because it spoils the contrast between ζῶσα and τυμβεύειν.

> And now he leads me thus by the hands, without marriage, without bridal rites, having no share in wedlock or in the rearing of children, but thus deserted by my friends I come alive, poor creature, to the caverns of the dead.

The cave is described here by Antigone both as the spot in which she will be reunited with her dead kin in a never-ending tie of φιλία (891–899) and as a place of total isolation, where she will be deprived of her legitimate hope of marriage and children (916–920). This distressing perspective is condensed in the image of 920: "I come alive, poor creature, to the caverns of the dead" (ζῶσ' εἰς θανόντων ἔρχομαι κατασκαφάς). Eventually, the ambiguous nature of the cave will be gruesomely confirmed by the suicides of Antigone and Haimon, which will transform it into a true, albeit perverted bridal chamber: "He lay, a corpse holding a corpse, having achieved his marriage rites, poor fellow, in the house of Hades" (κεῖται δὲ νεκρὸς περὶ νεκρῷ, τὰ νυμφικὰ / τέλη λαχὼν δείλαιος ἐν γ' Ἅιδου δόμοις, 1240f.).

From the moment Creon established the penalty for Antigone, enriching the meaning of the extra-scenic space with a further disquieting feature, the events are put in motion, and the characters with them. Two decisive scenic movements mark the tragic catastrophe that follows. The first is the moving final exit of Antigone, which expands to the dimension of an entire scene, mingling the traits of an anomalous funeral procession for a living creature with those of a no less disturbing wedding procession. Both aspects are highlighted by the Chorus-leader in the introductory anapests: "I see Antigone here passing to the bridal chamber where all come to rest" (τὸν παγκοίτην ὅθ' ὁρῶ θάλαμον / τήνδ' Ἀντιγόνην ἀνύτουσαν, 804f.). Antigone herself describes her exit as "the last journey" (τὰν νεάταν ὁδὸν στείχουσαν, 807f.) leading her to the abominable marriage with Hades (ἀλλ' Ἀχέροντι νυμφεύσω, 816). Of this movement towards her "strange tomb" (τάφου ποταινίου, 849), the spectators see the first part on stage, while the rest must be imagined in the extra-scenic space beyond *eisodos* B, whose meaning at this point in the drama is already well established in their minds. The conflation of wedding and funeral rites in Greek tragedy has been widely explored,[19] so that I have no need to insist on this point. What is important is that in this scene their unsettling overlapping takes Antigone's desperate isolation to an extreme. She has no φίλος who can pity her at this moment, and she is moving towards an even worse isolation, since she will experience in the cave the condition of dwelling with neither the living nor

---

19 See among others Segal 1981, 179–183; Seaford 1987; Rehm 1994.

the dead (βροτοῖς / οὔτε νεκρὸς νεκροῖσιν / μέτοικος, οὐ ζῶσιν, οὐ θανοῦσιν, 850–852).[20]

The second, decisive scenic movement, which gives form to the entire final section of the tragedy, is Creon's exit at 1114 in the same direction as Antigone (and Haimon before her), toward the extra-scenic space beyond *eisodos* B. Up to this point, the king has never abandoned the scenic space where he exercises his power over the city. But after Teiresias has spoken, the ruler's authority is irreparably undermined. The seer reveals that Creon's foolish behaviour, rather than protecting Thebes, is hurting it terribly. Through his speech in 998–1022, the spectators learn that not only the battlefield outside the walls but the whole space of Thebes is now polluted. Carrion from the corpse is clogging the city's altars (1016–1018):

βωμοὶ γὰρ ἡμῖν ἐσχάραι τε παντελεῖς
πλήρεις ὑπ᾽ οἰωνῶν τε καὶ κυνῶν βορᾶς
τοῦ δυσμόρου πεπτῶτος Οἰδίπου γόνου.

For our altars and our braziers, one and all, are filled with carrion brought by birds and dogs from the unhappy son of Oedipus who fell.[21]

Because of this pollution, the gods reject sacrifices and prayers: victims smolder with no flame and much smoke, birds produce sounds that are indistinguishable even for a skilled *oionomantis* like Teiresias. Moving from the plain to the city's sacred spaces, the contagion, although still confined to the extra-scenic space, is getting dangerously close to the royal palace.

Given this public disaster, the seer makes a request as simple as it is hard to swallow for Creon: "Give way to the dead man, and do not continue to stab him as he lies dead!" (ἀλλ᾽ εἶκε τῷ θανόντι, μήδ᾽ ὀλωλότα / κέντει, 1029f.). For a final time, the king reacts angrily, accusing Teiresias and all *manteis* of untrustworthiness and corruption, and pushing his boldness to an impious hyperbole. He cries that he would not give Polynices' corpse up for burial, even if the very eagles of Zeus should bear the carrion morsel to the divine king's throne, and affirms that mortals have no power to pollute the gods (1039–1044).[22]

---

20 For the motive of denied μετοικία, see also Creon's words at 890 (μετοικίας δ᾽ οὖν τῆς ἄνω στερήσεται: above note 17).

21 Teiresias' words echo the initial image of 29–30 οἰωνοῖς γλυκὺν / θησαυρὸν εἰσορῶσι πρὸς χάριν βορᾶς: what Antigone feared there has become real.

22 Segal 1981, 174 observes that though this general idea is "the sort of rationalistic principle that one might find in Protagoras or Prodicus … any rationality is undercut by the emotional

After a brusque stichomythia in which the king and Teiresias taunt one another, the seer is impelled to reveal what lies in wait for Creon. He will soon be bound to give in exchange for corpses the corpse of a child from his own loins, since he has subverted the relationship between the upper and the nether worlds (1068–1076):

> ἀνθ' ὧν ἔχεις μὲν τῶν ἄνω βαλὼν κάτω,
> ψυχήν τ' ἀτίμως ἐν τάφῳ κατῴκισας,
> ἔχεις δὲ τῶν κάτωθεν ἐνθάδ' αὖ θεῶν
> ἄμοιρον, ἀκτέριστον, ἀνόσιον νέκυν.
> ὧν οὔτε σοὶ μέτεστιν οὔτε τοῖς ἄνω
> θεοῖσιν, ἀλλ' ἐκ σοῦ βιάζονται τάδε.
> τούτων σε λωβητῆρες ὑστεροφθόροι
> λοχῶσιν Ἅιδου καὶ θεῶν Ἐρινύες,
> ἐν τοῖσιν αὐτοῖς τοῖσδε ληφθῆναι κακοῖς.

[...] in return for having hurled below one of those above, blasphemously lodging a living person in a tomb, and you have kept here something belonging to the gods below, a corpse deprived, unburied, unholy.[23] Neither you nor the gods above have any part in this, but you have inflicted it upon them! On account of this there lie in wait for you the doers of outrage who in the end destroy, the Erinyes of Hades and the gods, so that you will be caught up in these same evils.[24]

Everything is clear now: if Creon will not yield to the rights of the gods below, Death will impose itself upon him.[25] We can now fully appreciate the decisive meaning of the extra-scenic space for the development of the plot. Creon's

---

vehemence, by the scornful phrase, trembling in fear of a miasma, and especially by the staggering hybris of the sentence which precedes (1039–1040)".

23 The idea that the nether gods are offended by the presence of the unburied corpses is also present in Lys. 2.7, where the orator is praising Athens for its role in defending the rights of the Argive dead at Thebes (a passage probably influenced by Sophocles).

24 The possessive genitives Ἅιδου καὶ θεῶν express the persons whose wrongs will be avenged by the Erinyes (cf. πατρὸς or μητρὸς Ἐρινύς). Sophocles is probably alluding here to an ancient conception of these goddesses, who at *Il.* 19.418 are represented as putting an end to the unnatural phenomenon of a speaking horse. (Edwards 1991, 285 suggests that the poet was probably thinking of their function in punishing those who violated the rights of the gods.) I am not persuaded by the interpretation of the passage given by Zeroch 2015, 112–114, who considers Teiresias' words equivalent to a curse and interprets the Erinyes as a personification of its force.

25 It is significant that the decisive revelation about divine will comes from a *mantis*. As Parker 1999, 174 observes, "real insight into the will of the gods in Sophocles comes only from the interpretation by oracles and seers embedded in the plays". The poet does not want to leave any doubt about Creon's responsibility.

movement marks a complete reversal compared to the first part of the play. We see no more characters coming from offstage to him and confronting his authority before the royal palace. It is now he who hastily goes out in the direction connotated by his dangerous contempt for the boundary between life and death. His exit at 1114 is preceded by the anxious question "What must I do? Tell me, and I will obey!" (τί δῆτα χρὴ δρᾶν; φράζε· πείσομαι δ' ἐγώ, 1099), revealing the dismay of a king who is no longer able to decide. Roles have now been reversed: leaving aside his previous authoritarianism, Creon is forced to ask the old men of the chorus for advice. They exhort him to hurry, because the swift-footed Harms (Βλάβαι) of the gods can easily cut off foolish mortals from completing their course (1103f.),[26] and insist, with a direct and assertive tone, that he must not entrust this job to others: "Go, then, and do it, and do not leave it to others!" (δρᾶ νυν τάδ' ἐλθὼν μηδ' ἐπ' ἄλλοισιν τρέπε, 1107). This request fits Sophocles' dramatic plan perfectly: the displacement of Creon from scenic to extra-scenic space will in fact result in an individual experience of sorrow belonging only to him.[27] His final utterance before leaving the scenic space reveals an uncontrollable anxiety and a haste unbefitting a king (1108–1114).

> ὧδ' ὡς ἔχω στείχοιμ' ἄν· ἴτ' ἴτ' ὀπάονες
> οἵ τ' ὄντες οἵ τ' ἀπόντες, ἀξίνας χεροῖν
> ὁρμᾶσθ' ἑλόντες εἰς ἐπόψιον τόπον.
> ἐγὼ δ', ἐπειδὴ δόξα τῇδ' ἐπεστράφη,
> αὐτός τ' ἔδησα καὶ παρὼν ἐκλύσομαι.
> δέδοικα γὰρ μὴ τοὺς καθεστῶτας νόμους
> ἄριστον ᾖ σῴζοντα τὸν βίον τελεῖν.

I will go, just as I am! Come on, come on, my servants, present and absent, take picks in your hands and rush to the ground that you can see! Since my decision has been thus re-

---

26 We have here a transparent allusion to the role of *Atē* in the allegory of the Λιταί at *Il.* 9.502–507. The Βλάβαι run fast, like *Atē* in the Homeric passage, and harm is a direct consequence of the latter. For a detailed discussion of this allusion, see Cairns 2013, xxiii f., according to whom "the transparent evocation of this, one of the most salient and emblematic passages of the ancient world's most authoritative poetic archetype, comes at the point at which the balance between the sufferings that await Creon and those that he has imposed upon Antigone begins to become apparent".

27 Knox 1964, 64 and 75 regards Creon's change of mind as evident proof that he lacks the 'heroic temper' of stubborn figures such as Ajax, Antigone and Philoctetes, who never yeld to advice. But it is precisely this change of mind that makes him a deeply tragic figure, who realizes his mistake too late and undergoes an upsetting experience of learning and suffering. For Creon as a tragic figure in an Aeschylean and Aristotelic perspective, see Torrance 1965, 298f.; Winnington-Ingram 1980, 117–119; Di Benedetto 1983, 4–13; Griffith 1999, 27.

versed, I who imprisoned her shall myself be present to release her! I am afraid that it is best to end one's life in obedience to the established laws!

The dramatic significance of this exit is so great that Sophocles chooses to make Creon's movements offstage fully perceptible to the spectators, through the narration of a Messenger, who enters at 1155. A detailed description of relevant actions taking place in invisible parts of the dramatic space can be found elsewhere in Sophocles: compare for example Deianeira's farewell to her home and bridal bed (*Tr.* 899–946) or the description of the final moments of Oedipus' life at *OC* 1586–1666. Here, however, the playwright adds a crucial element, since immediately after the Messenger's narration, Creon comes on stage again, profoundly changed by the events he has witnessed offstage and with the corpse of Haimon in his arms. The Messenger's report may thus be regarded both as preparation for what the audience will see in the exodos and as a guide for interpreting what the king has suffered offstage.[28]

Aeschylus in the exodos of *Seven against Thebes* had already created a situation in which a character goes offstage through one of the *eisodoi* and then returns as a corpse, accompanied by a funeral procession. In picking up this Aeschylean pattern, Sophocles modifies it by introducing a decisive novelty: he brings the character back on scene still living but deeply affected by the events he witnessed offstage, and accompanied by another person's corpse. His extra-scenic movements thus become an essential part of the dramatic action and acquire paramount importance for the interpretation of the play.[29]

But let us return to the Messenger. The man begins his speech with some gnomic considerations about the power of τύχη and the wretched lot of those

---

28 A similar sequence (exit of a character — narration of his retro-scenic actions by an ἐξάγγελος — entrance of the same character devastated by what happened in the house) will again be exploited by Sophocles for the blinding of Oedipus (*OT* 1185–1307).

29 The scenic pattern of the *Antigone* is picked up and intensified three decades later by Euripides for the character of Antigone in the *Phoenissae*. The desperate run of the young girl together with her mother towards the battlefield, which begins onstage (1278–1283) and continues in the narration of a Messenger (1427–1479), is followed by her entrance with three corpses (Eteocles, Polynices and Jocasta) at 1480. The journey to-and-fro the extra-scenic space suddenly transforms Antigone in an adult woman, shattered by the horrible sequence of deaths which takes place under her eyes on the battlefield. The same pattern is again proposed by Euripides one or two years later in *Orestes*, where the protagonist, too feeble to walk, exits with the help of Pylades to reach the Assembly (806), and after the detailed report of a Messenger about the debate which has led to his condemnation (866–956), comes back onstage at 1012 in a state of deep prostration. For a discussion of the two scenic sequences see Medda 2013, 145–147 and 241–246.

who, like Creon, although they seem completely fortunate, suddenly experience the loss of everything dearest to them (1155–1165). The key passage of this introduction is 1165–1167: "When a man's pleasures have abandoned him, I do not consider him a living being, but an animated corpse" (τὰς γὰρ ἡδονὰς / ὅταν προδῶσιν ἀνδρός, οὐ τίθημ' ἐγὼ / ζῆν τοῦτον, ἀλλ' ἔμψυχον ἡγοῦμαι νεκρόν). The image of the "animated corpse" perfectly embodies the outcome of Teiresias' prophecy. The confusion between life and death is now tragically reproduced in the man who has caused it. His new condition is summarized by a few terrible words: "They are dead! And those who are alive are guilty of their deaths" (τεθνᾶσιν· οἱ δὲ ζῶντες αἴτιοι θανεῖν, 1173).

A little later the Messenger reports in detail the desperate extra-scenic behavior of the king. Creon and his men hastened first to bury Polynices' corpse, which had been torn by dogs (κυνοσπάρακτον σῶμα Πολυνείκους, 1198). After praying to Hekate and Pluto, they gave the corpse a purifying bath, collected and burned what was left of it, and eventually covered the ashes with a mound (1199–1203). Then they proceeded to Antigone's prison, where the sight of an upsetting scene of death was announced in advance by loud shrieks and wails (1206f.). Recognising Haimon's voice, Creon had a clear presentiment of the abyss of suffering waiting for him at the end of the road that had brought him from the palace to the cave: "O my unhappy self, am I a prophet? Am I traveling on the saddest path of all the ways I have come in the past?" (ὦ τάλας ἐγώ, / ἆρ' εἰμὶ μάντις; ἆρα δυστυχεστάτην / κέλευθον ἕρπω τῶν παρελθουσῶν ὁδῶν;, 1211–1213). It is particularly significant that Sophocles has made the protagonist himself describe his extra-scenic κέλευθος as the decisive passage of his destiny.

Inside the cave, Antigone had hung herself by means of her silky veil or girdle; the first man to enter saw a stunned Haimon desperately embracing the corpse. Pathos is at its peak, to the point that Creon's supplication to his son is reported as direct speech: "Come out, my son, I beg you as a suppliant" (ἔξελθε, τέκνον, ἱκέσιός σε λίσσομαι, 1230). Haimon reacted with a wild look, spat in his father's face and drew his sword. When Creon ran away, he turned it against himself and shed his blood over Antigone's body. Far from being dominated by the king, Death now totally overwhelms him.

The audience could now expect a view of the ruined protagonist returning from the prison/tomb. Sophocles, however, delays this a little, in order to fully exploit all the conventional means available to his stagecraft. Between the two parts of the Messenger's narration (1155–1179 and 1191–1243), in fact, he inserts the entrance from the house of Creon's wife Eurydike, announced by the Chorus-leader at 1179–1182. The Queen says that she was just opening the door and coming out to pray to the goddess Pallas when she heard a voice inside announcing a disgrace.[30] Despite the fear caused by this unexpected perception, she has decided to come out and learn what has happened, being well acquainted with suffering (κακῶν γὰρ οὐκ ἄπειρος οὖσ' ἀκούσομαι 1191). Her reaction to the Messenger's report of the deaths of Antigone and Haimon is to grow upset: without a word, she disappears into the house, arousing a worried conjecture in the Chorus (1251 f.). The Messenger then decides to follow her inside in order to determine if her "excessive silence" (τῆς ἄγαν ... σιγῆς, 1256) conceals the intention of hurting herself.

Euridike's movements, albeit confined to a short section of the play, acquire a paramount dramatic significance, since they mark the moment at which Death enters the royal palace and definitively contaminates the king's private space. The queen's desperation has no words that can be said in public: she lets her sorrow erupt only within the house, at the altar where she kills herself after mourning the death of her eldest son Megareus, sacrificed to ensure Thebes' salvation, and cursing Creon as the murderer of his children (σοὶ κακὰς / πράξεις ἐφυμνήσασα τῷ παιδοκτόνῳ, 1304 f.) All her actions behind the stage front, culminating in her suicide, are again narrated by the Messenger, who emerges from the house at 1277.

Everything is now ready for Creon's entrance with the corpse of Haimon in his arms,[31] a visual symbol of a disaster caused by his own ἁμαρτία, as the Chorus-leader points out in an anapestic announcement (1257–1260).

καὶ μὴν ὅδ' ἄναξ αὐτὸς ἐφήκει
μνῆμ' ἐπίσημον διὰ χειρὸς ἔχων,
εἰ θέμις εἰπεῖν, οὐκ ἀλλοτρίαν
ἄτην, ἀλλ' αὐτὸς ἁμαρτών.

Here comes the king himself, bearing in his arms an all too clear reminder. If we may say so, his ruin came not from others, but from his own error.

The audience in the theatre now witnesses the complete triumph of Death: coming from the extra-scenic space, it conquers the entire dramatic area and becomes visible in a scene that presents a peculiar variation on the traditional

---

30 Sophocles is exploiting here in a most refined way the widespread convention allowing a character who is inside the *skēnē* to hear the voices of other characters speaking outside. See Di Benedetto/Medda 2002, 54–57.

31 At 1258 the phrase διὰ χειρὸς ἔχων suggests that Creon is carrying his son's body himself, cf. 1298 ἔχω μὲν ἐν χείρεσσιν. It is also possible, however, that the corpse is carried by attendants, with Creon holding his hands on some part of it.

situation of the arrival of a corpse to be mourned on stage. A decisive novelty is
that the spectators' attention is called less to the mourning of the dead than to
the effect produced by death on the living Creon. The impious and contaminat-
ing mix of death and life he has culpably imposed on Thebes is now embodied
in his person. He addresses the old men of the chorus as "you who see those
who have killed and those of the same family who have been killed" (ὦ κτανό-
ντας καὶ / θανόντας βλέποντες ἐμφυλίους, 1263f.), emphasizing that the blood
tie between father and son, previously broken in the name of power, has been
recreated in the dimension of death and sorrow.[32]

But the wretched king has only time to begin his lament for Haimon, since
he must learn in addition what happened in his house. At the end of the first
strophic pair of the *kommos*, the Messenger emerges from the palace, telling
Creon that he will soon witness other disgraces: his wife is dead by suicide
(1277–1283). At this culminating point, Sophocles is not content with the common narrative convention that assigns the function of informing other characters on stage about retro-scenic action to someone who emerges from the house.
He wants to exploit the full impact of the vision of this second corpse as well,
which becomes visible at 1293, when the door is opened: "Ch.: you can see it! It
is no longer hidden indoors. Cr. Alas, I see this second disaster, miserable one!"
(ΧΟ. ὁρᾶν πάρεστιν· οὐ γὰρ ἐν μυχοῖς ἔτι. ΚΡ. οἴμοι, / κακὸν τόδ᾽ ἄλλο δεύτερον
βλέπω τάλας, 1294f.). This new irruption of Death from the retro-scenic space is
an intolerable burden for Creon, all the more so because the Messenger reports
Eurydike's curse to him as well.

What the spectators see and hear in the exodos of *Antigone* is the completion of a devastating process through which Death, like the red mask of a short
story by Edgar Allan Poe, breaks its banks and, coming from the extra-scenic
space, conquers all the other spaces involved in the dramatic action, annihilat-
ing Creon's family. The king is broken and left without even the authority to
decide the manner of his own death, as the Chorus-leader reminds him at 1337f.:
"Utter no prayers now! There is no escape from fated calamity for mortals" (μὴ
νυν προσεύχου μηδέν· ὡς πεπρωμένης / οὐκ ἔστι θνητοῖς συμφορᾶς ἀπαλλαγή).
The final scene is an eloquent demonstration that the gods may inflict an untol-
erable blow on men at any moment, as Creon shows he has understood in his
final utterance: "Fate hard to deal with has leapt upon my head" (τὰ δ᾽ ἐπὶ κρατί

---

32 Liapis 2013, 102–107 points out that in the course of the play Creon is subjected to a pro-
gressive assimilation to the Labdacids, "which becomes more pronounced towards the end of
the play in which the themes and patterns [...] of that doomed *oikos* are now associated with
Creon and his own *oikos*" (p. 102).

μοι / πότμος δυσκόμιστος εἰσήλατο, 1345f.). The spectators can now appreciate an unexpected and upsetting implication of what the Chorus said in the first stasimon, when they recalled the impossibility of man finding a remedy for Hades (Ἄιδα μόνον / φεῦξιν οὐκ ἐπάξεται, 361f.). Hades is indeed not only mankind's one inescapable limitation, but also the measure by which human frailty is assessed.

The close intertwining between the construction of the characters and that of dramatic space which characterizes *Antigone* offers a clear indication of Sophocles' primary dramatic idea. The axis around which the poet has constructed the story is the subtle and dangerous boundary dividing the spheres of life and death, which informs the theatrical space and creates a perfect balance between the movement of the characters and their tragic experience. All the other themes of the play, such as conflicts between law and individual freedom, between State and family, between father and son or male and female, although they seem the most relevant for modern interpreters, must be projected against the foil of this primary conception, which requires the audience to experience first of all the precarious situation of human beings when they face the overwhelming power of the gods.

When considered from this perspective, it becomes clear that *Antigone* cannot be reduced to a simple matter of right or wrong. Creon is right in his attempt to defend the collective safety and welfare of the *polis*, but tragically wrong in choosing the way to achieve his goal. Antigone is right in rejecting the authoritarianism of the king, but her position too is undermined by an unbalanced relationship with the underworld and by her αὐτόγνωτος ὀργά, deriving from her Labdakid origin. Her death is a consequence not only of the king's violence, but also of her being περισσή in her devotion to Hades and to the dead members of her family.[33] It is significant that the gods, despite Antigone's pious defence of the rights of the dead, do not take the trouble to save her. On the other hand, however, they make her death an instrument to bring the proud king to ruin, partially counterbalancing her downfall. Why they act as they do remains ob-

---

33 As Oudemans/Lardinois 1987, 115–117 point out, the lack of a correct appreciation of this aspect and of the obsession of the *Antigone* with pollution and perversion of rituals represents one of the main weaknesses in Hegel's interpretation: "The powers of which Antigone and Creon are the vehicles cannot be divided into just and unjust parts, nor can be harmonized in a final scene of higher justice. Their reckless acts, their ambiguous fates, their holy pollutions, are alien to coherent, separative or harmonious thought. Therefore, these protagonists cannot be incorporated into any philosophical system" (p. 117).

scure. As always in Sophocles, the divine will is left unexplained and the gods are seen, as Robert Parker puts it, "through a glass darkly".[34]

At the time he wrote *Antigone*, Sophocles was sensible to the issue of the refusal of burial to enemies, a theme he dealt with also in the second half of *Ajax*.[35] Moreover, we know that Aeschylus too, in his lost *Hektoros Loutra*, brought on scene the Iliadic episode of the mistreatment of Hector's corpse by Achilles. In one of the few preserved fragments (F 266 Radt²), Hermes says that the dead feel no joy or grief, so that it is unimportant whether one does them good or ill. Nonetheless, "our indignation, on the other hand, is more powerful, and Justice exacts the penalty for the wrath of the dead" (ἡμῶν γε μέντοι νέμεσις ἐσθ' ὑπερτέρα, / καὶ τοῦ θανόντος ἡ Δίκη πράσσει κότον, 4–5; transl. by A.H. Sommerstein). The Justice evoked here by Hermes seems to be quite the same as the "Justice who lives with the gods below" (ἡ ξύνοικος τῶν κάτω θεῶν Δίκη) summoned by Antigone at *Ant.* 451 against Creon's κήρυγμα. There is therefore some reason to suspect that the practice of denying burial, although accepted by the Athenians in certain cases, was a subject of discussion in the middle of the 5th century BCE,[36] and that Sophocles' choice of his mythic stuff for *Ajax* and *Antigone* had some political significance. Nonetheless, the treatment of the time-old story of the war at Thebes in *Antigone* was for him most of all an occasion to explore the delicate terrain on which men walk when they transgress the boundary between life and death and between men and gods. Sophocles reminds his spectators in any time and place that human existence, even that of mighty kings, is a dangerous path on the edge of an abyss, an obscure world which spreads its shadow over men's happiness even through a delicate, adamant figure like the Theban virgin devoted to death.

---

34 The phrase is borrowed from St. Paul, I *Corinthians* 13:12.

35 In *Ajax* too Sophocles' treatment of space is strictly connected with his construction of the character of the protagonist. In particular, the place where the hero commits suicide, untrodden by human feet and far from the camp of the Achaeans, is so strongly connected with Ajax's 'purification' that Sophocles, through a rare change of scene, makes it become the visible scenic space of the second half of the play. I have discussed the notoriously controversial staging of *Ajax* in detail in Medda 2013, 25–51 and Medda 2015).

36 Xen. *Hell.* 1.7.22 mentions an Athenian law that forbade the burial of traitors or temple robbers on Attic soil (cf. also Thuc. 1.138.6 on the hidden burial of the traitor Themistocles). For evidence of the practice of not burying enemies in historical times, see Rosivach 1983.

Bibliography

Battezzato, Luigi (2019), "Antigone e gli dèi", in: *Dioniso. Rivista di Studi sul Teatro Antico*, n.s. 9, 101–126.

Björk, Gudmund (1956), "Sophoclean Sarcasm (*Antigone* 888 'be in the tomb' or 'put in the tomb')", in: *Studi Italiani di Filologia Classica* 27, 55–58.

Burian, Peter (2010), "Gender and the city: Antigone from Hegel to Butler and Back", in: Euben, J.P./Bassi, Karen (eds.), *When Worlds Elide*, Lanham, MD, 255–299.

Butler, Jane (2000), *Antigone's Claim: Kinship between Life and Death*, New York.

Cairns, Douglas L. (2013), "Introduction. Archaic Thought and Tragic Interpretation", in: Cairns, Douglas L. (ed.), *Tragedy and Archaic Greek Thought*, Swansea, ix–liv.

Cairns, Douglas L. (ed.) (2016), *Sophocles: Antigone*, London.

Campbell, Lewis (1879), *Sophocles. The Plays and Fragments*. Second Edition, Revised, I, Oxford.

Carpanelli, Francesco (2008), "*Antigone*: la negazione dell'*oikos* e i suoi riflessi sull'organizzazione drammaturgica", in: Alonge, Roberto (ed.), *Antigone, volti di un enigma: da Sofocle alle Brigate Rosse*, Bari, 33–57.

Cartabia, Marta/Violante, Luciano (2018), *Giustizia e mito. Con Edipo, Antigone e Creonte*, Bologna.

Carter, David (2012), "*Antigone*", in: Markantonatos, A. (ed.), *Brill's Companion to Sophocles*, Leiden, 111–128.

Cropp, Martin (1997), "Antigone's Final Speech (Sophocles, *Antigone* 891–928)", in: *Greece & Rome* 44, 137–160.

Di Benedetto, Vincenzo (1983), *Sofocle*, Firenze.

Di Benedetto, Vincenzo/Medda, Enrico (2002²), *La tragedia sulla scena. La tragedia greca in quanto spettacolo teatrale*, Torino.

Easterling, Patricia E. (1987), "Women in Tragic Space", in: *Bulletin of the Institute of Classical Studies in London* 34, 15–26.

Edwards, Mark W. (1991), *The Iliad: A Commentary*, Volume V: *Books 17.20*, Cambridge.

Fisher, Roger S. (2014), *Antigone vs. Creon. Sophocles 'Antigone' as a Courtroom Drama*, Toronto.

Foley, Helene (2001), *Female Acts in Greek Tragedy*, Princeton.

Garrison, Elise P. (1989), "Eurydikes' Final Exit to Suicide in the *Antigone*", in: *The Classical World* 82, 431–435.

Greco, Giovanni/Belardinelli, Anna Maria (2010) (eds.), *Antigone e le Antigoni: storia forme fortuna di un mito*. Atti del convegno internazionale, Roma 13, 25–26 maggio 2009, Milan.

Griffith, Mark (1999), *Sophocles: Antigone*, Cambridge.

Griffith, Mark (2001), "Antigone and her Sister(s): Embodying Women in Greek Tragedy", in: Lardinois, André P.M.H./McClure, Laura (eds.), *Making Silence Speak: Women's Voices in Greek Literature and Society*, Princeton, 117–136.

Harris, Edward M. (2004), "Antigone the Lawyer, or the Ambiguities of Nomos", in: Harris, E.M./ Rubinstein, L. (eds.), *The Laws and the Courts in Ancient Greece*, London, 19–56.

Honig, Bonnie (2013), *Antigone, Interrupted*, Cambridge.

Irigaray, Luce (2010), "Between Myth and History: the Tragedy of Antigone", in: Wilmer, Stephen E./Žukauskaité, Audroné (eds.), *Interrogating Antigone in Postmodern Philosophy and Criticism*, Oxford, 192–211.

Jebb, Richard C. (1900³) (ed.), *Sophocles. The Plays and Fragments*, Part III, *The Antigone*, Cambridge.

Johnston, Sarah Iles (2006), "Antigone's Other Choice", in: Patterson, Cynthia B. (ed.), *Antigone's Answer: Essays on Death and Burial, Family and State in Classical Athens* (*Helios* Special Issue 33), 179–186.

Jouanna, Jacques (2007), *Sophocle*, Paris.

Kamerbeek, Jan Coenraad (1978), *The Plays of Sophocles*, Part III, *The Antigone*, Leiden.

Roselli, David Kawalko (2006), "Polinices' Body and his Monument: Class, Social Status, and Funerary Commemoration in Sophocles' *Antigone*", in: Patterson, Cynthia B. (ed.), *Antigone's Answer: Essays on Death and Burial, Family and State in Classical Athens* (*Helios* Special Issue 33), Athens, 135–177.

Knox, Bernard M.W. (1964), *The Heroic Temper: Studies in Sophoclean Tragedy*, Berkeley/Los Angeles.

Liapis, Vayos (2013), "Creon the Labdacid: Political Confrontation and the Doomed Oikos in Sophocles' *Antigone*", in: Cairns, Douglas L. (ed.), *Tragedy and Archaic Greek Thought*, Swansea, 81–118.

Lloyd-Jones, H. (1994), *Sophocles, Antigone, Women of Trachis, Philoctetes, Oedipus at Colonus*, Cambridge Mass./London.

Lloyd-Jones, Hugh/Wilson, Nigel G. (1990) (eds.), *Sophoclis Fabulae*, Oxford.

Löwe, Nick J. (1987), "Tragic Space and Comic Timing in Menander's *Dyskolos*", in: *Bulletin of the Institute of Classical Studies in London* 34, 126–138.

Mastronarde, Donald J. (1979), *Contact and Discontinuity. Some Conventions of Speech and Action on the Greek Tragic Stage*, Berkeley/Los Angeles.

McCall, Marsh (1972), "Divine and Human Action in Sophocles: The Two Burials of the *Antigone*", in: *Yale Classical Studies* 22, 103–117.

Medda, Enrico (2013), *La saggezza dell'illusione. Studi sul teatro greco*, Pisa.

Medda, Enrico (2015), "Uno spazio per morire. Riflessioni sceniche sul suicidio di Aiace", in: Most, Glenn W./Özbek, Leyla (eds.), *Staging Ajax's Suicide*. A Three Day International Conference, Pisa, Scuola Normale Superiore, 7–9 November 2013, Pisa, 159–179.

Montani, Pietro (2017²), *Antigone e la filosofia. Hegel, Kierkegaard, Hölderlin, Heidegger, Bultmann*, Rome.

Mueller, Melissa (2011), "The Politics of Gesture in Sophocles' *Antigone*", in: *Classical Quarterly* 61, 412–425.

Müller, Gerhard (1967), *Sophokles. Antigone*, Heidelberg.

Oudemans, Theodorus C.W./Lardinois, André P.M.H. (1987), *Tragic Ambiguity: Anthropology, Philosophy and Sophocles' Antigone*, Leiden.

Paduano, Guido (2008), "Antigone e la democrazia ateniese", in: Alonge, Roberto (ed.), *Antigone, volti di un enigma: da Sofocle alle Brigate Rosse*, Bari, 3–22.

Parker, Robert (1999), "Through a Glass Darkly: Sophocles and the Divine", in: Griffin, J. (ed.), *Sophocles Revisited.Essays Presented to Sir Hugh Lloyd-Jones*, Oxford, 11–30.

Raeburn, David (2017), *Greek Tragedies as Plays for Performance*, Chichester-Malden MA.

Rehm, Rush (1994), *Marriage to Death: The Conflation of Wedding and Funeral Rituals in Greek Tragedy*, Princeton.

Rehm, Rush (2002), *The Play of Space. Spatial Transformation in Greek Tragedy*, Princeton.

Rehm, Rush (2006), "Sophocles' Antigone and Family Values", in: Patterson, Cynthia B. (ed.), *Antigone's Answer: Essays on Death and Burial, Family and State in Classical Athens*, (*Helios* Special Issue 33), 187–218.

Rosivach, Vincent J. (1983), "On Creon, Antigone and not Burying the Dead", in: *Rheinisches Museum* 126, 192–211.

Schneidewin, Friedrich Wilhelm/Nauck, August (1880), *Sophokles,* Viertes Bændchen, *Antigone*, achte Auflage, Berlin.

Seaford, Richard (1987), "The Tragic Wedding", in: *The Journal of Hellenic Studies* 107, 106–130.

Seale, David (1982), *Vision and Stagecraft in Sophocles*, London.

Segal, Charles (1981), *Tragedy and Civilization. An Interpretation of* Sophocles, Cambridge, MA/ London.

Shapiro, H. Alan (2006), "The Wrath of Creon: Withholding Burial in Homer and Sophocles", in: Patterson, Cynthia B. (ed.), *Antigone's Answer: Essays on Death and Burial, Family and State in Classical Athens* (*Helios* Special Issue 33), 119–134.

Sourvinou-Inwood, Christiane (1989), "Assumptions and the Creation of Meaning: Reading Sophocles' *Antigone*", in: *The Journal of Hellenic Studies* 109, 134–148.

Strauss, Jonathan (2013), *Private Lives, Public Deaths: Antigone and the Invention of Individuality*, New York.

Stuttard, David (ed.) (2018), *Looking at Antigone*, Oxford.

Susanetti, Davide (2012), *Sofocle: Antigone*, Roma.

Taplin, Oliver (1984), "The Place of Antigone", *Omnibus* 7, 13–16.

Torrance, Robert M. (1965), "Sophocles: Some Bearings", *Harvard Studies in Classical Philology* 60, 269–327.

Wiles, David (1997), *Tragedy in Athens. Performance Space and Theatrical Meaning*, Cambridge.

Wilmer, Stephen E./Žukauskaité, Audroné (eds.) (2010), *Interrogating Antigone in Postmodern Philosophy and Criticism*, Oxford.

Winnington-Ingram, Reginald P. (1980), *Sophocles: An Interpretation*, Cambridge.

Zeroch, Sebastian (2015), *Erinys in Epos, Tragödie und Kult. Fluchbegriff und personale Fluchmacht*, Berlin/Boston.

Žižek, Slavoj (2001), *Did Somebody Say Totalitarianism?*, London.

Oliver Taplin

The Inference of Staging from Deictics, with some Pointers towards Sophocles' *Trachiniae*

Abstract: Deictic pronouns, especially the most immediate ὅδε etc., are far more frequent in plays than other poetic forms, because they embody the story rather than narrating it. It is argued that they indicate various possible or probable gestures, movements and stagings. They may be used of vividly envisaged people and events off-stage as well as those directly visible. The employment of deictics in Sophocles' *Trachiniae* is especially complex and interesting. This is because the past is vividly evoked, and because Iole is inside the house and Heracles is still away from home for most of the play. Deictics are also particularly used to speak allusively, and sometimes quite explicitly, of sexual matters, especially Heracles' driving passions. In contrast with the middle scenes, the final part when Heracles has returned uses hardly any deictics. This reflects his lack of emotion or regret over the victims of his monstrous lust, Deianeira and Iole. It is argued that this may bear on whether his ending on the pyre on Oeta is to be regarded as a reward or a punishment for his exploits.

Keywords: *Trachiniae*, deixis, off-stage, sex, monstrosity

The immediate "first person" or "proximal" deictic pronoun, ὅδε etc., had to wait until the invention of Tragedy for its greatest period in Greek narrative poetry. It was the theatre and its physical staging that transmuted its applicability from a narrator's evocation of presence to actual embodied presence.[1] And that, as I hope to show, opened up further dimensions of envisaging, re-enactment, implication, and even innuendo.

Warmest thanks to Piero Totaro, whose enthusiasm and organisational skills made the conference in Bari in May 2019 such an enjoyable reality. I am also indebted to Nancy Felson for helpful deictic advice.

1 For wider surveys of deixis in Greek, see Edmunds 2008, Bonifazi 2013, Felson/Klein 2013. Passmore 2018 is a good contribution, with full bibliography, on the *Odyssey*. On lyric D'Alessio 2008 is something of a classic.

https://doi.org/10.1515/9783111248028-003

At the risk of becoming tediously repetitive, I do not think it can be emphasised too often how great a narrative revolution theatre brought about: it was not a gradual development, it was a quantum leap.[2] There are, of course, important ways in which tragedy grew out of pre-dramatic epic and lyric,[3] but it was the physical enactment that created a vital new art-form, one that would sweep through the Greek world in the next two centuries. So far as we know there was no form of story-telling that was enacted, as opposed to narrated, before the late sixth century BCE. And this story-telling revolution brought with it a whole nexus of tangible innovations which revolutionised both the organisation of the performance and the audience's experience. Most obviously there are the actors and chorus-members who *become* the participant agents, no longer tethered in the world of the ambient occasion, but transported to the time and place of the story. The actors bring to this enterprise deployments of voice and gesture and body-language that go far beyond anything that could be achieved by even the most versatile of rhapsodes. And it is very likely that the physicality of the chorus was also far more expressive that any non-dramatic choral performance. In addition to all this, there is the whole range of resources that were provided by the *skeuopoios*; costumes, portable props, stage furniture, and so forth. Instead of being verbally evoked, however vividly, these are given solid physical substantiation.

Once it is appreciated that spoken deictics make the leap from being solely oral/aural to being physically directed, it is easy to see why ὅδε-deictics occur far more frequently in tragedy than in epic, let alone lyric.[4] The person, parts of their bodies, objects, altars, doors and so forth are all there, visible and tangible, so that they can be directly indicated. And the actors' accompanying gestures would, of course, be appropriately matched. Just one illustration of the kind of difference it would make. At *Iliad* 1.233ff. Achilles takes an oath that he will make Agamemnon regret his behaviour, swearing by the speakers' sceptre — ναὶ μὰ τόδε σκῆπτρον ... (*by this sceptre ...*). At the end of his speech the narrator tells how after these words Achilles threw the *skeptron* to the ground (245–246). A lively rhapsode might well have made a grand gesture of lifting up and dashing down an imaginary *skeptron*. But if this scene were to be dramatised in a tragedy, the actor of Achilles would be holding an actual *skeptron*

---

2 I have tried to convey the ramifications of this realisation in Taplin 2016 on props, Id. 2018 on masks, and Id. 2019 on Aristotle's failure to appreciate this point.

3 Herington 1985 is important (and undervalued) on this subject.

4 D'Alessio 2008, 101–102 makes some calculations and finds such deictics about once in every 70 lines in Pindar and once in every 10 in tragedy (most frequent in Sophocles).

(supplied by the *skeuopoios*), and will then have actually thrown it on the ground, most probably accompanying the action with words. Something like this can be seen when Cassandra throws off her prophetic paraphernalia at Aeschylus' *Agamemnon* 1264ff., employing deictics as she does so: τάδε καὶ σκῆπτρα καὶ μαντεῖα περὶ δέρηι στέφ ... τοῖσδε κόσμοις (... *this staff and ribbons round my neck ... this prophet's rigmarole.*)[5]

Some initial idea of the range of uses for ὅδε-deictics in tragedy may be gauged by looking at three passages in Sophocles' *Oedipus Tyrannos* before turning to *Trachiniae* for more detail. The great majority of the material uses of ὅδε in pre-dramatic poetry refer to people or things that are present — *ad oculos*[6] — in the here and now of the narrative. This is the case whether used by the narrator, or, as more often, a character in direct speech within the narrative. It is hardly surprising, then, that the same is true in the entirely direct-speech genre of Tragedy. What is more, because of the embodiment of the performance, this can be all the more effectively deployed. The kind of extra dynamic that can be reinforced by direct physicality may be seen in the passage in *Oedipus Tyrannos* where Oedipus is recalling how he killed a man — in fact his father Laius, of course — at the place where three tracks meet. At lines 810–812 he tells how he struck the old man:

συντόμως
σκήπτρῳ τυπεὶς ἐκ τῆσδε χειρὸς ὕπτιος
μέσης ἀπήνης εὐθὺς ἐκκυλίνδεται·
κτείνω δὲ τοὺς ξύμπαντας.

I struck him sharply with my stick; and knocked down by this hand of mine, he toppled headlong from the wagon. I kill them, every man.

In this vivid recollection (with the historic present verb κτείνω) there can be little doubt that the verbal deictic ἐκ τῆσδε χειρός would be expressed in action — translated from page to stage. At the moment of re-enactment Oedipus raises this very hand with which he struck back then. It is further likely, though not provable, that Oedipus holds up his *skeptron*,[7] symbol of the royal power which he has in a sense obtained through the violent prior use of his crude traveller's *skeptron* on the road.

---

5 All translations are my own. They occasionally differ from my published versions in order to bring out the particular points being made here.
6 His terminology and the distinction from "deixis am Phantasma" goes back to the landmark study of Bühler 1934.
7 Tragedy-related iconography almost invariably shows kings with a regal *skeptron*.

So-called "deixis am Phantasma", in distinction from "*ad oculos*", means the vivid conjuring of something that is not physically present but vividly present in the mind. There is relatively weak form of this that is known as "anaphoric", when the deictic simply resumes the reference to something that has been recently talked about or narrated. In drama, however, the physicality of the person speaking can add an extra degree of significance, often giving the deictic more than a textual reference, and calling for enacted expression on the stage. There is a good example a little earlier in the same speech of Oedipus in *OT*. At 798–804 he is telling his wife what happened after he left the Delphic oracle and set off in a direction away from Corinth. He recalls how he then encountered a man fitting the description of Laius at the specific place in the region of Phocis where three tracks meet, as mentioned by Jocasta:

στείχων δ' ἱκνοῦμαι τούσδε τοὺς χώρους ἐν οἷς
σὺ τὸν τύραννον τοῦτον ὄλλυσθαι λέγεις.[8]

And as I journey on, my path comes to that region where you say this king of yours was killed.

This is closely followed by another deictic signpost specifying τριπλῆς... κελεύθου τῆσδε ("this three-road place"). These may be classified as 'anaphoric' in that they refer back to a previously highlighted locality,[9] but there is more than that going on here. It is indicated again by the historic present verb (ἱκνοῦμαι) that there is an immediacy indicating that Oedipus is in effect re-living the events. He sees this place in front of him, and then this splitting of the ways. We can never know, of course, precisely how this was acted out on the Sophoclean stage, but it is most unlikely that there was no motion or gesture to reinforce these words. It may be that Oedipus took some steps as though approaching the spot; and it may be that he conveyed the junction by a forking gesture with his hands. The deictics must be treated as indications towards staging rather than precise instructions: the point is that the crucial event is not only being verbally narrated but also re-lived.

Occasionally there is a cluster of deictics that would be impossibly confusing in a narrative text, but with some staged clarification in terms of space and time they can be lifted off the page to make sense of them. Take, for example,

---

8 While οὗτος is sometimes indistinguishable in usage from ὅδε, there are other places where, as here, it is clearly more distanced — "this king of yours". This is well discussed by Ruijgh 2006; there are further examples below, especially on p. 37.

9 As duly noted by Finglass 2019 *ad loc.*

Iocasta's jubilant response at *OT* 946–949 when she has just learned that Polybus is dead:

> ... τοῦτον Οἰδίπους πάλαι τρέμων
> τὸν ἄνδρ᾽ ἔφευγε μὴ κτάνοι· καὶ νῦν ὅδε
> πρὸς τῆς τύχης ὄλωλεν οὐδὲ τοῦδ᾽ ὕπο.

For ages Oedipus has steered clear of that man for fear that he would kill him: and yet now this one has died by random chance, and not by this man's hand at all.

This man whom Oedipus so feared was τοῦτον, but now, with the immediacy of the news, he becomes ὅδε, which might well be accompanied by a gesture suggesting the corpse lying in front of her. And ὅδε has died, but not τοῦδ᾽ ὕπο, indicating the man immediately present in the house, who does actually emerge at that moment.

***

Trachiniae has been, I believe, relatively undervalued, although I would not be surprised if its concern with gender issues brings it fresh attention in the near future. It is also a play which is particularly rich in its use of deictic pronouns across the range of ὅδε, οὗτος, and ἐκεῖνος. This is no coincidence, since there is much that, instead of being directly shown, is conjured up or hinted at by the kind of gestural indications that these deictics imply.

There are at least four good reasons for this tendency. One is the central and unusual way that *Trachiniae* encompasses both the world of primal monsters — river gods, centaurs, the creatures that Heracles overcomes in his labours — and the world of family and domesticity, the here and now of Deianeira in Trachis, a household with all the security and anxiety of domestic life.[10] *Trachiniae* brings together these two worlds that prove incompatible, and which ultimately combine together to destroy each other. It is notable — though it has not perhaps been sufficiently noted — that Greek Tragedy, unlike many other performative traditions, hardly ever presents the monstrous as directly visible on stage — next to no dragons, giants, prodigies, fabulous beasts.[11] The only time such an phenomenon is brought on stage in *Trachiniae* is in the scene of Heracles suffering agonies from the poisoned robe. The monstrous is, however, much evoked

---

10 Kitzinger 2012 provides a good, brief account of the interpretation of the play, with (anglophone) bibliography.
11 The most obvious exception is the Erinyes in Aeschylus' *Eumenides*. Another was Pegasus in Euripides' *Bellerophon* and *Andromeda*. The only surviving play to present a varied sequence of the weird or monstrous is *Prometheus*.

through recollection, especially of Heracles' battle with Achelous, and the lust and death of Nessus.

Secondly, *Trachiniae* to an unusual extent (though by no means uniquely so) revolves around the reconstruction of past events. This calls for the kind of vivid evocation that exploits deictic immediacy, as has already been seen in the examples from *Oedipus*. Third, things that go on inside the house are extremely important in this play.[12] The use of deictics to refer to these makes the wall of the building have some permeability: the interior scenes are made into a kind of "here", as though almost visible. In particular the indoor presence of Iole after she has gone in at 334 is repeatedly and suggestively important. Inside the house there is also the matrimonial bed in the *thalamos*, the threatened territory where Deianeira kills herself.

This leads on to a fourth reason why deictics are so tellingly exploited in *Trachiniae*: their usefulness for a play where there is an unusual quantity — and quality — of allusion to sex and to the physical intercourse of male with female. Greek tragedy is seldom physiologically explicit about sex. Yet the physical act can still be brought to the foreground through euphemism or innuendo. There are conspicuous examples of this in the speech (531ff.) where Deianeira recognises the sexual rivalry that Iole threatens her with. She now sees, with a mildly obscene application of a standard marital metaphor, that Iole is κόρην ... οὐκέτ᾽, ἀλλ᾽ ἐζευγμένην (536: *and yet no more a simple girl, I think: a fully harnessed woman*). And so she foresees that in future Heracles will be nominally her πόσις, but in reality he will be τῆς νεωτέρας δ᾽ ἀνήρ (551: *in name my husband, ... the younger woman's male*).[13] There are two word-groups that are most used of sex, both of which tend to gather deictic insinuations, and are more than usually explicit in *Trachiniae*. One is γάμος / γαμεῖν, often much more specifically physical than is conveyed by the standard gloss of "marriage/marry" (let alone "wedding"). Secondly there is the wide range of periphrases that have to do with terms for the bed. Thus, for example, when the old Trachinian tells how Heracles had tried to get Iole as his κρύφιον...λέχος (360: *his secret bed*), that means, of course, as his secret bedfellow.

Within minutes of the start of the play we are faced with the first use of the proximal deictic to bring an experience of the past vividly into the present; it is moreover one laden with sexual innuendo. Deianeira tells how, when she was still an adolescent back in Pleuron, the river-god of Achelous came as a suitor for her hand, taking various frighteningly strange forms. Then in 15–17:

---

12 See Di Benedetto/Medda 2002, 49–69 on the general importance of "spazio retroscenico".

13 For a similar, even coarser, use of ἀνήρ, see the Nurse at Eur. *Hipp.* 491.

τοιόνδ' ἐγὼ μνηστῆρα προσδεδεγμένη
δύστηνος ἀεὶ κατθανεῖν ἐπηυχόμην,
πρὶν τῆσδε κοίτης ἐμπελασθῆναί ποτε.

Confronted with a bridegroom such as this, I prayed and prayed that I might die before he ever could climb on this bed of his.

This bed is τῆσδε, not, as might have been expected, ἐκείνης or τοιαύτης: the horror has stayed with her so vividly that it is as though she sees that repulsive couch in front of her. We cannot know what gesture accompanied this τῆσδε, but it is likely to have been some sort of two-handed suggestion of laying out a bed. Achelous had taken on various repulsive forms including a bull, so ἐμπελασθῆναί along with the deictic gesture is sexually more suggestive and graphic that merely "approach" (more like the innuendo of the English "mount", which is used of animals).

Instead of that prospect, Deianeira was awarded to the λέχος (27) of Heracles, a happy conclusion — εἰ δὴ καλῶς ("if happily it was"), as she presciently adds. Heracles did not fight Achelous out of high-minded chivalry: he wanted the young beauty for himself in his bed. One of the things that gives this play its power is the way that it does not mitigate the voraciousness of Heracles' sexual appetite, the bridge between his life with monsters and his domestic family life. It is so effective that Deianeira feels an instinctive affinity with Iole, before she knows who she is, because they are both, in fact, the sexual prize that Heracles has won through his violent exploits. A deictic euphemism hints at Deianiera's intuition that sexual experience is central to Iole's condition. This comes out in the very first words that she addresses to the as yet anonymous slave-girl (305–307):

ὦ δυστάλαινα, τίς ποτ' εἶ νεανίδων;
ἄνανδρος, ἢ τεκνοῦσσα; πρὸς μὲν γὰρ φύσιν
πάντων ἄπειρος τῶνδε, γενναία δέ τις.

Poor creature, who are you among these girls? Unmarried? or have you a child? Your manner seems to say you're not experienced in all these things — and that you are of noble birth.

Not "all that sort of thing", but "all these things", the inextricable experience of sex and family that means so much to her. And Heracles himself is, of course, the man who has already introduced Iole to "all this".

Iole is taken inside at 331, and is never seen on stage again.[14] There remains, though, a nagging awareness of her being just inside the house, just as there is a constant awareness of the imminence of the returning Heracles. The most frequent and most powerful uses of deictics in *Trachiniae* occur throughout the central section of some 400 lines between the exit of Iole and the return of Hyllus (at 734) with news of his father's fatal donning of the poisoned robe. The pronouns are employed to lay out the "triangle" of destructive forces that tie together Deianiera, Iole and Heracles. Deianeira is on stage throughout, except for the two brief but crucial times that she goes indoors, which are bridged by choral odes (498–530, 633–62). She interacts with Lichas, the Old Trachinian[15] and the women confidantes of the chorus; and constantly there are references to Iole inside, actually named only twice, and to Heracles who is on Euboea.

Heracles is almost invariably referred to by all speakers with (ἐ)κεῖνος. He has been away for over a year, his location is unfamiliar, his behaviour is grand and somewhat remote. So he is assigned the "third-person deictic", whether the speaker is the old man (353) or Lichas (479, 485, 488) or Deianeira herself (449, 495, 544, 603, 605, 608, 614, 719). This "distancing" is dropped in only one highly charged passage, when Deianeira recognises — too late — that the death-blood of the centaur Nessus cannot possibly have been a benevolent gift to her. There is a complex combination of deictics (not unlike that at *OT* 946–949, discussed on p. 33 above). The Hydra's poison, which was blended with his oozing blood, kills every creature (716–718):

ἐκ δὲ τοῦδ' ὅδε
σφαγῶν διελθὼν ἰὸς αἵματος μέλας
πῶς οὐκ ὀλεῖ καὶ τόνδε;

So, this dark poison welling from this one is bound to kill this man as well — is that not so?

Since this poison, ὅδε ... ἰός, which she recently smeared on the robe with her own hands, came out of this creature, ἐκ ... τοῦδε — distant in time and place yet so vividly recalled as to be re-embodied — how could it not kill καὶ τόνδε?

---

14 The identity of the person addressed in the instruction in 1275 at the end of the play — λείπου μηδὲ σύ, παρθέν', ἐπ' οἴκων ("You as well, young woman, do not stay behind at home") — is baffling. It might make good sense if this were addressed to Iole, telling her to participate in the final procession, but in the text as we have it there is nowhere she might be re-introduced on stage.
15 This character is conventionally called the *angelos*/Messenger, but he is more individualised and interventionist than that label suggests.

This τόνδε is the man who has been so consistently kept at mental bay by use of κεῖνος, but who now comes irresistibly close in her thoughts. Made vivid no doubt by some kind of gestural sign, her husband is virtually there in front of her.

The deictic indications pointing to Iole inside the house are completely different. She is always invoked with either ἥδε or αὕτη, never ἐκείνη. Whether the first-person or second-person pronoun is used is partly dependant on context, but more on who is speaking. Thus, the old Trachinian, who exposes Lichas' duplicity, almost invariably uses ταύτην/ταύτης (353, 362, 419, 428, 431). For all his lively, at times impertinent, manner, he is not close enough to Iole to use the more familiar τήνδε.[16] In the one exception,[17] which turns out to be the last line that he contributes, he insists that he heard Lichas say that it was Heracles' desire for Iole that destroyed her city, κοὐχ ἡ Λυδία / πέρσειεν αὐτήν, ἀλλ' ὁ τῆσδ' ἔρως φανείς (432–433: "it was not the Lydian queen who brought it down in ruin, but his intense desire for her, this girl"). His emphasis on Heracles' flagrant desire leads him to use the more direct, almost possessive, deictic pronoun τῆσδε.

The situation is different with Lichas, who has some responsibility for Iole's arrival in Trachis. At first, he refers with deictics to the whole group of slave women (244, 283), and it is only much later, after Deianeira's great plea for honesty, claiming to be complaisant about Heracles' amours, that he finally talks of Iole in a direct personal way. He admits (476–478) that it is true that ταύτης ὁ δεινὸς ἵμερός ("a fearsome passion for this woman") has thrilled through Heracles, and that it is τῆσδ' οὕνεκα ("for this one's sake") that he sacked the city of Oechalia. He pleads with Deianeira to treat Iole well, and to make good her tolerant words, concluding (488–489):

> ὡς τἄλλ' ἐκεῖνος πάντ' ἀριστεύων χεροῖν
> τοῦ τῆσδ' ἔρωτος εἰς ἅπανθ' ἥσσων ἔφυ.

> You see, that man who has exerted supreme power in everything has been completely conquered by his passion for this girl.

The trouble is that by being so frank about Heracles' ἵμερός and ἔρως, he twists the knife in Deianeira's wound, and pushes her, despite all her protestations of being "sensible", towards employing dark arts to keep Heracles' sexual desire for herself.

---

16 This is in keeping with the general argument of Ruijgh 2006.
17 The τῆσδε in 364 is simply anaphoric.

Deianeira's shifting emotions — between affinity and jealousy for Iole, desire and distaste for Heracles, between abandon and control towards human
sexuality — are a leading feature of the appeal of *Trachiniae*, for modern tastes
at least. She never names Iole, but the varying ways in which she refers to her,
and the four times that she uses the proximal deictic ἥδε, convey on the stage
much more than the words on the page.

When she learns the truth about Iole from the old Trachinian, that she is no
mere slave because Heracles ἐντεθέρμανται πόθῳ (368: "he's molten with desire"), her first response is to be lost in dismay (375ff.). Even when she first confronts Lichas, she simply asks τίς ἡ γυνὴ δῆτ' ἐστὶν ἣν ἥκεις ἄγων; (400: "Well
then, who is the woman that you brought?"); there is no gesture towards her
physical closeness yet. The old man takes over the interrogation, and it is only
when Lichas turns and appeals to her that Deianeira delivers her extraordinary
speech at 436–469. In this she makes the case in defence of Heracles' desire and
the consequential conclusion that she should accept Iole in her house. She
reasons that Eros is an irresistible power (445–448):

ὥστ' εἴ τι τώμῷ γ' ἀνδρὶ τῇδε τῇ νόσῳ
ληφθέντι μεμπτός εἰμι, κάρτα μαίνομαι,
ἢ τῇδε τῇ γυναικί, τῇ μεταιτίᾳ
τοῦ μηδὲν αἰσχροῦ μηδ' ἐμοὶ κακοῦ τινος.

So, if I were to hold my husband as to blame for having caught this fever, I'd be mad. And
I can't blame this woman, who bears no guilt for something shameful, nor for any malice
aimed at me.

If Heracles is afflicted τῇδε τῇ νόσῳ, this irresistible passion, then she should
not blame τῇδε τῇ γυναικί: at this moment the woman indoors becomes so vivid
to her that she gestures to her presence just the other side of the house-wall. She
goes on to admit that she knows well that Heracles has had sex with many
women,[18] and, since she has not resented them, she should not hold out against
this one either (462–465):

ἥδε τ' οὐδ' ἂν εἰ
κάρτ' ἐντακείη τῷ φιλεῖν, ἐπεί σφ' ἐγὼ
ᾤκτιρα δὴ μάλιστα προσβλέψασ', ὅτι
τὸ κάλλος αὐτῆς τὸν βίον διώλεσεν...

---

18 The verb ἔγημε in 460 is almost crudely physical, and carries no implication of marital
sanction.

Nor shall this one, not even if he's utterly consumed in his desire for her. I felt a special pang of pity for her on first sight, because her beauty has undone her life...

Despite the proximity gestured towards Iole by ἥδε, and despite her fellow-feeling, the heat of the expression κάρτ' ἐντακείη τῷ φιλεῖν[19] gives away that she is not totally convinced by her own argument. And the self-contradiction of her experience is then aggravated by the strong language of desire that Lichas expresses in the following lines at 488–489, quoted above on p. 37.

It is a mistake, I would maintain, to regard this speech as either true or false, sincere or duplicitous. There is no hint at all in the text that Deianeira is being deliberately deceitful: rather she is trying to persuade herself that she should adopt the worldly male attitude to their sexual appetites. The hints that she is not completely carried along by her own arguments prepare the way for her very different stance in the following scene at 531ff. It is only after she has been indoors that she fully recognises that this new sexual rival, far from being some passing amour or secret mistress, will be there sharing her household space. And that encompasses the connubial bed. Iole has been smuggled inside like some illicit cargo, καὶ νῦν δύ' οὖσαι μίμνομεν μιᾶς ὑπὸ / χλαίνης ὑπαγκάλισμα (539–540: "And now the two of us shall lie beneath a single coverlet, and wait to see which one he will embrace"). Deianeira cannot feel angry with him νοσοῦντι κείνῳ πολλὰ τῇδε τῇ νόσῳ ("when he is afflicted with this raging fever"), but she asks (546–547)

τὸ δ' αὖ ξυνοικεῖν τῇδ' ὁμοῦ τίς ἂν γυνὴ
δύναιτο, κοινωνοῦσα τῶν αὐτῶν γάμων;

yet what woman could bear living with this one here, and share in one man's making love?

This locates the τῇδε specifically in the bedroom. As Pat Easterling rather coyly puts it, "there is no need to limit her reaction to a concern for status": γάμων is, as often, much more physically explicit.

When she has told the chorus about Nessus — his lust, his dying gift to her, and its application to the robe she is going to send to Heracles — there is one last deictic allusion to the young woman inside her house. Deianeira says that she has no desire for using doubtful means, but... (584–586):

---

[19] This surely refers to Heracles' passion, not to Iole, as both Jebb 1892 and Easterling 1982 *ad loc.* claim to be more "natural". It is his lust that is the driving force throughout the play. The same applies to 444 (if genuine): it is Heracles' sex-drive that matters, not that of the female.

φίλτροις δ' ἐάν πως τήνδ' ὑπερβαλώμεθα
τὴν παῖδα καὶ θέλκτροισι τοῖς ἐφ' Ἡρακλεῖ,
μεμηχάνηται τοὔργον....

> but if I can in some way make this potion work on Heracles with charms that will outbid
> this girl, well then, the process has been set....

τήνδε...τὴν παῖδα here is not merely anaphoric, it conjures up the rival and her sexuality. At the same time, it may be that by using παῖδα, instead of the usual γυναῖκα, a hope is suggested that Iole is still, though not a virgin, an inexperienced παῖς, as Deianeira was herself when she first obtained the gift from Nessus (557). After this she will refer to Iole only one more time. When she tells Lichas to report to Heracles how tolerantly she had spoken about her, she carefully tones down her reference with the phrase τὰ τῆς ξένης.../ προσδέγματ' (627–628: "the way the stranger-woman was received"). Once she has heard from Hyllus of the terrible workings of the impregnated cloak on Heracles, Deianeira departs without a word (after 812). It is left for the sympathetic women of the chorus to draw out her motivation in the following choral lyric. They explain how she did not realise the fatal deceit of the Centaur, when faced by the threat of Iole's arrival, (842–844), μεγάλαν προσορῶσα δόμοισι / βλάβαν νέων ἀίσσου- / σαν γάμων κτλ. ("since she foresaw great harm / from his newly-made union / bearing down on her home"). It is not a new marriage that she so dreads, it is the novel prospect of the shared coverlet, the question of which of the two women Heracles shall choose from night to night. And in the closing stanza they sing of how Heracles' sacking of Oechalia has brought a θοὰν νύμφαν (857: "hasty bride"). But Iole is a νύμφη in a sexual rather than a legal or institutional sense: the women of the chorus do not shirk the carnality of Heracles' conquests.

This is even more luridly and strangely expressed when the old Nurse first breaks the news to them that Deianeira has killed herself. They respond in lyric dialogue and sing (893–895):

ἔτεκ' ἔτεκε μεγάλαν
ἁ νέορτος ἅδε νύμφα
δόμοισι τοῖσδ' Ἐρινύν.

> Just born, just born within this house, / this newly-wed has spawned / a mighty Erinys.

The vivid deictic ἅδε here was most probably accompanied by some sort of choreographic indication towards the house, so that they do not need to explain who they are referring to. They conjure a metaphor that is more macabre than has been generally recognised: when Iole was admitted into the house she was, they suggest, newly pregnant; and her progeny has turned out to be, not human, but an Erinys. Rather like the simile of the ship's captain who unwittingly takes on board a cargo (Deianeira at 537–538), Iole has smuggled the Erinys into the house in her womb.

★★★

The whole character of the final 300 lines of the play, after Heracles has arrived in all his agony, is utterly different. He displays no sign of personal affection or sorrow; he does not use deictics to bring anyone or anything absent vividly to mind; he shows no awareness of the house itself, which has been so important for the rest of the play. He never alludes to the fact that Deianeira is lying dead on the matrimonial bed just indoors, nor that his new conquest Iole is also in there. Indeed, the one and only reference to the house[20] with its private, domestic interior is made by Hyllus when he refers laconically to his mother's premonition of τοὺς ἔνδον γάμους (1139), a phrase that will be discussed below. The contrast with the portrayal of Deianeira, her varied emotions, her vivid evocations, her hopes and fears, could hardly be more extreme. The sensibilities of the two never meet.

In this final scene Heracles pays scarcely any attention to Deianeira, once he has found out that she is dead and he cannot kill her himself. He expresses no grief or regret, and he makes no allusion to the way that his lust for Iole has triggered the whole disastrous sequence of events. It falls entirely to Hyllus to make the connection, and to bring out that the true cause of what has happened was sexual. Despite Heracles' vengeful fury, Hyllus stands up in defence of his mother, and insists on explaining how it was through a mistaken but well-meaning motive that she sent the poisoned robe to Heracles (1138–1139):

στέργημα γὰρ δοκοῦσα προσβαλεῖν σέθεν
ἀπήμπλαχ᾽, ὡς προσεῖδε τοὺς ἔνδον γάμους.

Mistakenly she thought she had a love-charm over you, once she had seen your marriage-match indoors.

As Pat Easterling says *ad loc.* this is "a euphemistically vague reference to Iole", but γάμους is, I suggest, also physically explicit. What Deianeira foresaw inside her house was not just a "marriage", but the woman she would have to share

---

20 As already observed in n. 14 above, the reference of λείπου μηδὲ σύ, παρθέν᾽, ἐπ᾽ οἴκων (1275) in the final anapaests remains obscure.

the bed with — to put it bluntly, the prospect of Heracles and Iole having sex in her *thalamos*.[21]

Heracles does not show any personal feelings towards Iole either. This aspect of his portrayal has become increasingly alienating in recent times. His concern is not one of feeling, but of possession: he is determined that no other man should have contact with her body except for his son Hyllus. In pressing this unwelcome legacy on Hyllus he does use deictic pronouns and he alludes to his own intercourse with her, but both with a certain distance, coldness even. "Once I am dead", he commands, ταύτην... προσθοῦ δάμαρτα (*take that woman as your wife*), and (1225–1227):

> μηδ' ἄλλος ἀνδρῶν τοῖς ἐμοῖς πλευροῖς ὁμοῦ
> κλιθεῖσαν αὐτὴν ἀντὶ σοῦ λάβῃ ποτέ,
> ἀλλ' αὐτός, ὦ παῖ, τοῦτο κήδευσον λέχος.

> Do not let any other man but you possess her who has lain with me, her body pressed to mine. Reserve that bed of marriage for yourself, my son.

The language of "lying by my side" may be about as explicit as the generic decorum of tragedy normally admits, but τοῦτο κήδευσον λέχος has an unemotional impersonality about it in keeping with his distanced use of αὐτὴν instead of some warmer noun. The contrast with the vivid, emotion-laden language used by Deianeira is extreme. Heracles' making Hyllus marry Iole may, on one level, be explained by the pressure of dynastic myth, but does that require his expression of it to be so heartless?

It is worth considering, finally, whether the division of the play, which is marked by the contrasting use and absence of vivid and emotive deictics, may have some bearing on the much-discussed question of the significance of the pyre on Mount Oeta.[22] Has Zeus abandoned his far-from-perfect son to an appropriately grim death, a punishment even? Or does the name of Oeta cast a golden glow from beyond the conclusion, a reward and vindication for all his mighty deeds? Is it beyond question that Heracles' apotheosis and blissful immortality on Olympus outweighs, and even negates, all the human suffering? Or might his agonising death be a kind of corollary of his violent and libidinous life?

---

21 I even wonder if one letter might have got lost in transmission, and Sophocles might have had Hyllus make the prospect more vivid and more bitter by saying ὡς προσεῖδε τοὺσδ' ἔνδον γάμους — "once she had seen this marriage-match indoors".

22 See, for example, Easterling 1982, 9–12, 16–19; Holt 1989; Kitzinger 2012, 119–123.

A modern sensibility may tend to feel that Heracles' total lack of any feeling for Deianeira and for Iole should condemn him in the eyes of the audience. But this interpretation must face the objection that it is anachronistic, betraying present-day attitudes to gender in our age of "#MeToo". A defence of Heracles would counterclaim that this son of Zeus is no ordinary mortal, and he should not be judged by ordinary human standards. He is fuelled by more-than-human passions; and he makes no pretence to be super-virtuous as well. Whatever the colouring given to the ending of the play by the pyre on Oeta, Heracles is presented as, for all his flaws, indisputably the greatest human who has ever lived by the traditional measures of heroic greatness.

I do not believe, however, that this exoneration by appeal to "heroic" criteria is the end of the matter. As has been seen, Sophocles presents a keen stage-awareness of the division and incompatibility between the world of Heracles' labours and the world of Deianeira's house. The use of deictics to indicate the exposure of sexual tensions has played a part in this. It was Heracles' inordinate sex-drive that drew Deianeira into his bed, and that then destroyed an entire city in order to get Iole into his bed as well. So, it is poetic justice that it is the monstrous lust of the centaur Nessus which in the end kills him.

The prospect of Heracles' immortality (left less than certain) does not *redeem* his terrible end in the poisoned robe, the robe which was, ironically, meant to be aphrodisiac. Nor does it do anything to lighten or excuse the sufferings of the women whose lives have been dragged down by his sexual voracity. A more comfortable ending would have made this a less great play.

Bibliography

Bonifazi, Anna (2013), "Deixis", in: Giannakis, Georgios *et al.* (ed.), *Encyclopedia of Ancient Greek Language and Linguistics*. Vol. I, Leiden, 422–429.
Bühler, Karl (1934), *Sprachtheorie: Die Darstellungsfunktion der Sprache*, Jena.
D'Alessio, Giovan Battista (2008), "Alcune considerazioni sull'uso della deissi nei testi lirici e teatrali", in: Perusino, Franca/Colantonio, Maria (eds.), *Dalla lirica corale alla poesia drammatica*, Pisa, 95–128.
Di Benedetto, Vincenzo/Medda, Enrico (2002²), *La tragedia sulla scena*, Torino.
Easterling, Pat (1982) (ed.), *Sophocles. Trachiniae*, Cambridge.
Edmunds, Lowell (2008), "Deixis in Ancient Greek and Latin Literature: Historical Introduction and State of the Question", in: *Philologia Antiqua* 1, 67–98.
Felson, Nancy/Klein, Jared (2013), "Deixis in linguistics and poetics", in: Giannakis, Georgios *et al.* (ed.), *Encyclopedia of Ancient Greek Language and Linguistics*. Vol. I, Leiden, 429–433.
Finglass, Patrick J. (2019) (ed.), *Sophocles. Oedipus the King*, Cambridge.

Herington, John (1985), *Poetry into Drama*, Berkeley.

Holt, Philip (1989), "The End of *Trachiniae* and the Fate of Heracles", in: *Journal of Hellenic Studies* 109, 69–80.

Jebb, Richard (1892) (ed.), *Sophocles. The Trachiniae*, Cambridge.

Kitzinger, Margaret R. (2012), "The Divided Worlds of Sophocles' *Women of Trachis*", in: Ormand, Kirk (ed.), *A Companion to Sophocles*, Maldon, MA, 111–125.

Passmore, Oliver (2018), "From κεῖνος to ὅδε: deixis and identity in the *Odyssey*", in: *Cambridge Classical Journal* 64, 139–165.

Ruijgh, Cornelis J. (2006), "The use of the demonstratives ὅδε, οὗτος and (ἐ)κεῖνος in Sophocles", in: De Jong, Irene/Rijksbaron, Albert (eds.), *Sophocles and the Greek Language*, Leiden, 151–161.

Taplin, Oliver (2016), "Aeschylus 'Father of Stage-objects'", in: Coppola, Alessandra/Barone, Caterina/Salvadori, Monica (eds.), *Gli oggetti sulla scena teatrale ateniese*, Padova, 155–164.

Taplin, Oliver (2018), "The Tragic Mask and the Invention of Theatre", in: *Scienze dell'Antichità* 24.3, 1–9.

Taplin, Oliver (2019), "Aristotle *Poetics* and *skenikoi agones*", in: Damon, Cynthia/Pieper, Christoph (eds.), *Eris vs. Aemulatio. Valuing Competition in Classical Antiquity*, Leiden, 141–151.

Martin Revermann
Divinity on the Classical Greek Stage: Proposing a New Model

Abstract: What does the theatre *do* to divinity? By giving dynamic embodiment to gods the stage personalizes, localizes, emotionalizes, intensifies and, last but not least, creates discursive agents with whom other characters can interact. The kind of religious experience thus created is in no way derivative, as a 'Platonic model' would have it, but a 'first-order' experience, on par with (for instance) praying, sacrificing or taking part in a cultic procession. To describe these dynamics I use the analogy of the prism which generates spectral colours from seemingly monochromatic light. The model is therefore called 'Newtonian'. This approach not only leads to nuanced detailed analyses of deities in particular plays but also has significant broader implications for the relationship between theatre and religion.

Keywords: gods, Greek religion, Greek theatre, representation, religious experience

My lead question is as simple to articulate as it is complex to answer: what does the stage *do* to divinity? What exactly happens when a god or goddess, who exists, somehow, in the collective imagination, becomes a character on a stage, embodied by a human actor? By stark contrast with the topic of relations (the relation between myth and theatre, for instance, or between myth and ritual etc.), such questions about transitions and framing do not seem to be asked very often, at least not in particularly concrete terms. But the issue of the transformative power of theatre relative to people's religious imaginary is without doubt an important one, and I hope that even my brief and preliminary exploration in the present context will demonstrate some of its significance for a better understanding of the Greek theatre and the Greek religious imaginary alike.

Gods "in the flesh"

Embodiment is perhaps the first item that comes to mind when thinking about what the medium theatre does to divinity. It is an embodiment in the fullest, most corporeal sense: not a cult statue or a vase painting but a living, breathing

https://doi.org/10.1515/9783111248028-004

human adult male who appears on stage wearing a mask made of stiffened linen. The transition of the god or goddess from an imaginary or quite crudely material existence to a male living body acts as an equalizer of sorts in the sense that the god embodied by the male actor is now, like everybody else on stage, subject to the constraints of human physicality and physiology.

The fact that the Greek theatre tradition was able to embody the divine at all is remarkable in and of itself, also bearing in mind much more restrictive artistic practices in other religious systems (the Judaeo-Christian ones, for instance). Equally worth noting is the manner of this embodiment. While, to choose an illustrious example, Pheidias' chryselephantine seated Athena-turned-statue in the Athenian Parthenon articulated her divinity in part by sheer monumental size (Pausanias 1.24.5–7), there is no reason to hypothesize comparable strategies for any god-turned-character in Greek theatre art. The somewhat infamous high boot (*kothornos*) which was the subject of much discussion and speculation until the early 20th century has long been dismissed altogether as an entity that could be encountered on the Greek classical stage of the 5th and 4th centuries BCE. More importantly for the topic at hand, there is no evidence to suggest that this high boot, when it did start being used, ever functioned to set divinity apart from other stage characters (it is, on the contrary, associated with all characters in one particular *genre*, namely tragedy).[1]

Nor do extant theatre-related vases suggest a conspicuously different theatricality of the divine more generally. On the contrary: comedy-related vase paintings in particular, of both Athenian and Western Greek provenance, show full visual appropriation alongside the genre's distinct visual features for all characters, including divinity. And even if such vase evidence — an embodied divinity of unusually great size on a vase which appears to be inspired by tragedy, for example — were to present itself, the well-known and much-discussed methodological issues with inferring theatrical matters from theatre-related vase paintings, especially those related to tragedy, would hit with full force.

There is no textual or visual evidence to suggest that divine on-stage characters moved differently, spoke differently or used a different gestural language from human ones, while costume and props like a crown for a comic Zeus or a distinct cap (*petasos*) for Hermes were certainly deployed as distinct identifiers in the same way that a Heracles is identified by the club and the lionskin.[2] Not

---

1 A detailed discussion of the issue can be found in Pickard-Cambridge 1988, 205–208.
2 The Heracles figure on a (lost) Apulian bell crater (formerly Berlin Staatliche Museen F3046, 375 to 350 BCE, cf. Csapo/Wilson 2020, 416) or a Paestan bell crater (Rome, Vatican U 19 [inv.

even the upper spatial register can plausibly be argued to be the preserve of divinity: as has been realized for some time, both divine and human characters appear from high or on high, regardless of whether this might involve the crane or not.[3]

Material theatre and on-stage embodiment, then, appear to do nothing to divinity by way of overt and clearly marked differentiation. If anything, they combine to serve as an equalizer, bringing 'them' down to 'us' and making the gods 'relatable' by fully integrating them within the genre-specific performance matrix (including the comic matrix in the form of divinities that have been fully co-opted into the genre, like a comic Dionysus or Hermes). In fact, the most forceful differentiator may be the *absence* of embodiment altogether. The tragic Zeus appears to be an important case in point here. The possibility (not more than that) of an on-stage appearance in Aeschylus' *Psychostasia* or Euripides' *Alcmênê* set aside, there is currently no evidence for an embodied Zeus on the Greek tragic stage, although he is likely to have appeared regularly in comedies of the 'mythological burlesque' type and, perhaps, in some satyr plays.[4] A special case, to be sure, is the Jewish-Hellenistic *Exagôgê* by Ezechiel where the epiphany of the divine as a burning bush that talks (see esp. *Exagôgê* 92–99) replicates the biblical model narrative under stage conditions. And Zeus does have a central role as an embodied character in one fully preserved Roman Republican play, Plautus' tragi-comedy *Amphitruo*. It is, however, unknown what the Greek model for this play was or, indeed, whether such a model existed at all.[5]

Given this kind of environment, choosing alternatives to full-on embodiment may in fact be the much more powerful option for playwrights, as can for instance be seen in the somewhat eerie presence of Apollo in Sophocles' *Oedipus the King* which is generated by combination of several strategies: *persistent materialization* of the divine in the form a statue (prayed to by Iocasta about

---

17106], c. 350 BCE) are cases in point. On actors depicted on Attic and Western Greek comedy-related vases, see Csapo 2014, 104–116.

3 A good starting point into the the topic is Mastronarde 1990; cf. also Mastronarde 2010, 181–206 and Budelmann 2022.

4 On Euripides *Alcmênê*, see Collard/Cropp 2008, 102 with further literature; on Aeschylus *Psychostasia* see Taplin 1977, 431f. Zeus may well have appeared in satyr play, the best candidate in our evidence being Sophocles *Inachos* (even if this may have been the 'black Zeus', i.e. Hades), see Seidensticker 1999, 338f. and the other plays cited at 665. In comedy, on the other hand, there is no doubt that Zeus did appear on stage, for instance in Cratinus' *Nemêsis* (on which see Bakola 2010, 168–173 and 220–224 as well as Revermann 2006, 305).

5 Christenson 2000, 47–50 and Collard/Cropp 2008, 103.

two-thirds into the play at *OT* 919–923), its *vicarious representation* in the figure of Teiresias, and *ongoing reference* to divinity by way of the oracle which is being mentioned at several points in the script (with respect to Oedipus and to what is to be done with the murderer of Laius).

What kind of "religious experience" does the stage provide?

Integrated and levelling: as unspectacular as the embodiment of the divine on the Greek stage may initially seem to be, I would nonetheless like to explore the implications of all of this for what, since the publication in 1902 of a highly influential monograph by the American psychologist William James, has been labelled "varieties of religious experience".[6] In particular, I would describe the "variety of religious experience" provided by divinity on stage as characterized in the following ways: it is *doubly personalized* and *individualized*, doubly so in the sense that the experience is undergone both by the on-stage human character(s) who interact(s) with the divine (all watched by the audience) and with the spectator him- or herself (women, I believe, were indeed present in the classical Athenian theatre audience).[7] Secondly, the encounter is *localized* in peculiar ways because it delineates within different chronotopes: the world of dramatic fiction (be it the past world of myth or the contemporary world of many comedies) as well as the 'here-and-now' sphere of the actual embodied performance and the environmental space of the specific theatrical event (which takes place in a sanctuary that inter-connects with its surroundings); thirdly, the experience is *emotionalized* while also, fourthly, being made *interactively discursive* in that there is now an opportunity, embraced not infrequently by the playwrights, of human characters *talking back* to the divine; as a fifth and final aspect it must be emphasized that this particular experience is an *intensified* engagement with the divine which in tragedy is also characterized by unusually high stakes, even if these stakes are only vicariously experienced by the spectator. When making

---

6 A concept revived and re-explored more recently in the study of religion, and of Greek religion in particular, see Parker 2011, 224–264 and the discussion, informed by a cognitive approach, in Eidinow/Geertz/North 2022, 1–6 (where 'religious experiences' end up being defined, following Taves 2009, xiii, as 'experiences deemed religious', a notion which comes with its own set of problems).
7 On the (vigorously debated) issue of female theatre spectatorship, see Roselli 2011, 186–194 (with further literature).

these claims I postulate that divinity on stage is not a literary or performative trope or some kind of 'second-order' encounter, but a 'first-order' religious experience, on par in principle with making a prayer, participating in a sacrifice or taking part in a cultic procession. The Greek theatre, therefore, once again emerges as a site of remarkable significance and unusual versatility: as it gave voice to women or slaves, it gave voice, body and flesh to divinity, thereby creating unique opportunities for a wide range of affective and cognitive experiences. In other words, the theatre, qua being a medium which generates and shapes 'varieties of religious experience' of its own, must be regarded — like a temple, an altar or a cultic procession — as a(nother) site for encountering the divine 'first-hand'.

An attempt should therefore be made to describe and understand what kind of religious experience was provided by divinities embodied on stage, and how this experience differed from those made in other contexts of encountering the divine. This is part of a bigger issue. Theatre, to be sure, is on the radar screen of students of Greek religion, regardless of whether they approach the topic from a Durkheimian vista of symbolic interaction, with a structuralist-functionalist background, from the vantage point of cultural anthropology or guided by a cognitive approach.[8] But the focus tends to be on festival frameworks, myth and ritual rather than divinity embodied on stage, and even if what might be called 'theatrically embodied theology' is being discussed, the centre of attention is often not divinity but the tragic chorus as some kind of ritual agent. This is somewhat counter-intuitive: the sheer physical size of the theatre, its environmental embeddedness within places of worship, its ritual integration into festivals dedicated to the cult of particular divinities (often, but far from exclusively, Dionysus) and its prominent cultural position must mean that the theatre was a main site to encounter divinity and hence occupied an important place in people's religious experience overall. As a consequence, it is the modern interpreters' loss not to try to come to terms with divinity on the ancient Greek stage as a modality of first-order religious experience.

---

8 Six studies which exemplify these approaches, alone or working in tandem, are Parker's chapter on "Religion in the Theatre" in his *Polytheism and Society at Athens* (= Parker 2005, 136–152), Calame's book on tragic chorality and ritual (= Calame 2017), Chepel 2020 as well as Bowie's monograph on myth and ritual in Aristophanes (= Bowie 1993), Larson's introduction to a cognitive take on Greek religion (= Larson 2016) and, in a similar vein, Eidinow/Geertz/ North 2022 (for Greek drama in particular the chapters by Eidinow and Budelmann).

The case of Artemis

Constraints of space mean that there will have to be significant focus. One item I wish to zoom in on in this context is a particularly well-known scene from Greek tragedy, the ending of Euripides' *Hippolytus*. The staging of the divine in the play up to this point has been remarkable in that there has been a permanent material juxtaposition of the two opposing deities Artemis and Aphrodite. Not only have they been omnipresent on stage, but they have also been performatively engaged, hence explicitly been put 'in the spotlight', from the opening scene onwards where Hippolytus offered ritual acknowledgement to the statue of his deity Artemis while denying such acknowledgement to Aphrodite. Euripides' subsequent choice to embody Artemis at the very end creates the doubling, or mirror effect, of a divinity's dual synchronous presence both as statue and as embodied dramatic character.[9]

This dual presence of Artemis is all the more noteworthy on the grounds that it also highlights the corresponding absence of an embodied Aphrodite, even though it is important to point out that this rival deity is invoked, addressed and praised by the chorus immediately before Artemis' entry (at 1268–1281). This moment is an important reminder that the choral voice is another possible means of staging the divine, imaginatively through choral prayer and invocation. The emphasis by the chorus that Aphrodite *alone* (1281 μόνα) exercises her specific powers over everyone and everything is followed by the binary counterpoint of her embodied rival Artemis who now commands not only the visual but also the aural dimension of the stage: note her insistence, at the very start, that Theseus should "listen to her" (1284 ἐπακοῦσαι) and that she, Artemis, is "speaking" to him (1285 σ' Ἄρτεμις αὐδῶ). Once Hippolytus is being carried on stage, he is unaware of Artemis' presence on stage — until she eventually responds to his *kommos* (at 1399ff.).

The blocking and the details of staging the goddess at this crucial point in the play are of such importance to Euripides that he has inscribed them into the text with great clarity and precision. Note in particular the role of smell here: not only does Hippolytus thus recognize the presence of divinity more generally (1391 ἔα· / ὦ θεῖον ὀσμῆς πνεῦμα), but the olfactory recognition is so distinct

---

9 I take Artemis' statement "But I have *come* for this purpose, to demonstrate/the just mindset of your child" (1298–1299 ἀλλ' ἐς τόδ' ἦλθον, παιδὸς ἐκδεῖξαι φρένα / τοῦ σοῦ δικαίαν) to imply that she is visible to the audience (even if she may not be visible to the dying Hippolytus later on). But even if Artemis were 'only' audible and smellable throughout this scene, she would of course still be embodied in stage terms.

that the particular odour makes Hippolytus recognize this divinity as Artemis specifically (1393 ἔστ' ἐν τόποισι τοισίδ' Ἄρτεμις θεά). The ease and precision of recognition is a strong indication of the level of familiarity which characterizes the relationship between Hippolytus and Artemis, by interesting contrast with Prometheus who, in the *Prometheus Bound*, similarly smells the arrival of someone but is unsure as to whether this smell is "divine, mortal or a mixture of both" (*PV* 115f.; the newcomers turn out to be divine, namely the daughters of Okeanos).[10]

In the final moments of Artemis' encounter with Hippolytus, the body becomes the ultimate dividing line between god and human, driving home the point that while theatrically the divine body on stage may be the same as the human one, conceptually it never is (1335–1345). In a society which does not sequester the process of dying by relegating it to the high-tech machinery of an intensive care unit or the hallucinatory capabilities of palliative medicine, the reality of the death of a human being, not least its sheer physical manifestations over time, are all-too-familiar experiences that everyone in the audience has witnessed at some point. Note here in particular Euripides' striking emphasis on sight and seeing as a differentiator between the divine and the human: for Artemis it is "not proper to *see* the dead" (1437 οὐ θέμις φθιτοὺς ὁρᾶν), "stain *her eye*" (1438 ὄμμα χραίνειν) with the "breath of death" (1438 θανασίμοισιν ἐκπνοαῖς) now that she *sees* (1439 ὁρῶ) that Hippolytus is close to death (with this "breath of death" surely denoting what in modern medicine is referred to as "Cheyne Stokes breathing", a symptom of imminent death). Hippolytus, on the other hand, experiences darkness "reaching *my eyes*" (1444 κατ' ὄσσων κιγχάνει μ' ἤδη σκότος), and seeks physical contact with a fellow human, his own father. It is precisely the shared physicality, the common human body, which is being used on stage to articulate the unbridgeable ontological divide between divinity and humanity.

How can we describe, or approximate rather, the religious experience in this staging of Artemis' divinity? First of all, and at the most general level, it is a peculiar mix of modalities: doubly individual (on the one hand, the experience of Hippolytus the 'brilliant dynast' of old who encounters 'his' Artemis; on the other hand, the individual experience of each spectator who witnesses this encounter); collective (for the audience at large); mediated (by the stage);

---

10 It is, however, equally clear that incense was not exclusively associated with the divine, as the passage from *PV* also implies, cf. e.g. the court scene in Aristophanes' *Wasps* (860f.) and the *agôn* in *Frogs* (871) where the smell indicates solemnity more generally. On 'smellscapes' involving divinity in Greek culture, see Eidinow 2022.

embedded (by the ritual context, which in the Athenian scenario is the cult of Dionysus); cumulative (over the duration of the dramatic festival[s]); and polyphonal, hence potentially inconsistent or even contradictory (other plays and other playwrights may stage the same divinity quite differently). To zoom in on the scene just discussed, the ending of Euripides' *Hippolytus*, there is one aspect of this particular divinity on stage which stands out: Artemis is now a goddess of death, not so much by virtue of bringing death to Hippolytus but rather by being closely associated with his dying moments. This is not the Artemis as she would have been experienced elsewhere by the Athenians and the Greeks generally, namely as the goddess associated with birth, virginity, female initiation into marriage, hunting and dancing. Euripides has therefore created an Artemis 'à la carte' and not 'au menu', to use the memorable terminology suggested by the French (!) scholar Paul Veyne.[11] This shift from Artemis as someone important at the beginning of life and its early formative stages, especially that of women, to Artemis as a significant presence at the end of the life of a young male tragic hero, is a significant displacement from one end of the spectrum to the other.[12] It also forcefully illustrates what the stage can do to divinity: shift, displace, move, extend and invert. The theatre here is functionally similar to ritual localization in the sense that local cults too can 'shift' or 'extend' deities, for example in the case of Persephone as worshipped at Epizephyrian Locri.[13] This shift is made possible by Artemis' full and logical integration into the narrative of Hippolytus' tragic life and death. Its particularly impressive force and potential impact results from the fact that this narrative integration occurs not in the medium of an image, or a ritual, or a festival, or a rhapsode, but in the medium of the theatre, a medium which in its complexities and sheer multitude of communication channels exceeds any other media of its time. In addition, it is a fiercely competitive medium where playwrights are required and indeed expected to re-tell and re-shape the story in individually different ways rather than replicate the existing narratives in non-dynamic, iterative and

---

11 Veyne 1971, 141.

12 This shift towards a darker tone in the spectrum of a divinity is in some ways comparable to what Euripides (at *IT* 1462–1467) has the goddess Athena say about the cult of Iphigenia at Brauron, where Artemis was closely associated with childbirth. For, according to Euripides' Athena, after her death at Brauron (where she had become the guardian of the temple of Artemis) Iphigenia will receive the clothes of women who *die* in childbirth, cf. Scullion 1999–2000, 227 on this passage.

13 Parker 2011, 227–232 (with further literature).

more static ways.[14] In other words: Euripides' Artemis *has* to be different, somewhat and somehow.

The prism of theatre and the power of 'reverse engineering'

As a competitive 'super-medium', the theatre in no way inauthenticates, or otherwise detracts from, the religious experience, as is insinuated by what I would like to label the 'Platonic model' where gods in the theatre are 'less real' or even 'not real' (as 'literary fictions'), by somehow being several stages re-moved from their true existence. Instead, I would like to invoke the analogy of the prism. What theatre does to divinity can, I suggest, fruitfully be compared to what a prism does to seemingly monochromatic light. It brings out, unlocks, presents and re-directs the colours inherent in Greek divinity: those blues, greens, yellows, reds — and with them the black, white and greys of Greek god-desses and gods. One consequence of adopting this 'Newtonian', as I would like to call it, model of divinity on stage instead of the 'Platonic' one would, for in-stance, be that the question of whether a particular ritual mentioned in a dra-matic text existed in the ritual practice outside of the theatre not only loses its force: it loses its point.[15] The prism that is the theatre adds to divinity everything that comes with spectral colours: visibility, variety, emotion, intensity, fun, entertainment and, not least, a sense of awe. The gods appear 'in a different light': not less real nor less important than any other light the gods may appear in — and a light that *only* the theatre is able to cast on them.

Conversely, the theatre can itself shape the way in which a divinity is con-ceptualized more generally. A case in point is Dionysus who by the beginning of the 4th century BCE, surely under the growing and ever more wide-spread influ-ence of theatre festivals and dramatic competitions, has started to be associated with the notion of victory. Thus Dionysus, the god of theatre and patron deity of many dramatic festivals (especially in Attica), appears with *Nikê*, the winged goddess of victory, on two Attic oinochoe-vessels (a shape commonly associated

---

14 The notion of Greek theatre as competitive is more fully developed and explored in Rever-mann 2006 (not just for comedy but for all dramatic genres).
15 For this kind of discussion, see for instance Scullion 1999–2000.

with the Anthesteria festival) from the first decade of the 4th century BCE.[16] On a grander scale, the splendid red-figure volute crater commonly referred to as the Pronomos vase (produced in Attica around 400 BCE but found in, and perhaps specifically manufactured for, Ruvo in Apulia) persistently and programmatically combines the Dionysiac with the epinician element, especially in the form of the seated Dionysus who, together with his bride Ariadne, is placed in a pictorial environment which hammers home the victory theme (regardless of whether an actual victory underlies, somehow, the creation of this artifact).[17] In a similar vein, two Apulian bell-craters from a slightly later date (400–380 BCE) show naked youths with thyrsus rods respectively (among them possibly the young Dionysus himself) who are being crowned by a *Nikê*-figure.[18] An Attic calyx-crater from ca. 350 BCE, finally, shows Dionysus making a grand appearance on a chariot drawn by panthers.[19] Apart from the (winged) god Eros and two satyrs there is also a woman present (without wings) who conspicuously holds a bunch of grapes or a vine leaf over Dionysus' head, clearly to emphasize the victorious nature and mood of the god's triumphant epiphany.

Such an instance of 'reverse engineering' of divinity further supports the notion, central to my case for the 'Newtonian model', of theatre as a site of first-order site religious experience which, as a medium of religious practice, in turn shapes and re-models that very experience. Another important case in this context is the sanctuary of Asclepius in Epidaurus of which the well-known, magnificent theatre is a major part. Among the preserved sculptures from the Asclepius temple of this large and important pan-Hellenic sanctuary, most of which are on display in one room at the National Archaeological Museum in Athens, there is a conspicuous presence of *Nikê*-figures. Both pediments of this temple (built around 380 BCE) were adorned with them: five are preserved, two form the east pediment and three of the west pediment.[20] They functioned as so-

16 Green 2002, 122 nos. 6 and 7 (with further references). On *oenochoai* and the Anthesteria see Parker 2005, 297–301.
17 See Taplin/Wyles 2010 for a wide-ranging a detailed multi-authored study of the Pronomos vase, among which Csapo 2010, 108f. discusses the victory theme on it in particular. See also Biles/Thorn 2014 and Robinson 2014 (especially on the likelihood that the vessel was produced for a Peucetian, i.e. ethnically non-Greek, elite consumer with high competence in Greek culture).
18 Biles/Thorn 2014 figs. 11.11 and 11.12.
19 Zurich 3926, see the discussion (with pictures) in Isler-Kerényi 2015, 226–229 as well as the more detailed (and better illustrated) discussion in Isler-Kerényi 1982.
20 In Kaltsas 2002, 173–179 these are nos. 340 and 357 (from the right and left akroterion respectively on the east pediment) as well as nos. 352, 355 and 356 (from the central, left and right akroterion on the west pediment).

called akroteria, which are particularly visible and exposed ornamentations, placed on the top and the sides of each pediment. It seems safe to assume that the sixth (and lost) akroterion was also a *Nikê*-figure. The temple was thus architecturally framed, as it were, by six winged goddesses of victory. Situated right next to the sleeping hall where the god would demonstrate his healing powers over night, this was a temple of Asclepius in triumph! It fits into this overall scheme that a relief slab from an altar, probably dedicated to the Twelve Olympian Gods, also shows *Nikê*, in the company of either Asclepius or Zeus.[21]

Associating the god of health and healing with victory (over disease) is, of course, an obvious and logical step. But while the sheer presence of these *Nikê* figures in the Asclepius sanctuary of Epidaurus may be unremarkable, their quantity and especially their prominence certainly deserves attention. It is worth noting here that in preserved hymns associated with the cult of Asclepius at Epidaurus — the most famous of them being the paean to Apollo and Asclepius by Isyllus (from the last quarter of the 4th century BCE) — the explicit notion of victory is absent (although, of course, always implied in a sense).[22] Rather, Asclepius is being presented here as a source of joy, a kind and powerful protector against illness and bad fortune. In view of this, the prominent and highly visible connection of Asclepius with victory at his most important sanctuary appears to be something not generic but much more particular: a product of the *specific local* experience that was to he had at Epidaurus. This unique sanctuary experience of course emphatically included the spectacular theatre venue and everything offered by its performances which, as usual in the prestigious theatre business, were surely strongly competitive in nature (with much-coveted prizes for actors and productions).[23] The competitive theatre business therefore appears to have 'rubbed off' on the local perception and visual presentation of the healing god Asclepius at Epidaurus specifically. This meant not inventing new attributes but bringing out and amplifying a characteristic feature associated with and implied by this particular divinity: its ability to prevail (in this case against the adversity of illness). Once again, the prism of theatre has the power to see a god 'in a new light' — but more than that, in the specific local environment of Epidaurus where the theatre is so present and prominent, the theatre itself configures and engineers, at least partially, the very colour(s) in which that divinity is being seen and experienced here.

---

21 Kaltsas 2002, 178, no. 354.
22 A collection of these hymns can be found in section 6 of Furley/Bremer 2001.
23 On this kind of competitiveness in Greek theatre culture more specifically, see Revermann 2006, 5–7, 19–23, 73f. and 99, as well as Revermann 2017, 8–10.

Dark Athena

This 'Newtonian model' of theatre as a kind of prism for seeing divinity in a uniquely different light can further be illustrated by another scene, no less prominent or memorable than the previous one. In the chilling opening of Sophocles' *Ajax*, the goddess Athena demonstrates her power by driving Ajax mad and presenting him to his arch enemy, Athena's protégé Odysseus. The deranged Ajax, however, proudly boasting to have done away with his enemies in the Greek camp while Odysseus has been saved to be the object of the triumphant final kill, evokes in Odysseus not *Schadenfreude* but pity. The scene — a notorious and quite controversial one as far as the actual staging is concerned (Finglass 2011, 135–138 provides a good overview) — very much capitalizes on the interpretive possibilities which are opened up by embodying divinity as a dramatic character on stage: visibility and invisibility (the goddess Athena appears to be at least initially invisible to Odysseus, and she will make Odysseus invisible to Ajax by putting "darkness" [85] over his eyes); audibility (Athena has to call Ajax twice before he moves out of his tent); the expression of emotionality in the form of laugher (here in its extremely aggressive form as a sign of superiority: "Isn't it the most pleasant laughter to laugh at your enemies?," Athena asks Odysseus rhetorically [79]); the expression of power and power asymmetries by movement, blocking and the use of theatrical space more generally; and, very importantly, the interactively discursive nature of the encounter with the divinity, which entails Odysseus actually *talking back* at Athena (118–128). This particular exchange is deeply significant. Far from providing Odysseus with a sense of satisfaction, Ajax' divinely induced mental disorder makes him feel pity and empathy, a response which in turn prompts Athena to articulate strongly the uncrossable demarcation line between divinity and humanity (which had been so prominent in the final moments of Euripides' *Hippolytus* as well).

How does the opening of Sophocles' *Ajax* contribute to the colour spectrum of experiencing the divine? Athena describes herself as the "long-time guardian" of Odysseus (36 πάλαι φύλαξ), a role which in turn is used to justify and rationalize her brutal demeanour according to the zero-sum game logic of 'helping your friend by harming his enemy'. Athena's individually protective side, so well-known to any Greek audience from the tales of the Epic cycle in general and from the *Odyssey* in particular, is therefore now seen from a different perspective, that of the victim and the loser in this zero-sum game. Her kindness towards Odysseus comes with cruelty towards his enemies, the effects of which on Ajax, on his family and on the Greek army the audience will now be watching for the next two or so hours. In other words, the prism of Sophocles' theatre generates a colour spectrum of experiencing the guardian deity Athena which now shows different, more nuanced and most of all darker colours.

Bringing an Athenian localization into the equation makes this scene even more interesting. For if, as surely must be done, a performance in a deme theatre in Attica or especially at the Athenian Theatre of Dionysus is envisaged, further complexities emerge. As the guardian deity of Athens and Attica, the *phylax* of its population, Athena is prominently worshipped all over the region, not least on the Athenian acropolis at the southern slope of which the Theatre of Dionysus is located. This guardian Athena, be she worshipped in Athens as *parthenos* ("virgin"), *promachos* ("front-fighter") or *nikê* ("victory"), is a caring divinity who is strongly committed to the welfare of a community and its constituent members. By stark contrast, the Athena performatively experienced here by the Athenians in the mirror (quite literally!) of the Athenian stage during Sophocles' *Ajax* is a selfish and nepotistic Athena who undermines the community of the Greek aristocratic fighters in an attempt to protect her favourite one among them.

Most importantly, however, the Athenian audience — and any audience in the Greek cultural continuum where the play might be staged, for that matter — witness a deity in immediate action, exercising her divine power. Whereas in the various types of worship on the Athenian acropolis and elsewhere this divine power is usually *presumed*, on stage it is *actualized*. The deity is shown an agent of power instead of being seen an object of worship. Or, to deploy another metaphor borrowed from physics, what the stage does for divinity here is to show it not in an inertial system but in a dynamic one in which the focus is on the gods' agency rather than their presumptive but non-actualized power.

The spectral colours of comedy

Turning to tragedy's unruly rival genre, what colours does comedy contribute to the religious experiences generated by the prism-like medium theatre? The most obvious addition to the spectrum is that of the ridiculous and the laughable, bringing with it the distinct possibility, regularly exercised, that divinity becomes the object of comic abuse. That these trademark characteristics of the genre were fully and pervasively extended to its staging of divinity is not only borne out by the preserved playscripts themselves but, very importantly, by the visual evidence as well. A pertinent example, from Athens (!), are the fragments from a polychrome oinochoe found on the Athenian agora and dated to ca. 400

BCE.[24] Despite their poor status of conservation, the left figure whose name label is certainly to be restored as [DIO]NYSOS is clearly wearing the typically grotesque comic body suit, including what seems to be an unusually long and even spiralling phallus. These important vessel fragments, which are part of other precious visual evidence pointing in the same direction, strongly suggest that pervasive comedification of the divine on the stage of Attic comedy did extend fully to the visual dimension.[25]

The buffoon-god Dionysus is arguably the most prominent and striking example of comic divinity. Ignorant, slow, effeminate and cowardly, he becomes the target of verbal and physical abuse and violence, (for us) most aggressively so in Aristophanes' *Frogs*. But the picture is much more complex than might initially be thought. *Frogs* very much juxtaposes the ridiculous representation of the divine with extreme solemnity in the (second) chorus, the initiates of the Eleusinian mysteries. The comedy therefore, far from exposing, undermining or even critiquing the divine and the religious systems framing it, in fact re-asserts and reinforces its power, its relevance, its resilience and its validity.[26] In other words: ridiculing the divine is not a sign of vulnerability, doubt, criticism and dwindling overall-significance. The fact that the comic Dionysus — long spiralling phallus and all — can be abused and vilified like this in Athens in his own sanctuary, in front of his own priest and facing his own cult statue set up in the theatre (!), impressively underlines his power: divinity is ultimately beyond human ridicule and remains unaffected by it, hence has no need for retaliation either. Within the envelope of the theatre festival and sanctioned abuse (especially in Dionysiac rituals), humans can ridicule the gods with impunity, without having to fear divine retaliation against themselves and their communities.[27] This mode of experiencing divinity includes the physiological dimension of actual laughter in the theatre, an overt and publicly observable outlet of emotionality and personal experience.[28] Comedy, then, extends and broadens the colour spectrum of the religious experiences to be had in the theatre, resulting not only in a broader range but also new possibilities of contrasts with tragedy

---

24 Agora P 23985, best accessible via the website of the *American School of Classical Studies* at https://www.ascsa.edu.gr/resources landing/details?source=dc&id=Agora:Object:P%2023985.

25 See Revermann 2006, 145–159 on "comic ugliness", a notion of central importance for Piqueux 2022.

26 Perrone 2005 puts particular emphasis on this combination of the comically low and the solemn.

27 Revermann 2014b expands further on the issue of ridiculing the divine within religious frames.

28 Halliwell 2008 (especially ch. 5) is foundational on this topic; see also Halliwell 2014.

(note in particular the near-simultaneous juxtaposition of the Dionysus of Aristophanes' *Frogs*, first performed in 405 BCE, with the Dionysus in Euripides' *Bacchae*).

It is the phenomenon of making divinity ridiculous and laughable which also presents the perhaps greatest obstacle to the modern interpreter who often approaches the evidence with a mindset shaped, consciously or not, by Judaeo-Christian pre-conceptions (an ever-present danger in the modern study of Graeco-Roman religions more generally). As I have just argued, the ridicule of divinity does not undermine but in fact helps to strengthen the status of the gods as 'beyond', *hors concours* and 'set apart'. When laughing at Dionysus, the Athenian viewer is not bonding with a Dionysus who is, after all, 'one of us'. On the contrary: he or she — I believe, as previously mentioned, that women were indeed in the theatre audience at Athens and presumably elsewhere — experiences the strength of the god who ultimately remains completely unaffected by the abuse, unlike any human in the same situation. Comic ridicule cannot possibly 'get to the gods', which is why they emerge all the more powerful even when being the object of such ridicule. It is neither a 'laughing with' nor a 'laughing at' or 'laughing down' but, so to speak, a 'laughing up'.

Among the colours, dimensions and nuances added to the religious experience by comedy are elements of magic and the miraculous (hardly found in existing tragedy, the Euripidean Medea being a notable exception). Thus the rejuvenation of Demos, the personification of the people of Athens, who the *Knights* by Aristophanes is being "cooked young" by the sausage-seller, has this dimension, even if the playwright is careful not to attribute god-like attributes to the miraculously revived Demos himself (who is instead referred to as a "monarch" [*Knights* 1330] or "King of Greeks" [*Knights* 1333]). Things are different in the case of Ploutos, the god of wealth, in the Aristophanic play of the same title (the last of the preserved Aristophanic comedies). Here the healing of the wealth-god from his blindness by the fellow-deity Asclepius, which is not shown to the audience but narrated by the slave Cario in an extensive eye-witness narrative, is another one of the miracle healings for which Asclepius was famous and which, in the form of inscriptions, were put on display at the god's main sanctuary in Epidaurus (situated right next to the famous theatre). These were for visitors to read themselves or to be told about by priests, guides or others.[29] Both Ploutos and Demos are examples of comedy extensively dramatizing embodied abstracts of which the genre is very fond, especially in the

---

29 On these inscriptions, see for instance Kearns 2010, 304–308.

5th century BCE. A play by Cratinus features a chorus of "Wealth Gods" (*Ploutoî*).[30] In the Aristophanic *Peace* the statue of the peace deity (*Eirênê*) becomes the focal point of an entire comedy as the object of the comic protagonist's heroic quest: Trygaeus succeeds in bringing the divinity down (from heaven) and firmly establishing her in his, and the audience's 'here and now'.

Comedy, then, can do special, indeed unique, things to divinity on stage. Perhaps most striking in this context is its ability to *make* gods, as can be witnessed in the Aristophanic *Birds*. Creatively engaging with the theme, familiar from Greek myth, of gods battling and overthrowing each other, Aristophanes has the comic protagonist convince the chorus of their own status as bird-gods who, in a kind of comic ornithomachy, end up replacing the Olympians — under the leadership of a human-turned-(half)bird protagonist who triumphantly ends as a Zeus-like Supreme God married to Kingship (*Basileia*) itself. Conversely, comedy also has the capacity to un-make gods. The clouds in the play of the same title are initially launched as new divinities, proclaimed as such by themselves as well as Socrates and his followers. Eventually, however, the old-fashioned religious order to which Strepsiades adheres proves to be the goddesses' undoing (and that of the Socratic Thinkery which goes up in flames). Comedy here builds on, and expands, the range of the Greek religious imaginary, providing experiences where actors and their audiences can imaginatively 'play through' scenarios of fracture and destabilization. Making visible these colours of the Greek religious spectrum is something which only the prism of comedy can achieve.

A brief look ahead

I have made, and briefly explored some ramifications of, the claim that the stage and the performative medium theatre do not turn divinity into a literary-performative trope, a somewhat less authentic second-order religious experience but that they instead constitute an integral first-order part of the varieties of the Greek religious experience. To illustrate my point, I have prominently invoked the analogy of the prism, arguing that the prism-like qualities and powers of divinities embodied in the theatre, according to what I have termed the "Newtonian model," shed a nuanced and colourful light on the gods. It is significant that my point of departure was the "production-aesthetics" side of

---

30 See Bakola 2010 for discussions of this fragmentary play from various angles.

theatre and the performative embodiment of the divine, rather than other possible starting points like chorality, aetiology, ritual frames, myth or the cognitive apparatus presumed in ancient playgoers. The approach taken here suggests that, as embodied theophany, divinity on stage needs to be an integral and integrated part of the study of Greek religion. The classical Greek stage offered levels, ranges and modes of emotionalization, interactive discursiveness, intensification and localization that could not, or not to a similar degree, be experienced in ritual or myth.

This means, among other things, that there needs to be re-consideration of the value and status of Greek dramatic texts as evidence for the study of Greek religion. To adduce a blatant example (outside of the present focus on divinity on stage): if dramatic texts are indeed considered 'first-hand' testimony of religious experience, any discussion of the Thesmophoria festival in books or articles on Greek religion will have to devote space, attention and interpretive effort to the one preserved comedy which is completely centred around this very festival, the *Women at the Thesmophoria* by Aristophanes (instead of simply ignoring this play as evidence for Greek religion altogether, as is often done).

Comparatist vistas are likely both to deepen and to complicate the picture I have been sketching here. What insights does the cross-generic dimension contribute (i.e. the comparison of divinity in the medium theatre with divinity in, say, epic or lyric poetry)? Another road not taken here is the question of whether and how things are fundamentally different on the Roman stage (bearing in mind that this is, for us, essentially confined to Roman comedy and Senecan tragedy)? And what mileage is there in a cross-cultural perspective: in which cultures, for instance, is divinity ridiculed with impunity in similar ways?

It should also be noted that the points developed here as part of the prism-inspired 'Newtonian model' are consistent with, and complementary to, arguments about the nature of Greek religious experience made in the cognitive study of (Greek) religion in particular, for two main reasons. First, while the cognitive approach is not driven by 'production aesthetics' but the psychological and neuro-scientific processes underlying 'reception aesthetics', it nonetheless shares one crucial feature with the approach I have outlined here: this is a *focus on embodiment* and its importance for generating specific kinds of religious experience. Once such a focus is seriously established on either the production or the reception side of things (or, indeed, on both), a nuanced and multi-faceted picture is bound to emerge in any case. Secondly, both approaches see religion as the product of *interactive experiences* (between stage and audience, for instance). The processes, as described in both these paradigms, are therefore never seen as one-directional and static but as complex and ever-dynamic areas of contact, exchange, impact, osmosis and so forth.

This has not been the place to reflect at great length or in much detail on the relationship between actors and divinities, the stage and the gods, theatre and religion. But even within the narrower focus adopted in the present context one feature emerges with great clarity: once divinity on stage is seen as a foundational and integral part of the variety of the Greek religious experience, the enormous range, elasticity and appeal of those experiences available to ancient viewers can be better appreciated: the theatre expands, the theatre deepens, the theatre complicates. Most of all, perhaps, it is capable of generating its own kind of religious experiences, thus creating an environment which could be provided nowhere elsewhere but in and by the theatre.[31]

Bibliography

Bakola, Emmanuela (2010), *Cratinus and the Art of Comedy*, Oxford.

Biles, Zachary/Thorn, Jed (2014), "Rethinking Choregic Iconography in Apulia", in: Eric Csapo *et al.*, 2014, 295–231.

Bowie, Angus M. (1993), *Aristophanes: Myth, Ritual and Comedy*, Cambridge.

Budelmann, Felix (2022), "Belief, Make-Believe, and the Religious Imagination: The Case of the Deus ex Machina in Greek Tragedy", in: Eidinow/Geertz/North 2022, 96–117.

Calame, Claude (2017), *La Tragédie Chorale: Poésie Grecque et Rituel Musical*, Paris.

Chepel, Elena (2020), *Laughter for the Gods: Ritual in Old Comedy*, Liège.

Christenson, David M. (2000), *Plautus: Amphitruo*, Cambridge.

Collard, Christopher/Cropp, Martin (2008), *Euripides*, VII, *Fragments: Aegeus—Meleager*. Cambridge, MA.

Csapo, Eric (2010), *Actors and Icons of the Ancient Theatre*, Malden, MA/Oxford.

Csapo, Eric/Goette, Hans Rupprecht/Green, J. Richard/Wilson, Peter (2014) (eds.), *Greek Theatre in the Fourth Century BC*, Berlin/Boston.

Csapo, Eric/Wilson, Peter (2020), *A Social and Economic History of the Theatre to 300 BC*. II: *Theatre Beyond Athens. Documents with Translation and Commentary*, Cambridge.

Easterling, Pat/Hall, Edith (2002) (eds.), *Greek and Roman Actors. Aspects of an Ancient Profession*, Cambridge.

Eidinow, Ester (2022), "Ancient Greek Smellscapes and Divine Fragrances. Anthropomorphizing the Gods in Ancient Greek Culture", in: Eidinow/Geertz/North 2022, 69–95.

Eidinow, Ester/Geertz, Armin W./North, John (2022) (eds.), *Cognitive Approaches to Ancient Religious Experience*, Cambridge.

Finglass, Patrick J. (ed.) (2011), *Sophocles: Ajax*, Cambridge.

---

31 I wish to thank Rachel Mazarra and Kenneth Yu for helpful and incisive comments.

Furley, William D./Bremer, Jan Marten (2001), *Greek Hymns. Selected Cult Songs from the Archaic to the Hellenistic Period* (I–II), Tübingen.

Green, J. Richard (2002), "Towards a Reconstruction of Performance Style", in: Easterling/Hall 2002, 93–126.

Halliwell, Stephen (2008), *Greek Laughter. A Study of Cultural Psychology from Homer to Early Christianity*, Cambridge.

Halliwell, Stephen (2014), "Laughter", in: Revermann 2014, 189–205.

Isler-Kerényi, Cornelia (1982), "Il Trionfo di Dioniso", in: *Quaderni Ticinesi/Numismatica e antichità classiche* 11, 137–160.

Isler-Kerényi, Cornelia (2015), *Dionysos in Classical Athens: An Understanding through Images*, Leiden.

Kaltsas, Nikolaos (2002) (ed.), *The Sculpture Collection in the National Archaeological Museum Athens*, Los Angeles.

Kearns, Emily (2010), *Ancient Greek Religion: A Sourcebook*, Malden, MA/Oxford.

Larson, Jennifer (2016), *Understanding Greek Religion: A Cognitive Approach*, London.

Mastronarde, Donald (1990), "Actors on High: The Skene Roof, the Crane, and the Gods in Attic Drama", in: *Classical Antiquity* 9, 247–294.

Mastronarde, Donald (2010), *The Art of Euripides: Dramatic Technique and Social Context*, Cambridge.

Parker, Robert (2005), *Polytheism and Society*, Oxford.

Parker, Robert (2011), *On Greek Religion*, Cornell.

Perrone, Serena (2005), "Aristofane e la religione negli *scholia vetera* alle *Rane*", in: Montana, Fausto (ed.), *Interpretazioni antiche di Aristofane*, La Spezia, 111–229.

Pickard-Cambridge, Arthur W. (1988), *The Dramatic Festivals of Athens*. 2nd ed., revised with addenda by John Gould and D.M. Lewis, Oxford.

Piqueux, Alexa (2022), *The Comic Body in Ancient Greek Theatre and Art, 440-320 BCE*, Oxford.

Revermann, Martin (2006), *Comic Business: Theatricality, Dramatic Technique and Performance Contexts of Aristophanic Comedy*, Oxford

Revermann, Martin (2014a) (ed.), *The Cambridge Companion to Greek Comedy*, Cambridge.

Revermann, Martin (2014b), "Divinity and Religious Practice", in: Revermann 2014a, 275–287.

Revermann, Martin (2017) (ed.), *A Cultural History of Theatre. I: Antiquity*, London.

Robinson, Edward (2014), "Greek Theatre in Non-Greek Apulia", in: Csapo *et al.* 2014, 319–332.

Roselli, David K. (2011), *Theater of the People: Spectators and Society in Ancient Athens*, Austin.

Scullion, Scott (1999/2000), "Tradition and Invention in Euripidean Aitiology", in: Cropp, Martin/Lee, Kevin/Sansone, David (eds.), *Euripides and Tragic Theatre in the Late Fifth-Century* (*Illinois Classical Studies* 24–25, 217–233).

Taplin, Oliver (1977), *The Stagecraft of Aeschylus: The Dramatic Use of Exists and Entrances in Greek Tragedy*, Oxford.

Taplin, Oliver/Wyles, Rosie (2010), *The Pronomos Vase and its Context*, Oxford.

Taves, Ann (2009), *Religious Experience Reconsidered: A Building-Block Approach to the Study of Religion and Other Special Things*, Princeton.

Veyne, Paul (1971), *Comment on écrit l'histoire. Essai d'épistémologie*, Paris.

Eric Csapo

Victory Ritual and the Performance of Victory in Aristophanes' *Exodoi*

Abstract: The endings of Aristophanes' plays often offer an imaginary transition from the world of the play to the world of the dramatic competition. The victory of the comic hero is frequently accompanied by words and actions that are appropriate to rituals that celebrate the victory of the comic poet and performers. In particular I draw attention to the pragmatic relations between the play endings and two such customs: the invitations to a feast at the end of *Peace* and *Ecclesiazusae* and their suggestive anticipation of the epinician feast held in the Sanctuary of Dionysus; and the raising of the comic hero onto the shoulders of the chorus in *Acharnians* and *Peace* and its suggestive anticipation of the *periagermos,* a congratulatory processing, about and out of the theatre, of the victor after the judging.

Keywords: Aristophanes, endings, dramatic competition, victory, performance

It would be very difficult to find something new to say about the staging and the imagery of Aristophanes' *exodoi*. This is particularly true since 2013, the date of the appearance of the excellent and comprehensive *Scene finali di Aristofane* by Marta Di Bari.[1] My contribution looks only at a couple small details of the performance of some *exodoi*. In particular I am interested in the *exodos* as a transitional space between the play and the comic competition, and in the victory imagery that *exodoi* share with choregic art. Specifically, I wish to show how two recurrent motifs in Aristophanic *exodoi* playfully anticipate victory rituals that took place at the Dionysia and Lenaea: one is the official victory party or

I thank J.R. Green and Peter Wilson for advice on many of the topics touched on in this essay. I am most grateful to Piero Totaro for the invitation to the colloquium in Bari and to Piero and Tiziana Drago for their very generous hospitality during my stay in Bari. This research was made possible through the support of a Marie Sklodowska-Curie FCFP Senior Fellowship at the Freiburg Institute of Advanced Studies (FRIAS).

1 Di Bari 2013 (with extensive reportage of previous scholarship).

https://doi.org/10.1515/9783111248028-005

epinikia, and the other is an unofficial procession from the site of victory to the site of celebration.[2]

Epinikia

In the *exodos* of Aristophanes' *Peace* and *Ecclesiazusae* the chorus invites the audience to "follow along" as they withdraw from the theatre.[3] It promises supporters a share in a feast. There is more literal truth to this than generally recognised.

Official celebrations called the *epinikia* were celebrated at the Dionysia and Lenaea for all choral victories. By "official" I mean that the city provided at least part of the food for the party. Victorious circular choruses at the Dionysia were almost certainly awarded an ox, in addition to the tripod, as a prize, and this ox was intended for the epinician sacrifice.[4]

The function of the oxen is clear when one compares the Panathenaic prize list, an inscription of the 380s BCE detailing expenditures for the prizes of the Panathenaia.[5] It lists prizes for choral and team competitions organised by the tribes (*pyrrhiche, euandria,* torch-race, boat-race; probably also the lyric choruses and *anthippasia*). There are also prizes for second-place finishers. All received oxen. The inscription specifically names the oxen as 'prizes' (*niketeria*) and they are expressly given "to the winning tribe." The winners of the boat race receive three (?) oxen plus "[200 drachmas] *also for the feast.*" The obvious reference is to the *victory feast.*[6] As Michael Jameson put it (speaking of the representation of Nikai with oxen on the reliefs decorating the Nike parapet on the Athenian Acropolis): "the sacrifice celebrates victory and accompanies the

---

2 Possible metatheatrical connections with the victory celebrations of the festivals are mentioned by Di Bari only in passing (2013, 28–29 n. 39). On this theme, see the excellent treatment by Biles 2011, 83–94.

3 Ar. *Pax* 1357–1359 (ὦ χαίρετε χαίρετ᾿ ἄν- / δρες· κἂν ξυνέπησθέ μοι, / πλακοῦντας ἔδεσθε); *Ec.* 1145–1148 (καὶ τῶν θεατῶν εἴ τις εὔνους τυγχάνει, / καὶ τῶν κριτῶν εἰ μή τις ἑτέρωσε βλέπει, / ἴτω μεθ᾿ ἡμῶν· πάντα γὰρ παρέξομεν). Cf. Pherecr. *fr.* 101 and Di Bari 2013, 454f.

4 Simon. 27 P. (= 141 Bergk, *Anth. Pal.* 6.213); *Suda* s.v. *taurophagon; schol.* Plat. *Resp.* 394c; *schol.* Ar. *Ra.* 357 etc.; the evidence is thoroughly reviewed in Csapo/Wilson (forthcoming).

5 *IG* II² 2311, ll. 71–81; Shear 2003, 104, ll. 82–93a.

6 Shear 2003, 104, ll. 91–92. Parker (2005, 256) thinks the prize oxen are for the tribal banquet, but the tribal banquet more probably took place just after the sacrifices following the procession and before the competitions (Schmitt-Pantel 1997, 126–130), or, at the Dionysia, possibly after the dithyrambic contests as suggested by Wilson 2008, 116.

erection of trophies ... what we know about *niketeria* shows that they were so-cial occasions, an opportunity, whether the victory was military or agonistic, for the victors to provide a generous feast."[7]

It was also with a view to the victory feast, *epinikia*, of the tribal choruses that oxen were given as prizes for men's and boys' choruses at the Dionysia. It is for this reason that choregic monuments often show Nikai sacrificing bulls.[8] At Cyrene the bull prize for each dithyrambic and tragic chorus explicitly came with cooks and some instructions for preparing the meat.

The tradition that names a goat as a prize for victory in tragedy is much less reliably attested (it may be an etymologising historical fiction contrived by the ancient Atthidographers).[9] Dionysian tragic choruses were not tribally organ-ised (the comic ones were only from some time in the 4th century),[10] and this may have made an animal prize less obviously suitable. If an animal prize was not given for tragedy, we can nonetheless be certain that there were ample con-tributions of food for dramatic victory celebrations. Aristophanic meta-reference tempts us to guess that the priest of Dionysus provided wine and cakes for the feast.[11] Other meta-reference makes it clear that substantial contributions from the choregoi and others were expected.[12] Major contributions to the feast from the choregos were doubtless a norm rather than a requirement. We do have inscrip-tions from the 2nd and 1st centuries BCE where choregoi are honoured for feeding all citizens and visitors.[13] In Megara a choregos for *pyrrhiche* provided sacrifice and a meal "for the citizens, those from neighbouring townships, the resident Romans and their sons, slaves and wives, and for the female citizens, neigh-bouring townswomen, female slaves and girls."[14] The inscriptions unfortunately make no reference to *epinikia*, but their inclusiveness is suggestive.

---

7 Jameson 1994, 313.
8 Csapo 2010, 82–84, 126–130.
9 Csapo/Wilson (forthcoming) **I Avii 2**.
10 [Arist.] *Ath.* 56.3.
11 Ar. *Ach.* 1085–1095 (ἐπὶ δεῖπνον ταχὺ / βάδιζε τὴν κίστην λαβὼν καὶ τὸν χοᾶ. / ὁ τοῦ Διονύ-σου γάρ σ' ἱερεὺς μεταπέμπεται. / ἀλλ' ἐγκόνει· δειπνεῖν κατακωλύεις πάλαι. / τὰ δ' ἄλλα πάντ' ἐστὶν παρεσκευασμένα, / κλῖναι, τράπεζαι, προσκεφάλαια, στρώματα, / στέφανοι, μύρον, τρα-γήμαθ', — αἱ πόρναι πάρα, — / ἄμυλοι, πλακοῦντες, σησαμοῦντες, ἴτρια, / ὀρχηστρίδες, τὸ Φίλταθ' Ἁρμόδι' οὗ, πάλαι. / ἀλλ' ὡς τάχιστα σπεῦδε); *Ra.* 297 (ΔΙ. ἱερεῦ, διαφύλαξόν μ', ἵν' ὦ σοι ξυμπότης); Biles 2011, 85–86.
12 E.g. Ar. *Ach.* 886–887, 1150–1152; *Pax* 1017–1022; *Pelargoi* fr. 448 K.-A. Cf. Plat. *Sym.* 173a, schol. Ar. *Nu.* 339g, and Wilson 2000, 102–103, 347–348 (who however fails to distinguish fully the *epinikia* from the victory party, setting of Plato's *Symposium*, see below).
13 *IG* XII 7, 389; *IG* XII 5, 721 (add. p. 336 + *SEG* 3, 748); Schmitt Pantel 1997, 366–367.
14 Wilhelm 1907, 19 ll. 19–22.

It seems poets too made contributions to the feast. Plato's *Symposium* states that "(Agathon) and his choreuts made the epinician sacrifice" (173a). The absence of any mention of the choregos in the quotation may suggest that Agathon made a large contribution in his capacity as poet. Ion of Chios, at the celebration of his tragic victory, gave "a jar of Chian wine to every Athenian."[15]

The evidence of the *Symposium* indicates that the epinician sacrifice took place in a public space in which the public were also present. Nearly all the guests at Agathon's dinner party are assumed to have been present the night before at the *epinikia*: Socrates, Pausanias, Aristophanes, "and most of the others." They would have been part of the indeterminate mob (*ochlos*) from which Socrates fled in panic and in which Agathon was unable to find his friends to issue invitations to his private dinner party.[16] This can only have taken place in the Sanctuary of Dionysus Eleuthereus immediately south of the theatre.

The amount of food certainly suggests that far more than the victorious choruses, choregoi and poets were involved. We do not know if the *epinikia* for all four choral contests were held on the same day — the only clue I know is Aristophanes' presence at the *epinikia* of Agathon and his words αὐτός εἰμι τῶν χθὲς βεβαπτισμένων which makes it sound as if Aristophanes was a contestant, though not necessarily a winner (even if there is no allusion to Eupolis' *Baptai*).[17] On most reconstructions, at least, both dithyrambic contests were run on the same day, and the dithyrambic *epinikia* included at least two oxen from the official contribution: thus, a big feast for the *epinikia* of the lyric choruses is likely, but possibly the dramatic choruses also celebrated on the last evening of the Dionysia. Note that two decent ancient oxen could feed 1600 normal portions of beef.[18] If all the victorious choregoi added an equal contribution to the same event, there was potentially meat for 4800 people. But as the examples of Agathon and Ion (above) show, there could be contributions from poets too. This being the case, the *Acharnians* chorus that complains that Antimachus left them dinnerless at the Lenaea need be adopting the persona neither of the poet nor of the (somehow recycled) chorus but may retain the persona of Acharnians, i.e. ordinary Athenians. I would argue that the "if you follow me, you will eat cakes" in *Peace* is both metaphorically and literally true: anyone in the audience

---

15 Athen. 1.3f (cf. *Suda* ι 487; *schol.* RV Ar. *Pax* 835): ὁ δὲ Χῖος Ἴων τραγῳδίαν νικήσας Ἀθήνησιν ἑκάστῳ τῶν Ἀθηναίων ἔδωκε Χῖου κεράμιον.

16 Plat. *Symp.* 174a, e, 176a-b.

17 As argued by Storey 2003, 104–105 n. 18.

18 McInerney 2010, 175f. estimates an average of 150–200 kilos of meat per bovine (about 27–45% less than modern beef cattle). As these were special oxen, worthy of serving as prizes, I take the upper estimate x 2 (= 400 kilos at 250 grams per serving).

who wants to follow the victory *komos* (once the judges announce victory) is very likely to find something to eat and drink. It is, after all, assumed in Plato's *Symposium* not only that most people at Agathon's party had attended the *epinikia* but that they had all there drunk to excess (176a), and yet none but Agathon, and perhaps Aristophanes, had actually participated in a production, successful or otherwise. The *epinikia* were not only open to all, but had food and drink in abundance for all who wanted to attend.

Periagermos

Unlike the *epinikia*, the second ritual we will look at is informal. It is the victory procession that goes from the site of victory (in this case the theatre) to the site of the *epinikia* (the Sanctuary of Dionysus). Most of our comic *exodoi* are happy and somewhat disorderly processions, whence the alternative (modern) name of *komoi*. Two Aristophanic *exodoi* are of particular interest. In *Acharnians* the hero is carried out by the chorus (*Ach.* 1224 ὡς τοὺς κριτάς με φέρετε). The staging here is important. Lamachus and Dikaiopolis sing a kind of echo duet. Lamachus orders his servants to carry him out in a stretcher to the hospital (θύραζέ μ' ἐξενέγκατ' εἰς τοῦ Πιττάλου / παιωνίαισι χερσίν);[19] this low exit contrasts with Dicaeopolis' high exit, carried out of the theatre by members of the chorus as it sings the victory song. In the *exodos* of *Peace,* the victorious hero is again raised aloft by the chorus as it leads him out singing his wedding song (1341f. ἀράμενοι φέρωμεν οἱ προτεταγμένοι / τὸν νυμφίον, ὦνδρες, "Those men in the front rank [of the chorus], let's lift and carry the groom!"). How are the heroes carried? Our first clues come from descriptions of victory rituals at athletic competitions.

Athletic victors are raised up in an informal ritual called the *periagermos*. Dio Chrysostom (*Or.* 9.14, written ca. 100 AD, but fictionally set in the 4th century) describes a *periagermos*:

> Afterwards he (Diogenes the Cynic) saw someone coming out of the racetrack with a great crowd and he was not even walking upon the earth, but carried high by the crowd, and some of them followed and shouted, others jumped for joy and raised their arms towards the sky, while yet others threw garlands and ribbons. When he was able to get near he asked someone "what happened and why all the racket around this man?" He answered "We won, dear fellow, the two-hundred yard dash!"

---

19 Cf. Olson 2002, 365 [*ad* Ar. *Ach.* 1231]; Biles 2011, 87–88.

This same ritual is described by Cicero, Plutarch and Pausanias in connection with the boxer and Olympic victor Diagoras whose sons were both victorious at the Olympic games of 448 BCE. We are told how the victorious sons carried their father about as virtual victor while the crowds showered him with flowers and declared him blessed on account of his sons.[20]

For athletes all stages of the ritual are well attested in literature.[21] It took place at the games in the immediate aftermath of a victory, though the petal-showers and possibly ribbon-tying would be repeated at the time of his home-coming, giving those not present at the victory an opportunity to congratulate the victor.[22] The ribbon-tying and petal-showers are also well attested in art.[23] Note, for future reference, that in the art the athletes who receive ribbons and petal or leaf showers frequently hold sprigs of foliage in their hands to signify the phyllobolia, even though, one can also sometimes clearly see a flurry of branches, petals, and leaves filling the air about them.[24]

Custom extended the *periagermos* and petal-showers to mythical heroes,[25] and popular practice extended petal-showers and ribbon-tying to victorious politicians and generals.[26] There seems however to be no explicit description of such victory rituals applied to the winners of musical or dramatic competitions.[27] Our earliest sources on these practices, Plato[28] and Eratosthenes[29] show

---

20 Cic. *Tusc.* 1.111; Plut. *Pel.* 34.6; Paus. 6.7.2–3 νικήσαντες δὲ οἱ νεανίσκοι διὰ τῆς πανηγύρεως τὸν πατέρα ἔφερον βαλλόμενόν τε ὑπὸ τῶν Ἑλλήνων ἄνθεσι καὶ εὐδαίμονα ἐπὶ τοῖς παισὶ καλούμενον.
21 Pind. *P.* 8.124; Simon. *PMG* 506; Eratosth. *FGrHist* 241 F 14; Dio Chrys. *Or.* 9.14; Paus. 6.7.2–3; Clem. Alex. *Paed.* 2.8.72.13; Ps.-Didymus, *On Problematic Words in Plato* 47; Phot. π 628 Theod.; Blech 1982, 112 n. 17.
22 See e.g. Slater 1984, 241–248; Currie 2005, 139–142.
23 Giglioli 1950; Kefalidou 1999, 110–117.
24 A fine example is provided by the Attic red-figure lekythos by the Bowdoin Painter, ca. 480 BCE (Paris BN 487 = Kafalidou 2009, 41 fig. 3).
25 Pind. *P.* 4.240; Eur. *Hec.* 573; Callim. *Hecale* fr. 260.11–15 Pf.; Ps.-Didymus, *On Problematic Words in Plato* 47; Phot. π 628 Theod.; Blech 1982, 124.
26 Blech 1982, 113 n. 20; Kefalidou 1999, 103–104; Currie 2005, 142; Kefalidou 2009, 41–42.
27 Nero's triumphant return from the Greek games, despite Blech 1982, 112 n. 17, refers to quite a different ritual, for which see Slater 2013 and cf. *P.Oxy.* 5202.
28 Plat. *Resp.* 621d καὶ ἐπειδὰν τὰ ἆθλα αὐτῆς κομιζώμεθα, ὥσπερ οἱ νικηφόροι περιαγειρόμενοι, καὶ ἐνθάδε καὶ ἐν τῇ χιλιέτει πορείᾳ, ἣν διεληλύθαμεν, εὖ πράττωμεν.
29 Eratosth. *FGrHist* 241 F 14 from *schol.* Eur. *Hec.* 573 (cf. Phot. π 628 = *Suda* π 1054). Ἐρατοσθένης γὰρ περὶ τῆς φυλλοβολίας φησὶν ὡς πάλαι χωρὶς ἄθλων ἀγωνιζομένων τῶν ἀνθρώπων τῶι νικήσαντι καθάπερ ἔρανον εἰσφέροντες ἔρριπτον τῶν θεατῶν ἕκαστος ὅπως ηὐπόρει. οἱ μὲν οὖν ἐμπορευόμενοι (?) διάφορα δῶρα ** τῶν δὲ λοιπῶν οἱ μὲν ἐγγὺς καθήμενοι στεφάνους ἐπετίθεσαν, οἱ δὲ ἀπωτέρω τοῦτο ὅπερ ἦν λοιπὸν ἔβαλλον τοῖς ἄνθεσι καὶ φύλλοις,

that the point of the ceremony was a kind of curtain call, to allow the victor to gather applause and gifts. Both Plato and Eratosthenes refer to "contest winners" generally. Eratosthenes, at least, is thinking primarily of athletes, since he goes on to speak of the origins of the practices at the Olympic games.

Tainiosis

There is some scholarship for the ribbon-tying ritual. Since Passow in 1902 it has been knowable that ribbon tying was very much part of the culture of Dionysian choral victory. It is alluded to in the mystic chorus of *Frogs* and in the Alcibiades episode of Plato's *Symposium*. Scholars have generally ignored this evidence for different reasons.

The chorus in *Frogs* (348–393) makes a prayer for victory:[30]

Δήμητερ, ἀγνῶν ὀργίων   [Str.]
   ἄνασσα, συμπαραστάτει,
καὶ σῷζε τὸν σαυτῆς χορόν,
καί μ' ἀσφαλῶς πανήμερον
   παῖσαί τε καὶ χορεῦσαι·

   καὶ πολλὰ μὲν γέλοιά μ' εἰ-   [Antistr.]
πεῖν, πολλὰ δὲ σπουδαῖα, καὶ
   τῆς σῆς ἑορτῆς ἀξίως
παίσαντα καὶ σκώψαντα νι-
κήσαντα ταινιοῦσθαι.

Demeter, Lady of the Holy Rites, stand beside me and save your chorus, and (allow) me to jest and dance with everything going as it should all day long; and (allow) me to say many funny things, and many serious, and after jesting and mocking to win and be ribboned.

The meaning of this passage has been obscured by the scholia that claim that "be ribboned as the victor" means "to be crowned". The "ribbon," they argue, is

---

<ὡς> καὶ νῦν ἐπὶ τοῖς ἐπιφανῶς ἀγωνιζομένοις προβάλλουσι ζώνας, πετάσους, χιτωνίσκους, κρηπῖδας. διὸ σύνηθες ἦν κύκλωι περινοστοῦντας ἀγείρειν τὰ διδόμενα. ἕως μὲν οὖν ἒν ἀγώνισμα κατὰ τὴν Ὀλυμπίαν ἦν, δαψιλὴς ἐγίνετο ἡ τῶν δώρων δόσις, πολυπλασιαζομένων δὲ τούτων ταῦτα ἐμειοῦτο εἰς πολλοὺς καταμεριζόμενα, καὶ τέλος ἡ φυλλοβολία κατελείφθη. ταῦτα οὖν παρὰ τοὺς χρόνους Εὐριπίδης· ὀψὲ γάρ ποτε ὁ ἀγερμὸς <ἀντὶ> τῆς φυλλοβολίας ἀπελείφθη.
30 For anticipations of victory in the choral lyrics generally, see Revermann 2006, 113–118, 256; Wilson 2007, 268–284; Biles 2011, 88–94.

what ties the crown together (ταινιοῦσθαι: ἀντὶ τοῦ στεφανοῦσθαι. ταινία γὰρ τὸ ῥάμμα τοῦ στεφάνου). This is nonsense. The scholia are improvising to make sense of "ribboned" in this passage where "crowned" was expected.

Both colloquial and official Attic speech are careful to distinguish "ribbons" (ταινίαι) from "crowns" (στέφανοι): they are completely different in material, shape and function.[31] Crowns are of foliage or flowers, circular and awarded by the festival officials; ribbons are long bands of coloured fabric, tied in bows with long streaming ends to the head, arms and legs of the victor and given by friends, family and admirers. The chorus in *Frogs* speak of being ribboned in anticipation of what for most was surely the climactic moment of victory, when the community offered its tokens of congratulation.

The Alcibiades episode in *Symposium* clearly gives us the context. When Alcibiades appears at Agathon's house he is "garlanded with a thick *stephanos* of ivy and violets and wore a great many ribbons (*tainiai*) on his head."[32] Alcibiades wants to tie a ribbon on Agathon in celebration of his victory but his words upon entering Agathon's house make it clear that the appropriate moment for ribbon-tying would have been at the "official" *epinikia* the day before: "I was not able to come yesterday, but now I have come with ribbons on my head, so that from my head I can bind — so I proclaim it — the head of the wisest and most beautiful man" (χθὲς μὲν οὐχ οἷός τ᾽ ἐγενόμην ἀφικέσθαι, νῦν δὲ ἥκω ἐπὶ τῇ κεφαλῇ ἔχων τὰς ταινίας, ἵνα ἀπὸ τῆς ἐμῆς κεφαλῆς τὴν τοῦ σοφωτάτου καὶ καλλίστου κεφαλὴν, ἀνειπὼν οὑτωσί, ἀναδήσω). Alcibiades' words ἀνειπὼν οὑτωσί significantly reproduce the official language of proclamation of victory by the herald as if replaying the cue that normally triggers these rituals.[33] The value of this evidence has often been missed because of confusion in the mind of scholars between Agathon's private party and the *epinikia*. The right time to tie a ribbon is during the *komos* that follows the announcement of victory or during the course of the feast at the Sanctuary of Dionysus. Untenable, incidentally, is the interpretation that the Lenaea (where the *Frogs* was first performed and where Agathon, according to Athenaeus 5.217a–b, won the victory

---

31 On the rare occasions where Attic decrees crown people with both "crowns" and "ribbons" the language is careful to specify "a crown along with a ribbon:" *IG* II² 1292, ll. 11–12 (215/14 BCE); Vanderpool 1968, 6; Robert 1969, 22–23; Clinton 1974, 107 n. 49.
32 Plat. *Symp.* 212d–e.
33 Dover 1980, 160; Biles 2007, 26 n. 38. Hermann's emendation of the manuscripts' (and *P.Oxy.* 843's) banal ἐὰν εἴπω is surely right. For the general imitation of the Dionysian festival program in *Symposium*, see Sider 1980, Biles 2007.

celebrated in *Symposium*) differed from the Dionysia in awarding ribbons rather than crowns.[34] As Passow long ago observed: "Tänien-Agone gab es nicht!"[35]

The ribbon ceremony has been well studied by Zachary Biles.[36] He drew attention to the delayed *tainiosis* ritual in the *Symposium* and the scene depicted on a series of some thirty-three reliefs known (misleadingly) as the "Icarius Reliefs."[37] These reliefs are thought to copy a neo-Attic relief of the 2nd century BCE which in turn copies a 3rd-century BCE votive.

Fig. 1: Marble Relief, 1st c. AD copy of a probably 3rd-c. BCE original, London BM 1805,0703.123. © Trustees of the British Museum.

The scene is set in a sanctuary of Dionysus — there is no obvious reproduction of the topography of The Sanctuary in Athens — but details make it perfectly clear this is sacred space. Chief among these is the appearance of votive reliefs (*pinakes* of the type dedicated by dramatic *choregoi*), seen on pillars, one in the

---

34 Reasonable doubts exist about the accuracy of Athenaeus' information. The circumstances described by the *Symposium* are better suited to the Dionysia: see Taplin 1993, 4 n.12.

35 Passow 1902, 9.

36 Biles 2007, 21–23.

37 Pochmarski 1990, 297–301; Bacchielli 1996.

foreground and one in the background to the right of the satyr.[38] The man on the couch has food and drink before him. Under the couch are four comic masks mounted on boxes. Because of the masks, scholars have usually identified the figure on the couch as a poet,[39] though he could just as well be an actor or any-one else who might win a Dionysian victory. He is clearly the god's guest, but there is a bit of a role reversal. Dionysus appears at the head of a *komos* and he is carrying a ribbon in his hand, obviously to tie on the victor's head. There is another couch beside the victor's, awaiting Dionysus.

The relief is of the sort that we know dramatic choregoi dedicated at the Sanctuary of Dionysus Eleuthereus to commemorate a victory (comparable to the *pinakes* depicted in the relief itself). The composition borrows and plays with the typical imagery of choregic reliefs.[40] Andrew Stewart has recently pub-lished what he supposes to be a terracotta sculptor's model for a choregic mon-ument for dithyramb from 330–300 BCE, just a little before our hypothesised choregic relief for a dramatic victory.[41] It shows Dionysus leaning against a tri-pod holding a cornucopia from which dangles a ribbon, ready to be tied on a victor. Evidently the motif of Dionysus performing a *tainiosis* was a known feature of late 4th-century Athenian choregic art. The cornucopia alludes to the plenitude of the festival generally, but in combination with the ribbon, it probably alludes more specifically to the plenitude of the victory feast.

Vase-painting also amply attests a ribbon-tying ritual for choral victories. Over fifty Attic black- and red-figure vases render images of the choregic tripods given as prizes for the dithyrambic choruses at the Dionysia.[42] (Tripods were given out as prizes in Athens only for dithyrambic victories.) One of the most common motifs is a Nike or Eros flying towards a choregic tripod, ribbon in hand; otherwise tripods are frequently shown already tied with ribbons on legs and rings. Dionysus famously is sometimes depicted wearing the victor's *tainia* wrapped around his own head.[43]

---

38 For the dedication type, including a more detailed discussion of the relief in London, see Csapo 2016.
39 A scholarly reflex since Picard 1934, 141 and Picard 1964, 188–193 specifically identified the reclining figure as Menander.
40 Picard 1934; Micheli 1998; Csapo 2010; Heinemann 2011, 398–403; Csapo 2016.
41 Stewart 2013, 622–623 no. 7 fig. 8.
42 The list in Csapo 2010, 125–130, needs several supplements.
43 Most spectacularly on the Apulian bell-krater, ca. 390 BCE, in the Cleveland Museum of Art (inv. 1989.73).

Iconographic Evidence for the *Periagermos* in Dionysian Competitons

The distance from the theatre of Dionysus to the Sanctuary is very short. In order to give time to supporters to press through the crowd to bring ribbons of congratulations to the victors, athletic victors might make an extra lap of the stadium, walking, or frequently, as our textual sources suggest, being carried slowly about on the shoulders of friends. I know of no depictions of athletes being carried about this way,[44] but I have found four examples for choral victors.

The image on an unattributed Attic red-figure oinochoe of ca. 425 BCE (Fig. 2) is centred upon a mounted tripod monumentalising a dithyrambic victory.[45] What appears to be leaching white paint on the tripod was probably underlay for gilding. To the (viewer's) right of the tripod appear a pair of naked youths. The larger youth is in three-quarter profile, probably to indicate his ecstatic state. He carries on his shoulders another youth, whom he secures with his left hand, in his right he holds an oinochoe, probably containing wine to drink in celebration. The youth on his shoulders wears a crown around his head (the artist has taken care to show leaves at the front of his head and a few moving towards his temples and the back of his head). He holds out a sprig of, possibly, ivy in his right hand. It is an allusion to the phyllobolia (see above). A figure to the left directs his gaze, not to the tripod as is usual in this group of vases, but to the pair of youths. He offers a garland to the youth who is carried upon the other's shoulders. He wears ornate and formal dress, in contrast to the nakedness of the youths, and he also wears a crown around his head (there are articulated leaves at the front, side and back). The filmy white residue covering most of the crown may also be the remains of underlay for lost gilding (originally echoing the tripod). His crown and dress suggest that he can be understood to be the victorious choregos who graciously congratulates his chorus on their victory. We have the essential ingredients of the *periagermos* ritual as described by our sources: a representative of the chorus being carried aloft by a friend and receiving garlands and sprigs of foliage.

---

44 With the possible exception of charioteers in Roman art, see Dunbabin 1982, 68 n. 23.
45 Louvre CA 1354; van Hoorn 1951 no. 839, fig. 136; Amandry/Ducat 1973, fig. 13.

Fig. 2: Attic rf oenochoe, ca. 425, Louvre CA 1354. Photo ©RMN-Grand Palais (Musée du Louvre) / Hervé Lewandowski.

A second example is not Dionysian, but at least related to choral competitions in Athens. A relief on a choregic dedication for victory in the *pyrrhiche* at the Panathenaia has long been connected with the *periagermos*.[46] A naked youth carries a

---

[46] Athens NM 3854; Wilson 2000, 236–237, fig. 21; Agelidis 2008, 55–56, no. 102, pl. 11a. The base is interpreted as a *periagermos* by Poursat 1967, 109–110; Tzachou-Alexandri 1989, 210 no. 100; Valavanis 1990, 354–355 n. 152.

second youth, possibly the chorus leader, standing on his shoulders, and still bearing the arms that he carried in his performance. The supported youth adopts a kind of Promachos pose. A third figure, also bearing arms, follows close behind them. The relief does not show the chorus in performance. The naked youth who carries the other on his shoulders wears no costume (one would have expected the helmet at least). In any case there is no parallel for a dance performance that involves choreuts standing on other choreut's shoulders.

Fig. 3: Attic marble choregic relief, National Archaeological Museum, Athens 3854. Photo: Dimitrios Yalouris. © Hellenic Ministry of Culture and Sports / Archaeological Receipts Fund.

My third illustration of a *periagermos* is for a dramatic victory. It is a terracotta relief dated to the 4th century that was excavated in Kepoi on the Taman Peninsula (Russian Black Sea) in 1967, but first fully published in 2012.[47] The relief is probably of local manufacture but the region of the Cimmerian Bosporus had certainly received theatre culture by the time of the artifact's manufacture and the indications are that Bosporan theatre was strongly influenced by Athens.[48] The relief is a reasonable size for a choregic *pinax* (66 by 37 cm.) — note that the head of the figure who is being carried rose up above the upper frame of the *pinax*. Breaking through the frame is sometimes an iconographic index of exultation. If it is not itself a choregic dedication, it is a copy of the kind of imagery we would expect to

---

47 State Historical Museum, Moscow ГИМ 17322, Оп.Б 33/20; Zhuravlev/Lomtadze 2007; Zhuravlev/Lomtadze 2012 (Russian publication); Zhuravlev/Lomtadze 2013. I am most grateful to Dr. Denis Zhuravlev for sending me photographs of this relief.
48 Csapo/Wilson 2015, 374–378; Braund/Hall 2014, 382–386.

find on a dramatic choregic *pinax*. We do not have independent evidence for a choregic system in the Cimmerian Bosporus, but we do have evidence for an agonothete for theatrical competitions at Nymphaion as early as 389 BCE and at Hermonassa later in the same century; both agonothetes observed the custom of making dedicatory monuments.[49] That a Bosporan agonothete or choregos made a commemorative dedication for a dramatic victory is a likely possibility.

Fig. 4: Terracotta relief from Kepoi, State Historical Museum, Moscow ГИМ 17322, Оп.Б 33/20. © State Historical Museum, Moscow (Photo: I.A. Sedenkov).

---

49 Csapo/Wilson 2020, **IV Fiii**.

Two men wearing comic costume raise a third man onto their shoulders. The first publication, by Zhuravlev and Lomtaze in 2012, identified the costumed figures as satyrs, but the figures must be comic, the ears are odd, but not pointy, as one would expect to see on satyrs, and, more definitively, there are no tails. On the contrary, the leggings, limp and enlarged phalloi, rounded bellies and buttocks and the short tunics are standard costume for comic performers. The masks too appear to be different, so the figures represent a cast rather than specifically the chorus. The performer on the left wears the crown of victory around his head. The raised man wears regular clothing and has hair long enough to touch his preserved right shoulder. The first publication argues that the figure is Dionysus. The evident effort of the artist to show the details of the dramatic costumes suggests, however, that this is no mythical scene and, besides, there is no hint of any attribute like a thyrsos or a kantharos to recommend this interpretation. But, whoever the character on top, the scene alludes to the victory ritual of raising and carrying the victor about; here the performers possibly process the choregos himself.

Fig. 5: Terracotta relief, State Historical Museum, Moscow ГИМ 114745/181, Оп.Б 2151/181, ГК 14984551. © State Historical Museum, Moscow.

This pinax has a parallel in a much smaller and cruder terracotta plaque purchased by the Moscow State Historical Museum from a dealer in Kerch antiquities.[50] The head of the central figure is there also missing so it does not help establish his identity. Both appear to imitate a common model which we might reasonably guess to have been a well-known monument. The details of the comic costume, especially the belly padding and the exposed phalloi, would place the original relief no later than about 340 BCE, if Attic, and perhaps 330–320 BCE, if of local manufacture. The details appear to be different in this much cruder piece, but the schema is the same. Two comic performers carry a third figure, who is not wearing comic costume, about on their shoulders, in the manner of the *periagermos*.

To conclude: this evidence confirms that, once the victory was announced, and possibly after the official crowning by the Archon or Priest of Dionysus, it was normal practice for supporters to raise up the victorious choregos, or poets or even choreuts and parade them about while well-wishers showered them with leaves and petals and tied ribbons to their arms legs and heads. This procession led from the theatre, site of the victory, to the Sanctuary of Dionysus, site of the epinician feast. All who wished to come were welcome and could not in any case be kept out. There was food and drink for all provided by the state, by the priest of Dionysus, by the choregoi and at least sometimes by the poets. The raising of the hero in the final *komos* of *Acharnians* and *Peace* alludes to this victory ritual as do the invitations to the audience to dine in *Peace* and *Ecclesiazusae*.

Bibliography

Agelidis, Soi (2008), *Choregische Weihgeschenke in Griechenland*, Bonn.
Amandry, Pierre/Ducat, Jean (1973), "Trépieds déliens", in: *Bulletin de Correspondance Hellénique* Suppl. 1, 17–64.
Bacchielli, Lidiano (1996), "Un nuovo rilievo con la raffigurazione della 'Visita di Dioniso ad Ikarios'", in: Picozzi, Maria Grazia/Carinci, Filippo (eds.), *Studi in memoria di Lucia Guerrini*, Rome, 145–147.
Biles, Zachary (2007), "Celebrating Poetic Victory: Representations of Epinikia in Classical Athens", in: *Journal of Hellenic Studies* 127, 19–37.
Biles, Zachary (2011), *Aristophanes and the Poetics of Competition*, Cambridge.
Blech, Michael (1982), *Studien zum Kranz bei den Griechen*, Berlin.

---

50 State Historical Museum ГИМ 114745/18, Оп.Б 2151/18, ГК 14984551; Zhuravlev/Lomtadze 2013, 22 fig. 5.

Braund, David/Hall, Edith (2014), "Theatre in the Fourth-Century Black Sea Region", in: Csapo, Eric/Goette, Hans-Rupprecht/Green, J. Richard/ Wilson, Peter (eds.), *Greek Theatre in the Fourth Century B.C.*, Berlin, 371–390.

Clinton, Kevin (1974), *The Sacred Officials of the Eleusinian Mysteries*, in: *Transactions of the American Philosophical Society* 64.3, Philadelphia.

Csapo, Eric (2010), "The Context of Choregic Dedications", in: Taplin, Oliver/Wyles, Rosie (eds.), *The Pronomos Vase and its Context*, Oxford, 79–130.

Csapo, Eric (2016), "Choregic Dedications and What They Tell Us about Comic Performance in the Fourth Century BC", in: *Logeion* 6, 252–284.

Csapo, Eric/Wilson, Peter (2015), "Drama Outside Athens in the Fifth and Fourth Centuries BC", in: Lamari, Anna (ed.), *Dramatic Reperformances: Authors and Contexts*, Berlin/Boston, 316–395.

Csapo, Eric/Wilson, Peter (2020), *A Social and Economic History of the Theatre to 300 BC*, Vol. 2, *Theatre Outside Athens*, Cambridge.

Csapo, Eric/Wilson, Peter (forthcoming), *A Social and Economic History of the Theatre to 300 BC*, Vol. 1, *Theatre in Athens*, Cambridge.

Currie, Bruno (2005), *Pindar and the Cult of Heroes*, Oxford.

Di Bari, Marta F. (2013), *Scene finali di Aristofane: Cavalieri, Nuvole, Tesmoforiazuse*, Lecce.

Dover, Kenneth J. (1980), *Plato: Symposium*, Cambridge.

Dunbabin, Katherine M.D. (1982), "The Victorious Charioteer on Mosaics and Related Monuments", *American Journal of Archaeology* 86, 65–89.

Giglioli, Giulio Q. (1950), "Phyllobolia", *Archeologia Classica: rivista della Scuola naz. di Archeologia, pubbl. a cura degli Ist. di Archeologia e Storia dell'arte greca e romana e di Etruscologia e antichità italiche dell'Univ. di Roma* 2, 31–45.

Heinemann, Alexander (2011), "Ein dekorativer Gott? Bilder für Dionysos zwischen griechischer Votivpraxis und römischem Decorum", in: Schlesier, Renate (ed.), *A Different God? Dionysos and Ancient Polytheism*, Berlin, 391–412.

Jameson, Michael H. (1994), "The Ritual of the Athena Nike Parapet", in: Osborne, Robin/ Hornblower, Simon (eds.), *Ritual, Finance, Politics: Athenian Democratic Accounts presented to David Lewis,* Oxford, 307–324.

Kefalidou, Eurydice (1999), "Ceremonies of Athletic Victory in Ancient Greece: An Interpretation", in: *Nikephoros* 12, 95–119.

Kefalidou, Eurydice (2009), "The Plants of Victory in Ancient Greece and Rome", in: Morel, Jean-Paul/Mercuri, Anna Maria (eds.), *Plants and Culture: Seeds of the Cultural Heritage of Europe*, Bari, 39–44.

McInerney, Jeremy (2010), *The Cattle of the Sun: Cows and Culture in the World of the Ancient Greeks*, Princeton.

Micheli, Maria Elisa (1998), "Rilievi con maschere, attori, poeti. Temi di genere e/o ispirazione poetica?", in: *Bollettino d'arte del Ministero per i beni culturali e ambientali* 103–104, 1–32.

Olson, S. Douglas (2002) (ed.), *Aristophanes. Acharnians*, Oxford.

Parker, Robert (2005), *Polytheism and Society at Athens*, Oxford.

Passow, Wolfgang (1902), *Studien zum Parthenon*, Philologische Untersuchungen 17, Berlin.

Picard, Charles (1934), "Observations sur la date et l'origine des reliefs dits de la 'Visite chez Ikarios'", in : *American Journal of Archaeology* 38, 137–152.

Picard, Charles (1964), "Comment nommer le poète hellénistique qui passa pour avoir reçu, un jour, la visite solennelle de Dionysos?'", in: *Revue Archéologique* 3, 188–193.

Pochmarski, Erwin (1990), *Dionysische Gruppen: eine typologische Untersuchung zur Geschichte des Stützmotivs*, Vienna.

Poursat, Jean-Claude (1967), "Une base signée du musée national d'Athènes: pyrrichistes victorieux'", in: *Bulletin de Correspondance Hellénique* 91, 102–110.

Revermann, Martin (2006), *Comic Business: Aspects of Theatricality and Dramatic Technique in Old Comedy*, Oxford.

Robert, Louis (1969), "Inscriptions d'Athènes et de la Grèce Centrale", in: *Archaiologike ephemeris*, 1–58.

Schmitt-Pantel, Pauline (1997), *La cité au banquet: Histoire des repas publics dans les cités grecques*, Rome.

Shear, Julia L. (2003), "Prizes from Athens: The List of Panathenaic Prizes and the Sacred Oil", in: *Zeitschrift für Papyrologie und Epigraphik* 142, 87–108.

Sider, David (1980), "Plato's *Symposium* as Dionysian Festival", in: *Quaderni Urbinati di Cultura Classica* 33, 41–56.

Slater, William J. (1984), "Nemean One: The Victor's Return in Poetry and Politics", in: Gerber, Douglas E. (ed.), *Greek Poetry and Philosophy: Studies in Honour of Leonard Woodbury*, Chico, 241–264.

Slater, William J. (2013), "The Victor's Return, and the Categories of Games", in: Martzavou, Paraskevi/Papazarkadas, Nikolaos (eds.), *Epigraphical Approaches to the Postclassical Polis: Fourth Century B.C. to Second Century A.D.*, Oxford, 139–163.

Stewart, Andrew (2013), "Sculptors' Sketches, Trial Pieces, Figure Studies, and Models in Poros Limestone from the Athenian Agora", in: *Hesperia* 82, 615–650.

Storey, Ian (2003), *Eupolis: Poet of Old Comedy*, Oxford.

Taplin, Oliver (1993), *Comic Angels*, Oxford.

Tzachou-Alexandri, Olga (1989) (ed.), *Mind and Body. Athletic Contests in Ancient Greece*, Athens.

Valavanis, Panos (1990), "La proclamation des vainqueurs aux Panathénées", in: *Bulletin de Correspondance Hellénique* 114, 325–354.

Vanderpool, Eugene (1968), "Three Inscriptions from Eleusis", in: *Archaiologikon Deltion* 24, Chron. A', 1–9.

Wilhelm, Adolf (1907), "Inschrift aus Pagai", in: *Jahreshefte des Österreichischen Archäologischen Instituts* 10, 17–32.

Wilson, Peter (2000), *The Athenian Institution of the Khoregia*, Cambridge.

Wilson, Peter (2007), "Nike's Cosmetics: Dramatic Victory, the End of Comedy and Beyond", in: Kraus, Christina/Goldhill, Simon/Foley, Helene/Elsner, Jas (eds.), *Visualizing the Tragic: Drama, Myth, and Ritual in Greek Art and Literature: Essays in Honour of Froma Zeitlin*, Oxford, 257–287.

Wilson, Peter (2008), "Costing the Dionysia", in: Revermann, Martin/Wilson, Peter (eds.), *Performance, Iconography, Reception: Studies in Honour of Oliver Taplin*, Oxford, 88–127.

Zhuravlev, Denis V./Lomtadze, Georgii A. (2007), „Терракотовый рельеф V в. до н.э. с изображением 'несения Диониса' с Таманского полуострова (предварительная информация)", in: Zuev, Vladimir Y. (ed.), *Боспорский феномен: сакральный смысл региона памятников, находок,* St. Petersburg, 199–207.

Zhuravlev, Denis V./Lomtadze, Georgii A. (2013), "A Terracotta Relief with a Dionysiac Motif from Kepoi", in: *Ancient Civilizations from Scythia to Siberia* 19, 13–31.

S. Douglas Olson

Some Staging Issues and Their Consequences in Aristophanes' *Clouds*

Abstract: This paper focuses on three specific issues raised by the first scene in the surviving version of Aristophanes' *Clouds*: (1) the character of Strepsiades' bed and how it is put to use later in the action; (2) the costuming of Strepsiades and Pheidippides, and of the Just Argument and the Unjust Argument, who, I suggest, recall them in the second half of the play; and (3) the number of actors the text requires. I use these arguably minor points in an attempt to shed light on a number of structural and interpretative aspects of the play, on the relationship between *Clouds I* and *Clouds II*, and on the way that we today talk about and interpret Athenian comedy.

Keywords: *Clouds*, staging, props, Three Actors Rule, costuming

My topic of this chapter is Aristophanes' *Clouds*, a comedy first performed at the City Dionysia in Athens in 421 BCE. In particular, I consider a complex bundle of issues connected with the staging of the play; with the text as we have it today; and with the history of that text, which we know was reworked in antiquity by the poet himself. Most of my discussion is devoted to the opening scene, the finale, and the long confrontation between the two personified Socratic Arguments in the second half of the play. There is much about *Clouds* that we do not know and probably cannot know, which is to say that I will be working within difficult argumentative and historical parameters. I nonetheless hope to extract a bit more sense from an opaque and perhaps incompletely revised text regarding both what went on onstage in the Theatre of Dionysus in 421 BCE and how Aristophanes attempted to revise his comedy afterwards. But I will also offer some larger closing arguments about the fragility of such supposed "knowledge" and the extent to which it is tied to our contemporary concerns as critics and readers.

Thanks are due Piero Totaro, who conceived and organized the conference that formed the basis for this volume. It is a pleasure to publish this chapter in a collection that also features work by Oliver Taplin, whose book on Aeschylus first taught me to how to think about ancient dramatic texts as live theatre. Most of the arguments put forward here are implicit in rather different forms in Olson 2021.

https://doi.org/10.1515/9783111248028-006

I begin with a brief excerpt from Kenneth Dover's justly famous and influential Oxford University Press commentary, on the very beginning of the play: "From the other side of the theatre" (by which Dover means the right-hand side) "two beds are carried in and placed in front of the skene, somewhat to the right of the central door. In each bed there is a person covered with blankets. The men who have carried the beds in go away. The play begins ... One of the two [men] remains motionless. The other tosses and turns with increasing violence, and finally sits upright with a gesture of despair. We see from his mask that he is an old man".[1] Some details of this reconstruction are patently conjectural, but also insignificant. There is no way to know, for example, whether the beds in question are on the right- or the left-hand side of the stage, and which it is makes no difference to our understanding of the play. But other points of Dover's reconstructed staging are more concrete and more significant. There are two beds, which are bulky enough that they must be carried on- and off-stage by prop-men, so that what we have is a Taplinesque "canceled entrance", meaning that the audience knows that it should ignore all this as meaningless stage-business, and can accept that when the real action of the play begins, the characters have been sleeping — or trying unsuccessfully to sleep — perhaps for hours. Dover makes no comment here or elsewhere on the costuming of the individuals in the beds, who are in any case mostly invisible at this point.

At 18–29, the old man (eventually identified as Strepsiades) calls for a slave to bring him a lamp and his account books, since it turns out that what is keeping him awake is anxiety about how to repay the debts he has incurred to allow his son to have race-horses and chariots. The Slave speaks only one-and-a-half lines, but Dover (p. lxxix) identifies him as the fourth actor, to whom he also gives the parts of the Student who shows Strepsiades around Socrates' school later on, the Just Argument and the First Creditor, so that the man in question is onstage for 100s of lines and has a number of important roles. When Strepsiades grows annoyed with the Slave, supposedly for using the wrong lamp, he attempts to hit him, although Dover comments (on 58) "No doubt the slave in fact keeps out of danger, and runs indoors". In the meantime, the other sleeping character, Pheidippides (Strepsiades' son) has awoken momentarily, protesting (35–36, 38) "Really, father; why are you being difficult and tossing and turning all night long? Let me sleep a bit, sir!" After more complaining to the audience about his financial troubles, Strepsiades decides to wake up Pheidippides once and for all, in order to ask him to enter the Thinkery as a student, so that he can learn to talk in a sufficiently clever and misleading fashion to baffle the jurors

---

1 Dover 1968, 91.

and get his father out of paying his debts. When Pheidippides refuses, Strepsiades decides to go to school himself. I return to all these points later on. For the moment, some introductory remarks of a different sort are necessary.

As already noted, the original *Clouds* was a failure (thus the second *Hypothesis*), and the version of the comedy we have appears to be a rewrite (thus the first *Hypothesis*) produced a few years later on, in the early 410s BCE.[2] Just enough fragments of *Clouds I* are preserved to allow us to be certain that it was different from *Clouds II* at least occasionally on a line-by-line level, and the first *Hypothesis* informs us that the text was reworked and rearranged throughout, and in particular that the parabasis is completely different from the old one, and that the confrontation between the two Arguments and the final scene are additions to the text. To make matters more difficult, there are enough odd points in the argument and enough issues regarding staging practicalities to suggest that Aristophanes' revision of *Clouds* was incomplete, at least on what appear to be the standard rules of ancient staging, to which I return below. We are thus in the awkward position of attempting to make theatrical and literary sense of what is partially a performance text but perhaps partially also a text intended only for reading. But *Clouds* clearly got more attention from Aristophanes than most of his other plays did, since he returned to it for a second time and speaks about it at *Wasps* 1043–1048 with great — if admittedly self-serving — conviction as the most significant of his comedies up to that point, all of which suggests that we should at least begin with the assumption that it is coherent on an argumentative and dramatic level. In what follows, I focus on three specific issues raised by the first scene in the surviving *Clouds*: (1) Strepsiades' bed; (2) the costuming of Strepsiades and Pheidippides, and of two other characters I will suggest recall them in the second half of the play; and (3) the number of actors the text requires. My larger goal is to use these arguably minor points to shed light on a number of structural and interpretative aspects of the surviving play; on the relationship between *Clouds I* and *Clouds II*; and on the way that we today talk about and interpret Athenian comedy.

To return to the opening scene of the play and (1) the question of Strepsiades' bed: Dover (quoted above) suggests that there are in fact two beds, which are carried on by prop-men in the guise of slaves and then carried off again once Strepsiades and Pheidippides are up, to clear the stage. Dover further suggests that we are to understand that the night is cold, which is part of why Strepsiades

---

2 Detailed discussion of the question at Dover 1968, lxxx–xcviii; Di Bari 2013, 194–239. See also Hubbard 1986; Olson 1994, whose exchange ultimately has little effect on our overall understanding of the problem.

says at 10 that Pheidippides is wrapped in five blankets, and as is not unreasonable (in real-world terms) for Dionysia-time, in early spring. We might begin by asking "Why two beds?", particularly if staying warm is an issue. One bed would do, and it is accordingly worth noting that Pheidippides complains not about Strepsiades talking or having a light on in the same room, but about him tossing and turning, making it impossible for his son to sleep. This all implies that Strepsiades and Pheidippides share a single bed at the beginning of the play, and one reasonable interpretation of Dover's comments to the contrary would seem to be that they reflect an unconscious, culturally bound assumption that people do not sleep together unless they are married, and that fathers and sons in particular do not do so. Second, as for the prop-men who supposedly carry the bed on and off, we might also ask why Strepsiades and Pheidippides cannot do this themselves and then lie down, allowing the Theatre audience to "cancel" *that* little bit of arguably less puzzling stage-business — unless the bed was too heavy to make this possible. I discuss (and reject) the latter possibility below. But here I will merely suggest that we may have another problematic assumption at work in Dover's commentary on these lines, which is that Aristophanes' characters are sleeping on something approaching what we today would call "furniture", as opposed to a simple low, light cot or the like. Third, as to whether the slave who brings Strepsiades his account-book is a full-fledged actor: One standard principle developed by modern scholars to make sense of late 5th-century Athenian drama is the so-called "Three Actors Rule", which specifies that only three speaking characters can be onstage at one time, although an individual actor can go offstage, don a different costume and mask, and return as someone else. In the case of comedy, this rule is generally expanded to "Three Actors Plus", meaning that virtually every Aristophanic play contains a number of minor parts that require a fourth speaking character, and that these lines are routinely assigned to "extras", i.e. non-professionals who could be taught to pronounce a verse or two of stage-Greek properly and coached on how to get on and off without doing too much damage to the production as a whole. Dover in his Introduction (pp. lxxxviii–lxxxix), in a highly unconventional move, rejects the "Three Actors Plus Rule" for *Clouds* on the basis of the Arguments-scene and the play's finale (to which I return below), and indeed argues that the rule in general is a weak modern assumption that reflects a lack of imagination about how to stage the other ten surviving comedies. For the moment, I merely note that a four-actor staging is unnecessary for the opening scene of *Clouds*, which can in fact be staged assuming only three actors and no extras (since only Strepsiades and Pheidippides are onstage at this point, and no one else will appear for almost 100 lines). I also note that

Dover has taken the first step down a slippery and problematic argumentative slope, since if we are willing to allow comedy four actors, why not five? or even ten? And why, on the other hand, should it be the case that the other ten comedies neatly accommodate the "Three Actors Plus Rule", if this is merely a failure of modern critical thinking? Finally, I observe in passing that Dover's claim that Strepsiades' fist or stick never comes in contact with the slave finds no positive support in the text, while other evidence (including Ar. *Pax* 741–747) leaves little doubt that Athenian audiences found it wildly amusing to see slaves howl in pain. Once again, this looks more like an example of modern sensibilities imposed on the text than a dispassionate reconstruction of what went on onstage in 421 BCE.

I discuss the bed in more detail below. Before doing so, however, I turn briefly to (2) the question of costuming.[3] 497–498 shows that Strepsiades is by that point in the play wearing a heavy outer robe (a *himation*), since Socrates tells him that he must remove it in order to enter the Thinkery, while at 856–858 Pheidippides mocks his father for being without his robe, and indeed his shoes as well, since Socrates has kept them. It is accordingly worth asking what, if anything, Strepsiades is wearing when the play begins. Eustathius at one point early on in his commentary on the *Odyssey* (p. 1398.59) insists that "the ancients" slept naked, which is probably in the first instance a reference to Telemachus taking off his clothes when he goes to bed at the end of Book One. But Blepyrus in Aristophanes' *Ecclesiazusae* has also taken off his outer robe to go to sleep, which is why his wife is able to steal it when she goes off to the Assembly dressed as a man (*Ec.* 314–315, 526–527). It may accordingly be the case that Strepsiades at the beginning of *Clouds* is either stage-naked or at least half-naked, i.e. dressed only in a tunic (or *chiton*), as he certainly is throughout much of the action, given that we know he turns his *himation* over to Socrates. If this is right, there must be a bit of unmarked stage-action somewhere in the first fifty lines or so of the text, as the old man pulls on his clothing after he gets out of bed and prepares to face the world — a reminder, if we needed one, that our texts preserve only what was said onstage and not what sometimes went on between the words. Of more concern for my argument is the quality of Strepsiades' clothing. At 68–72, the old man makes intriguing comments on related issues when he offers what he appears to regard as a telling anecdote from Pheidippides' youth: his unnamed and now-absent wife wanted their son to grow up to wear a fancy saffron-dyed *xystis* and drive a chariot up to the Acropolis,

---

3 The standard work on Aristophanic costuming (examined on a comprehensive, item-by-item basis) is Stone 1981. See also (more recently) Compton-Engle 2015; Piqueux 2022.

like his uncle Megacles, while Strepsiades wanted him to put on a rough leather *diphthera* and drive goats in from the countryside, like his father. Clothing style is thus thematized early on in *Clouds*, and already at 14 Strepsiades has referred to his son's long hair, which is part of his physical self-presentation as an aspiring, aristocratic knight who has emphatically followed his mother's suggestions about what sort of a person he should become, rather than his father's. The text does not expressly tell us what Pheidippides is wearing. But it is an easy conclusion from the information it does offer that Pheidippides is costumed differently from Strepsiades, at least by the time he stalks indignantly off at the end of the opening scene: Pheidippides "dresses rich", meaning that Strepsiades dresses poorer, and perhaps much poorer, given that he is said at 858 to have been wearing rough, heavy, working-class boots (*embades*). Pheid-ippides' robe, not Strepsiades' (as Dover *ad loc.* assumes), is thus probably the one the old man points to at 54–55 as evidence of his wife's tendency to produce cloth of excessively high quality.

Dover on 91 argues that the bed (or beds) upon which Strepsiades and Pheid-ippides are lying when the play begins are quietly removed from the stage by prop-men somewhere in the course of the next scene, as the old man talks first with Socrates' student and then with Socrates himself. Once again, there are other — seemingly more efficient and interesting — solutions to the problem. At 254, Socrates orders his new student to sit on a previously unmentioned σκίμπους, which Dover suggests was left onstage after the other props representing the interior of the Thinkery (revealed via removal of a hypothetical screen at 184) were cleared. This σκίμπους seems generally to be imagined as a stool or θρόνος, and thus as a key element in what is often interpreted as an imitation of a mock-initiation into Corybantic rites or the like.[4] In fact, a σκίμπους is a rough, low bed — Dover on 254 notes that "Plato's Socrates slept on one at home (Plat. *Prt.* 310c)" — and the simplest conclusion would seem to be that this is the same prop as the one used in the opening scene, which was never cleared from the stage at all. A different word for the same object, according to Pollux 6.9; 10.35, is ἀσκάντης, and at 633–634 Strepsiades hauls an ἀσκάντης onstage from the Thinkery, complaining that it is full of bedbugs, something he punningly insisted was also true of the bed in the opening scene, although what he was being bitten by there was a demarch, i.e. a local official involved in the surrender of security for the repayment of debts (37, cf. 12–14). Once again, the simplest conclusion is that this is the same prop, which was taken into the Thinkery after the initiation scene, along with everything else onstage at the

---

4 Thus Dover on 254. The thesis is pushed to extravagant conclusions by Edmonds 2006.

point, at the beginning of the parabasis at 510, forcing Strepsiades to drag it back into view here — and incidentally confirming that the item is light and small enough that no prop-men are needed to move it.

Why this bed is needed onstage at this point is initially unclear. What has happened in the play so far is that Strepsiades, desperate to find a way to escape his debts, has asked Pheidippides to enter the Thinkery; Pheidippides has refused; Strepsiades has been introduced to the school and the Clouds, and has gotten a general idea of the nature of Socratic thinking; and he has finally enrolled as a student himself. At 627, after the parabasis, Socrates emerges from the Thinkery, complaining that Strepsiades is a fool who forgets his lessons even before he learns them. Strepsiades then comes out of the Thinkery as well, dragging his ἀσκάντης with him. What follows is not the next logical step in the action, however, but an onstage reprise of what must have gone on inside the house immediately before this. Socrates — despite having just disowned Strepsiades as a student — now asks what the old man would like to learn (636–638), and when Strepsiades proves, of course, unable to understand or absorb anything, Socrates (694–695) tells him to lie down on the bed and work matters out for himself. Strepsiades then tosses and turns, trying to come up with a plan. But in the end Socrates charges him once again with forgetfulness and stupidity (790), just as he did when he entered, and stamps out. The chorus now finally intervene, suggesting that Strepsiades recruit Pheidippides to study in the Thinkery instead (794–796), and with no other options left, the old man agrees (799–803). What has happened, in other words, is that the plot of Aristophanes' comedy has come full circle: we are back exactly where we were at the beginning of the play, and Strepsiades now takes the path he did not follow then, by requiring Pheidippides to get a Socratic education.

Plot "doublings" of various sort are common in Aristophanic comedy. *Lysistrata* and *Wealth*, for example, are both built around two fundamentally conflicting conceptions of the central action — will the war be stopped via a sex-strike, or via occupation of the Acropolis, in *Lysistrata*?[5] and will everyone be made rich, or will the good be made rich and the bad be made poor, in *Wealth*?[6] — while *Knights* and *Frogs* consist mostly of a repeated series of very similar contests, all of which come to the same conclusion although only the last one proves decisive. *Clouds*, by contrast, seems to be constructed as two mirror-image half-plays, both of which begin with Strepsiades lying uncomfortably in bed, seeking to discover a brilliant plan by means of which he can satisfy his

---

5 Hulton 1972.
6 Olson 1990.

creditors. In both half-plays, a student is chosen (Strepsiades the first time around, Pheidippides the second); the student is offered a preliminary introduction to Socratic studies and their benefits (with Socrates instructing Strepsiades in the first half-play, and Strepsiades instructing Pheidippides in the second); and "real instruction" follows (offered by Socrates in the first half-play, and by the two Arguments in the second; but see more on this below).

This brings us again to question (3), the number of actors that *Clouds* requires. At 885, Socrates, Strepsiades and Pheidippides — i.e. three actors — are onstage together, and Strepsiades declares his intention of turning Pheidippides over to Socrates to get an education. Given what goes on in the first half-play at this point, one would expect Socrates to take Pheidippides and enter the Thinkery, or Strepsiades to leave the two of them alone and go into his own house, or perhaps both. Instead, at 886–887 Socrates unexpectedly announces that Pheidippides will be instructed by the Arguments themselves and exits (presumably into the Thinkery), and at 889 the two Arguments are onstage. Socrates is actor #1. There is no time for between 887 and 889 for him to get offstage, change costume and return as one of the Arguments, so the Arguments must be actors #2 and #3. Strepsiades and Pheidippides, finally, are onstage throughout the confrontation between the Arguments, so they are actors #4 and #5. This is a striking violation of the "Three Actors Plus Rule", and already in antiquity it was hypothesized that a choral song had been lost between 887 and 888 (thus *schol.* **RVE** *ad loc.*), allowing the actor playing Socrates to return as one of the Arguments. But this still leaves us with four actors with major speaking parts in the play, hence Dover's decision to give the part of Strepsiades' slave in the opening scene not to an extra but to the supposed fourth actor.

One intriguing aspect of the "actor problem" in *Clouds* is the existence of similar difficulties in the final scene, in which Strepsiades burns down the Thinkery. Pheidippides (actor #1) has just refused to turn on Socrates (1475). Strepsiades (actor #2) then calls for a slave named Xanthias — normally taken to be a mute extra — to fetch a ladder and a mattock and to climb onto the Thinkery's roof and begin to destroy it (1485–1489). He also orders a second slave — doubtless another mute — to bring a torch so that he himself can personally set fire to the building (1490). At 1493, someone Dover identifies as a student appears (from the Thinkery?) and excitedly asks Strepsiades what he is doing, to which the old man snidely replies "Having a subtle conversation with the beams of the house"; at 1497 someone Dover identifies as a second student appears (again from the Thinkery?) and asks who is setting the house on fire, to which Strepsiades pointedly responds "The person whose *himation* you're wearing"; and at 1502 a character Dover identifies as Socrates (actor #3) appears and asks "You there on the roof, what are you doing?", which earns the mocking answer "I'm walking on air and contemplating the sun", recalling something Socrates himself said when he first appeared in the first half of the play (225). The staging of this scene is extremely complicated, and Dover's interpretation of the action seems to require that Strepsiades go up the ladder (so that he can be addressed in 1502 as "you there on the roof") but then come immediately back down (in order to chase Socrates and his students offstage at the end of the action). I return to these issues at the end of this chapter. The crucial point here, however, is that even if we hypothesize that actor #1 (who played Pheidippides just before this) returns as one of the Students, we still need at one least one extra, or on Dover's analysis a fourth actor, to make the scene work. Only one other section of the play — the confrontation between the two Arguments in the presence of Strepsiades and Pheidippides — involves this degree of staging complexity, and we know from the first *Hypothesis* that both sections were added to *Clouds II* and were not in the original. The problems with the "Three Actors Plus Rule" in *Clouds* are thus confined to the revised version of the play, and there is no reason to believe that they were also found in the staged version. Dover's suggestion that we should consider dividing the parts in the other ten comedies among four actors (or even more) is thus almost certainly to be rejected.

With all that in mind, I return to the confrontation between the Arguments, this time from a different angle, with attention to (2) costuming and its implications. What the Arguments say and represent is carefully discussed by Dover (pp. lvii–lxvi): the Just Argument is a puritanical lover of "ancient virtue" who nonetheless displays an obvious, leering interest in young boys, while the Unjust Argument is a morally vacuous exponent of hedonism, but also intellectually much faster on his feet than his opponent. As a consequence, the Unjust Argument ultimately makes a fool of the Just Argument and takes charge of Pheidippides. What the Arguments look like, on the other hand, appears not to have been considered, despite explicit evidence in the text, as well as the fact that when the Just Argument summons his opponent onstage, he tells him "Show yourself to the spectators!" (889–890), as if there were a significant visual aspect to the way the latter character, at least, is presented. The Just Argument implicitly characterizes himself as old, in that he claims to remember how life was "back in the day" (esp. 961–962, cf. 1028–1029), while the Unjust Argument refers to him directly as a τυφογέρων (908), as ἀρχαῖος (915) and as a Κρόνος (929). Some of this language might be dismissed as figurative. But given the volume of it, the simplest conclusion is that the Just Argument's mask is that of an older man, with the Unjust Argument's, by contrast, being that of a younger one. In addition, the Unjust Argument sneeringly says to the Just Argument αὐχμεῖς αἰσχρῶς ("you're shamefully squalid") (920), to which the Just Argument responds σὺ δέ γ᾽ εὖ πράττεις, καίτοι πρότερόν γ᾽ ἐπτώσευες ("Whereas *you* are doing very well, although you were previously a beggar") (920–921), suggesting a costuming contrast as well: the Just Argument wears shabby clothing, while the Unjust Argument is richly dressed. Not only can we recover important aspects of the costuming and masking of these characters from the text, therefore, but the contrast between them recalls the contrast between the old, ill-costumed Strepsiades and the young, richly appareled Pheidippides at the beginning of the play. Put another way, the confrontation between the two Arguments must be read on some level as a reprise or repetition of the conflict between father and son that is a basic organising principle of Aristophanes' play as a whole.

As for the two versions of *Clouds,* and the number of actors the preserved *Clouds II* in particular requires, I noted above that the first *Hypothesis* informs us that the confrontation between the Arguments was added to the revised version of the text. The problems with the "Three Actors Plus Rule" may thus reflect the fact that the poet has either failed to think the staging through completely or is aiming at readers rather than a theatrical audience; this is in any case very weak evidence for altering our view of standard comic stage practice. As also noted above, the staging problem in the Arguments-scene has been partially dealt with since antiquity by means of the theory that a choral song is missing between Socrates' exit at 887 (after Strepsiades agrees that Pheidippides should become Socrates' student) and 889 (when the Arguments enter), allowing the scene to be staged with four actors rather than five. But since this is all a rewrite, another striking set of parallels is worth noting, between 876–885 (where Strepsiades turns Pheidippides over to Socrates), on one end of the Arguments-scene, and 1107–1112 (where Strepsiades turns Pheidippides over to the Unjust Argument), at the other end. This is the same action, carried out twice; and it is thus worth considering the possibility that what we see here is evidence not for a hypothetical lacuna in the text, as has traditionally been believed, but for the fact that the Arguments-scene has been dropped clumsily into the revised version of the text. In the original version of the play, in other words, Socrates may have taken Pheidippides into the Thinkery, precisely as he did with Strepsiades at the same point in the action in the first half-play, after which — in place of the intrusive Arguments-scene in *Clouds II* — there may have been an onstage education scene between Socrates and Pheidippides similarly parallel to the one in the first half, although in the second half-play with a more intelligent student.

These final points are speculative, and my goal in this chapter is not to claim to be recovering solid, verifiable "facts" about a vanished text. *Clouds I* is lost, and the most we can do today is use the scattered bits and pieces that survive of it to produce hypotheses that potentially satisfy other questions, in this case about the significance of some obvious peculiarities of the surviving *Clouds II.* My real conclusions are thus simultaneously broader and more specific than this.

First: the general purpose of this volume is to consider how staging realities intersect with textual issues, even — or perhaps especially — in cases such as this one, where our primary evidence is an obscure and perhaps corrupt document whose performance status is uncertain. I have argued that a number of aspects of *Clouds II*, especially in the opening scene and the confrontation between the two Arguments, become clearer when considered from this angle. At the same time, I have attempted to show that seemingly pedestrian details, such as the kind of bed Strepsiades and Pheidippides are sleeping in and how that prop moved about the stage, or what father and son are wearing when the play begins, bring out larger structural and argumentative features of the text, including the division of the action into two parallel but ultimately contrasting half-plays, on the one hand, and the way that costuming renders the Just Argument reminiscent of Strepsiades, and the Unjust Argument reminiscent of Pheidippides, on the other. Those observations in turn offer insights into the history of the text of the play and the nature of the ancient rewrite, confirming what the first *Hypothesis* says about the addition of the Arguments-scene and the new finale, while allowing for some informed speculation about what the Arguments-scene replaced. They also allow us to reject Dover's request that we reconsider the "Three Actors Plus Rule" for staging late 5th-century comedy: *Clouds II* is an exceptional text and thus provides an insufficient basis for rejecting an otherwise effective interpretative paradigm.

Second, and perhaps more provocatively: reconstructions of staging, like all attempts to read the past, are inevitably bound up with modern presuppositions, which have their most powerful effect when they are not articulated or expressly argued for. At the beginning of this chapter, I noted two examples of this phenomenon in the opening scene of the play. Dover assumes two beds, even though this creates active difficulties in the interpretation of the text, apparently because he finds it unthinkable that Strepsiades and Pheidippides share one. And he argues that the Slave avoids a beating seemingly because that "would not be funny" and subordinate characters should be allowed a bit of dignity or even the chance to turn the tables on their nominal social betters. A third, more controversial example comes at the end of the play. At 1475, Pheidippides, after saying he will not join Strepsiades in attacking his teachers

(1467), exits somewhere; Dover comments "probably into Strepsiades' house". Perhaps; or perhaps he goes into the Thinkery, which is where he belongs at this point in the action. Christian Kopff argued many years ago that this means either that Pheidippides is one of the anonymous Students (on Dover's division of the lines) who emerge from the burning Thinkery at the very end of the play, or — even more disturbing — that he is *not* one of the students, in which case the implication is that he perishes in the fire.[7] F.D. Harvey responded to Kopff by saying essentially "This is unthinkable; comedies do not end in death, and comic fathers do not kill their sons".[8] I find myself instinctively on Harvey's side in this dispute. It is nonetheless the case that the text as we have it is unclear in this regard; that *Clouds II* is not a typical comedy, and perhaps not even a "real comedy", in the sense that it may never have been put on in the Theatre of Dionysus or anywhere else in ancient Attica; and that ultimately our judgments in this case as well are informed and controlled by where we are located today culturally, politically and socially. I will add that a subset of the staging problems involving Strepsiades' movement in the finale might be resolved by having the slave Xanthias (who is certainly on the Thinkery's roof) speak some of the lines traditionally given to his master, including the crushingly amusing "I'm walking on air and contemplating the sun". This is in one sense "impossible" and "unthinkable", since slaves have only limited agency in Aristophanic comedy, except when they do not — as in the case of another Xanthias in *Frogs*, for example — meaning that our answers to this question as well arguably have at least as much to do with what we believe as with what an ambiguous text can tell us. In any case, in the case of Aristophanes' surviving *Clouds*, the ancient page and ancient stage are productively read together, even if they ultimately offer us more questions than answers.

Bibliography

Compton-Engle, Gwendolyn (2015), *Costume in the Comedies of Aristophanes*, Cambridge.
Di Bari, Marta F. (2013), *Scene finali di Aristofane*, Lecce.
Dover, Kenneth J. (1968) (ed.), *Aristophanes. Clouds*. Edited with introduction and commentary, Oxford.
Edmonds, Radcliffe G. (2006), „To Sit in Solemn Silence? *Thronosis* in Ritual, Myth, and Iconography", in: *American Journal of Philology* 127, 347–366.

---

7 Kopff 1977.
8 Harvey 1981.

Harvey, F. David (1982), *"Nubes* 1493ff: Was Socrates Murdered?", in: *Greek, Roman, and Byzantine Studies* 22, 339–343.

Hubbard, Thomas K. (1986), "Parabatic Self-Criticism and the Two Versions of Aristophanes' *Clouds*", in: *Classical Antiquity* 5, 182–197.

Hulton, Angus O. (1972), "The Women on the Acropolis: A Note on the Structure of the *Lysistrata*", in: *Greece & Rome* 19, 32–36.

Kopff, E. Christian (1977), *"Nubes* 1493ff: Was Socrates Murdered?", in: *Greek, Roman, and Byzantine Studies* 18, 113–122.

Olson, S. Douglas (1990), "Economics and Ideology in Aristophanes' *Wealth*", in: *Harvard Studies in Classical Philology* 93, 223–242.

Olson, S. Douglas (1994), *"Clouds* 537–544 and the Original Version of the Play", in: *Philologus* 138.1, 32–37.

Olson, S. Douglas (2021) (ed.), *Aristophanes' Clouds. A Commentary*, Ann Arbor.

Piqueux, Alexa (2022), *The Comic Body in Ancient Greek Theatre and Art, 440–320 BCE*, Oxford Studies in Ancient Culture and Representation, Oxford.

Stone, Laura M. (1981), *Costume in Aristophanic Poetry*, New York.

Giuseppe Mastromarco
Sexy Mutes on the Aristophanic Stage

Abstract: In seven of Aristophanes' comedies (*Acharnians, Knights, Wasps, Peace, Birds, Lysistrata, Thesmophoriazusae*), one or more beautiful *sexy mutes* play active roles on the stage. Authoritative scholars maintain that these characters appear completely nude. On the base of a detailed textual analysis, I argue that: (a) Dardanis (in *Wasps*), Theoria (in *Peace*), Reconciliation (in *Lysistrata*), Fawn (in *Thesmophoriazusae*) were indeed completely nude; (b) the two prostitutes (in *Acharnians*), Thirty-Year-Truce (in *Knights*), Procne (in *Birds*) wore skimpy clothing; (c) Opora (in *Peace*), Princess (in *Birds*) wore bridal dresses.

Keywords: sexy mutes, Aristophanes, *Acharnians, Knights, Wasps, Peace, Birds, Lysistrata, Thesmophoriazusae*

The majority of the eleven extant Aristophanic comedies contain scenes in which κωφὰ πρόσωπα, *mutae personae,* play "one or more beautiful nude females, who normally come into the possession of a male character towards the end of the play, to be used at and for his pleasure. These, however, are always either divine or quasi-divine beings (like Theoria in *Peace*) or else professional sex-workers (*hetairai*)".[1] According to Henderson, these "sexy mutes" are active not only in *Lys.* 1115ff. (Diallaghe), but in "*Eq.* 1390ff. (Spondai), *Pax* 525, 847ff. (Opora and Theoria); cf. *Av.* 1706ff. (Basileia). Other appearances of naked girls are *Ach.* 1198ff., *V.* 1342ff., 1373ff., *Av.* 667ff., *Th.* 1174ff., *Ra.* 1305–1306".[2] Whether these female characters were played by actual nude women in flesh and blood or by male performers wearing padded bodysuits painted with nipples, a navel and pubic hair, is a question that remains unresolved today. The arguments that have been adopted in favour of either hypothesis are subject to significant objections.[3] Throughout this contribution I will accordingly speak of

---

1 Sommerstein 2009, 239–240.
2 Henderson 1987, 195. Sommerstein 1998, 235–236 (cf. Sommerstein 2009, 250–251) has advanced, albeit with caution, the theory that girls who were active as mute characters in the finale of *Ecclesiazusae* were also nude (I discuss this in Mastromarco 2021).
3 Let us recall just two of them: (i) in favour of the theory that such characters were played by male actors who wore *somatia,* it has been argued that, at the Lenaea, which took place in the winter month of Gamelion (between January and February), the frigid climate would not have allowed a girl to act on stage for a long time while remaining completely nude (cf., for example, Holzinger 1928, 37–54); (ii) that nude female characters were played by flesh-and-blood women

https://doi.org/10.1515/9783111248028-007

"nude women" without intending to take a position for or against either hypothesis. I propose instead to subject the scenes cited above (with the exception of *Frogs* 1305–1308) to rigorous textual analysis in order to ascertain whether or not Henderson's claim that *all* the sexy mutes active in such scenes were in fact nude.[4]

(i) During the finale of *Acharnians*, at 1198, Dicaeopolis returns from the symposium — to which he had been invited by the priest of Dionysus (cf. 1085–1094*a*) — and appears on stage in a state of inebriation.[5] In this condition, he moves forward with difficulty, supported by two sexy mutes playing the role of prostitutes: Dicaeopolis fondles their breasts and exchanges kisses and lustful bites. One can glean this from 1199, in which the old man exclaims: τῶν τιτθίων, ὡς σκληρὰ καὶ κυδώνια ("What breasts! How firm, like quinces!"). Similar information appears in 1200–1201, where he addresses the two girls in these terms: φιλήσατόν με μαλθακῶς, ὦ χρυσίω, / τὸ περιπεταστὸν κἀπιμανδαλωτόν ("Kiss me softly, my two jewels, one kiss broad, one kiss deep"), and later, in 1209, where he asks one of the two girls: τί με σὺ κυνεῖς; ("Why do you kiss me?"), and the other: τί με σὺ δάκνεις; ("Why do you bite me?"). The comedy comes to an end shortly after this, in 1234, when Dicaeopolis, the two girls and the Chorus, singing and dancing, leave the orchestra.

The text therefore presents *explicit references* to the girls' breasts (1199) and implicit references to their mouths (1200–1201, 1209). References to other erogenous areas of their bodies are missing. Major scholars nonetheless share the opinion that the two girls were nude.[6] And yet, this opinion may be subject to

---

is a theory put forth on the basis of pictures on vases, for example, a red-figure *skyphos* from 350–325 BCE that depicts a comic actor and a seminude acrobat ostensibly played by a girl (cf. Compton-Engle 2015, 35). As Taplin 1993, 74 observes, however, "it may be that the painters have felt free to create a composite figure with no direct counterpart in the theatre". On the *status quaestionis*, see Stone 1981, 147–150; Zweig 1992, 76–81; Revermann 2006, 157–159; Di Bari 2013, 163–166; Compton-Engle 2015, 28–37; Carey 2017, 57–64.

4 I do not examine *Frogs* 1305–1308, in which the Muse of Euripides appears. In contrast to Henderson (cf. already Willems 1919, III 96), I maintain that she was not played by a naked girl, since there are no references to any naked parts of her body. Moreover, Dionysus' reaction to her entrance (οὐκ ἐλεσβίαζεν, οὔ, "she certainly wasn't part of the Lesbian tradition!" 1308) should be interpreted to mean that "she did not perform [...] 'Lesbian' sexual acts [...] – presumably because she is, and always was, so ugly that no man, even when drunk, would fancy her" (Sommerstein 1996, 274; and cf. Totaro, in Mastromarco/Totaro 2006, 682–683, n. 208).

5 As he himself confirms, "I am first to drain my pitcher" (1202).

6 See most recently Henderson 1991, 62 ("Dicaeopolis enters with two naked girls"); and Olson 2002, 359, who maintains that the two girls were played by "a pair of naked prostitutes (most likely played by elaborately costumed men)".

doubts. The declaration Dicaeopolis makes in 1199 regarding the girls' breasts (ὡς σκληρὰ καὶ κυδώνια) proves that the sexual activities of the old man should consist not only of kissing and biting, but also of fondling their breasts, which would appear to require that they be nude, as 1185 of *Thesmophoriazusae* shows. As we will see later, the Scythian Archer fondles the breasts of Fawn only after the girl has undressed herself. But is it not also possible that fondling can take a dressed woman as its object, as in *Lysistrata*? In this play, Calonice, addressing Lampito, comments: ὡς δὴ καλὸν τὸ χρῆμα τῶν τιτθῶν ἔχεις ("What a splendid pair of tits you've got!", 83), to which the Spartan responds: "Really, *you're feeling me over* (ὑποψαλάσσετε) like a victim for sacrifice (ἅπερ ἱαρεῖον)" (84). From the moment Lampito fastened her Spartan peplum, it was clear that her breasts *were not nude*. It is therefore possible that Dicaeopolis does *not* fondle the *nude* breasts of the two girls. Furthermore, since the text contains no explicit references to other sexualised parts of the girls' bodies, it seems legitimate to consider the hypothesis that they were not nude, but were wearing revealing clothing.

(ii) In the finale of *Knights* (1390–1408), we do not know whether the Σπονδαὶ τριακοντούτιδες (Thirty-Year-Truce) on stage are played by one or more sexy mutes. The number of *mutae personae* that take this role is in fact a point of controversy,[7] since the term Σπονδαί is defective in the singular.[8] The hypothesis that thirty girls are present on stage, one for every year of the peace,[9] has been subject to many objections. There is instead evidence that the spectators would not have had time to count the Σπονδαί, nor would there have been sufficient space in the orchestra to contain all twenty-four *choreutae* together with the actors.[10] Moreover, "sembra scarsamente plausibile — e drammaturgicamente poco economico — che trenta fanciulle entrassero in scena dall'apertura centrale della *skené*, effigiante la casa di Demo, in cui Σπονδαί erano state celate (1393) e da cui è lecito supporre che dovessero anche apparire".[11] In any case, if it is true that the "silence" of the text does not permit the *reader* to establish how many *mutae personae* were active in the role of Σπονδαί, for which reason some scholars cautiously refer to an unspecified number of girls,[12] it is *also* true that important if not decisive arguments have been adopted in favour of the presence

---

7 For bibliographic references relevant to this *vexatissima quaestio*, cf. Di Bari 2013, 165–166, nn. 167–71.

8 For Σπονδαί = "Truce", cf. Di Bari 2013, 116.

9 See in particular Pohlenz 1952, 123 (= 1965, 539).

10 Cf. Gil Fernández 1995, 230.

11 Di Bari 2013, 166.

12 See recently Dover 1972, 46; MacDowell 1995, 105.

of just one woman: "In *Wasps* 1361, the defective αἱ δεταί is represented by a single torch, as shown in lines 1330 and 1372. Also, the erotic comment 'Is it possible to belt them thirty times?', made by Demos as he runs his hand over the Σπονδαὶ τριακοντούτιδες, 'Thirty-Year-Truce', clearly alludes to a single maiden. Hence, the rejuvenated Demos, 'smelling sweetly of peace' (1332), gets one girl and no more: likewise, the Spartans and Athenians in *Lysistrata* 1114–1121 are awarded the maiden 'Reconciliation' alone".[13]

What emerges clearly from 1388–1393, in which Demos and the Sausage-seller comment on the presence of Σπονδαί, is that these verses contain no explicit reference to erogenous parts of her (or their) body/bodies, but speak generically of her/their beauty (cf. ὡς καλαί, 1390), beauty that incites the reinvigorated Demos' sexual impulses, as he expresses a desire "to satisfy my thirty-year itch with them (κατατριακοντουτίσαι)" (1391). In contrast to scholars who assert that the Σπονδαί may have been played by one or more nude girls,[14] therefore, it appears to me that the *muta persona* (or *mutae personae*) that plays/play the role would have been wearing scanty clothing, which would suit women the scholiasts identify as ἑταῖραι ὡραῖαι.[15] Ultimately, I share Russo's conclusion: "The term σπονδαί, defective in the singular, is to find physical expression in *one* maiden alone, beautiful maybe, but not nude."[16]

(iii) At 1324 of *Wasps*, the protagonist, Philocleon, returning from a symposium, enters from an *eisodos* holding a torch in his hand (cf. 1330). With this torch, he illuminates the dark street, it now being evening. The old man who "stumbles forward" (1324) since, as his slave Xanthias confirms (cf. 1300, 1322), he is drunk, is accompanied by a mute character, the flute-girl Dardanis, to whom he makes crude sexual advances (1341–1347). Following this, at 1360, Bdelycleon enters, accusing his father of having stolen the flute-girl from the other guests (1368–1369). But Philocleon, not yet having noticed the young man's arrival, entrusts the torch to the girl (cf. 1361–1362*a*: ἀλλ' ὡς τάχιστα στῆθι τάσδε τὰς δετὰς / λαβοῦσ'), intending to render what he is about to say credible – that is, that Dardanis is not a flesh-and-blood woman, but one of the torches that burn in the square for the gods (1372). Bdelycleon and Philocleon then engage in a lively altercation, in which the son, pointing to the girl's erogenous zones, denies that they could possibly belong to a torch, while Philocleon

---

13 Russo 1994, 84.
14 Cf. e.g. Gould/Lewis, in Pickard-Cambridge 1968, 153 n. 1; Henderson 1991, 67.
15 Cf. *schol. vet. ad* 1390a Mervyn Jones.
16 Russo 1994, 84; also Wilamowitz 1927: among the nude *mutae personae* listed at pp. 186–187, Σπονδαί is not cited.

argues, against all evidence, that they do indeed belong to one. From their altercation in 1373–1377 it emerges that Dardanis is certainly nude:

ΒΔ.	δὰς ἤδε;
ΦΙ.	δὰς δῆτ'. Οὐχ ὁρᾷς ἐσχισμένην;
ΒΔ.	τί δὲ τὸ μέλαν τοῦτ' ἐστὶν αὐτῆς τοὐν μέσῳ;
ΦΙ.	ἡ πίττα δήπου καομένης ἐξέρχεται. 1375
ΒΔ.	ὁ δ' ὄπισθεν οὐχὶ πρωκτός ἐστιν οὑτοσί;
ΦΙ.	ὄζος μὲν οὖν τῆς δᾳδὸς οὗτος ἐξέχει.

BD.	This a torch?
	PHI. Certainly it's a torch. [*Pointing between Dardanis' legs*] Don't you see where it's split?
BD.	[*looking there*] Well, what's this black patch in the middle?
PHI.	It's the pitch coming out of the torch as it burns, of course.
BD.	And this round behind – it's a bum, isn't it?
PHI.	No, it's a knot sticking out of the wood.[17]

In these verses the erogenous areas of the flute-girl are in fact indicated, either implicitly or explicitly. When, in 1373, Philocleon asserts that the supposed torch "is split (ἐσχισμένην)", he most likely refers to the girl's vulva;[18] and when, in 1374, Bdelycleon points out τὸ μέλαν τοὖν μέσῳ, the reference must in all likelihood be to Dardanis' pubic hair.[19] Finally, in 1376, we find an explicit reference (evident in the staging from the deictic οὑτοσί) to the girl's πρωκτός.

(iv) At 520 of *Peace*, the choreutae bring the god Peace, represented by a statue, out from the cave where she had been hidden at the outbreak of war. As can be seen from 523, two mute female characters are next to her: Opora (Fullfruit), the personification of agricultural products (crops and fruit), and Theoria (Showtime), the personification of public festivals.[20] The two girls, to whom the text makes explicit reference in 706–717, when Hermes invites Trygaeus to take Opora as a wife and to bring Theoria back to the Council, remain on stage (or rather, in the sky) until 728, when they leave in the company

17 The translations of the passages from Aristophanes cited throughout this essay are those of A.H. Sommerstein.
18 "The discussion in 1374–1377 is so insistently focused on sexually interesting portions of her anatomy that it is difficult to believe that the reference here is not to her vulva in one way or another" (Biles/Olson 2015, 479–480).
19 Cf. MacDowell 1971, 310; Sommerstein 1983, 239; Henderson 1991, 143; Biles/Olson 2015, 480.
20 For an analysis of these two characters, cf. Newiger 1957, 108–111.

of Trygaeus (cf. 726*b*–728), with whom they reappear on stage (or rather, on earth) at 819.

It is generally accepted that during 520–728 Opora and Theoria "are probably nude, like Διαλλαγή at *Lys.* 1114–1118."[21] In my opinion, however, it is unlikely that in the course of this dramatic segment, over two hundred verses long, the two girls remain nude on stage without Trygaeus and Hermes mentioning any sexualised parts of their bodies. It accordingly appears reasonable to me to maintain that, from 520 to 728, the two girls are dressed. It goes without saying that, if this hypothesis is correct, when they reappear on stage in 819, Opora and Theoria must have on the same clothing that have been wearing since 728, when they left the stage.

At 847, Trygaeus' Slave, turning his attention to the two girls, asks his master: "Where did you get them from?" And following Trygaeus' response ("Where from? From heaven"), the Slave replies: "I wouldn't give three obols for the gods after this, if they go in for pimping just like us mortals" (848–849). It has been reasonably observed that the two interventions by the Slave prove that "she [i.e. Opora] cannot be dressed like a matron or a maiden. Her appearance suggests sexual availability. She may be naked. But there is no specific allusion to her body. Therefore, her body is probably exposed rather than nude. That is, she may be wearing a thin garment which reveals the contours of the padded female body".[22] In 856, the Slave, on Trygaeus' orders,[23] leads Opora inside the house, and in 869*b*, re-entering the stage, he confirms that he has done what his master told him to.[24] Later, reacting to Trygaeus' assertion that it is necessary to hasten to return Theoria to the Council (ἴθι νυν ἀποδῶμεν τήνδε τὴν Θεωρίαν / ἀνύσαντε τῇ βουλῇ, 871–872*a*), the Slave, in 872*b*–874, responds with these words: τίς αὑτηί; τί φῄς; / αὕτη Θεωρία 'στίν, ἣν ἡμεῖς ποτε / ἐπαίομεν Βραυρω-νάδ' ὑποπεπωκότες; ("What? This girl here? What did you say? Is this the Show-time we used to have when we'd screw our way to Brauron after a few drinks?"). There are good grounds to claim that Theoria is nude at this point. This is proven by the Slave's comment in 875*b*–876, when he points to her derriere (ὦ δέ-σποτα, / ὅσην ἔχει τὴν πρωκτοπεντετηρίδα, "Oh, master, what a big quadrennial bum she's got!"), as well as by the exchange of gags between Trygaeus and the

---

21 Olson 1998, 183.

22 Carey 2017, 57.

23 Cf. 842–844: "But now [*bringing Fullfruit forward*] take this girl and take her inside right away, rinse the bathtub and heat water, and spread the nuptial couch for her and me".

24 "The girl's been bathed, and her bottom part's in order. The flat-cake has been baked, sesame-balls are being shaped, and absolutely everything else is ready. Only the prick's missing!" (869*b*–870).

Slave that follows in 879–880. In these verses, the master asks: οὗτος, τί περι-
γράφεις; ("Here, you, what's that zone you're marking out?", 879*a*), to which
the Slave replies: τὸ δεῖν᾽, εἰς Ἴσθμια/ σκηνὴν ἐμαυτοῦ τῷ πέει καταλαμβάνω
("Well — er — actually — I'm staking a claim to camping space for my prick for
the Isthmian games", 879*b*–880). The Slave's reply alludes to a well-established
custom among Athenians who went to Corinth to join the Isthmian games, and
to the fact that many who did not manage to find accommodation in the city
pitched their tents on the outskirts. It is therefore evident that the Slave is
'drawing' (with his theatrical phallus?) a circle around the part of Theoria's
body (her vagina) that he would like to use as a 'tent' for his penis.[25] Later, at
891*a*, Trygaeus invites the Councillors, who occupy a section of the Theatre
reserved for them, to look at the "oven" (τουτὶ δ᾽ ὁρᾶτε τοὐπτάνιον), or rather
Theoria's vulva, highlighted by the deictic τουτί.[26] This invitation elicits the
enthusiastic reaction of the Slave in 891*b* (οἴμ᾽ ὡς καλόν, "My, how beautiful!"),
who in his next remark (διὰ ταῦτα καὶ κεκάπνικεν ἄρ᾽, "ah, that's why it's got all
smoky black", 892) referring to Theoria's pubic hair. Later (889–904), Trygaeus
emits a series of *double entendres* that allude to the various *figurae Veneris* the
Councillors will be able to practice on Theoria, who finally leaves the stage in
906 and "probably takes a seat in the βουλευτικόν and remains there until the
play is over."[27]

Thus, if the precise references made by Trygaeus and the Slave to the erogenous areas of Theoria's body demonstrate that the girl is nude throughout the
course of the scene starting from 869*b*, it is legitimate to wonder when she undressed. It is not easy for a *reader* to offer an answer to this question, since the
text provides nothing that might clarify the development of the scene's staging.
But that Theoria's denuding took place starting from 886 was suggested by
Meineke, who, in place of the transmitted line (ἄγε δὴ σὺ κατάθου πρῶτα τὰ
σκεύη χαμαί), which is identical to *Knights* 155, proposed reading ἄγε δὴ σὺ

---

25 "Comparison with *Th.* 647–648 suggests that part of the joke is that the 'isthmus' in question is located in Theoria's crotch" (Olson 1998 *ad l.*, *Addenda* 2003, 320); cf. Henderson 1991,
137. I would therefore exclude the possibility that the Slave's sexual advances were made
"probably from behind" (Carey 2017, 63).
26 That the "oven" metaphorically refers to the "female genitals" already appears in ancient
annotations to texts: τὸ αἰδοῖον αὐτῆς δείκνυσι (*schol. vet. Tr. ad* 891a Holwerda); and see
Taillardat 1965, 76–77; Henderson 1991, 142–143. A similar oven-vulva metaphor is evident in
ancient Latin literature (see Adams 1982, 86–87). For the double-meaning of oven/female
genitalia in the playful *Capitolo sopra il forno* by monsignor Giovanni Della Casa, see Sonnino
2012, 72–73, and in general in Italian literature, Boggione/Casalegno 2000, 207.
27 Olson 1998, 243.

κατάθου πρῶτα τὴν σκευὴν χαμαί[28] so as to interpret 886 as an order given by Trygaeus to Theoria to drop her clothes to the ground and reveal her naked body: "sequentia ostendunt aperte, iubere Trygaeum Theoriam ut nudam sese spectandam praebeat".[29] Meineke's suggestive conjecture, even if accepted by many scholars,[30] has neverthless been reasonably contested by Olson ("the fact that we do not know what this 'baggage' or 'equipment' is [schol. **RV** suggests cooking gear] is no ground for adopting Meineke's τὴν σκευὴν)"[31] and Sommerstein, who, after having accepted Meineke's conjecture into the text on the ground that "this gives full value to the following line — the councillors are being invited to gaze on Showtime's full beauty, now for the first time revealed",[32] has subsequently rejected it "since 875–880 makes it overwhelmingly probable that Showtime has no clothes to remove".[33] If Theoria appears nude to the spectators from 869*b* onwards, it is thus reasonable to assert that her undressing took place between the Slave's exit from the stage (855) and his return (in 869*b*), during the melic interlude between the Chorus and Trygaeus from 856 to 867. By contrast, Opora, wearing traditional bridal wear, re-enters the stage at the end of the comedy at 1329, when she *comes out of the house, escorted, as bride, followed by attendants who distribute lighted torches to the chorus.*"[34]

In conclusion, I would argue that Opora remained dressed throughout her appearance on stage, even if in the two scenes 520–728 and 819–855 she, like Theoria, put on revealing clothing that encouraged the Slave to claim that the two girls were prostitutes. It is certain that there are no explicit references to the erogenous areas of her body, the only exception being 869*b*, where the Slave marvels at Opora's rear (τὰ τῆς πυγῆς καλά). But this occurs when the girl is off-stage, and there are grounds to claim that Opora wears bridal dress in the finale

---

28 Cf. Meineke 1860, lxxv, 254.

29 Meineke 1865, 47; Droysen 1835 had given a similar interpretation of 886, but without the intervention on the transmitted τὰ σκεύη, in the stage directions accompanying his translation of the verse "Sie entkleidet sich und wird dem Publikum in ihrer Schönheit gezeigt".

30 Cf. Van Herwerden 1897, I 73; Willems 1919, II 59; III 389–390; Seager 1981, 244–245; Mastromarco 1983, 102–103, 626; Sommerstein 1985, 86, 175.

31 Olson 1998, 240. Regarding the σκεύη Theoria carries, Wilson 2007b, 110 observes: "If Theoria can be taken as including not just visits to sporting events (cf. 894–906) but delegations to religious centers, then she might carry offerings that would be appropriate to pilgrims".

32 Sommerstein 1985, 175.

33 Sommerstein 2001, 276; and τὰ σκεύη in Wilson 2007a, I 319.

34 This is the stage direction Sommerstein (1985, 131) gives in the margins of his translation.

of the comedy.[35] Theoria, by contrast, appears nude to the audience during the
part of the scene that runs from 869b to 908. Insofar as she is the personification
of Festivals, she represents the pleasures (sex, food, wine) that make up the
collective imaginary of Athenians in relation to festivities, and that are, moreover, fundamental elements of Aristophanic poetry. It is certainly significant that
in 873–874 the Slave asks Trygaeus if the girl was the same Theoria with whom
they had sex on the occasion of the Brauronia, the celebration in honour of
Artemis in the village of Brauron.

(v) At *Birds* 667, the *muta persona* Procne leaves Hoopoe-Tereus' dwelling
wearing a nightingale mask. Her beauty, made clear by Peisetaerus (ὡς καλὸν
τοὐρνίθιον· / ὡς δ' ἁπαλόν, ὡς δὲ λευκόν, "What a lovely birdie! How fair, how
tender!", 667b–668a), arouses the desires of Euelpides (ἐγὼ διαμηρίζοιμ' ἂν
αὐτὴν ἡδέως, "I'd have great pleasure in spreading her legs for her", 669). But
there is no explicit reference to the erogenous parts of Procne's body, unless we
consider the hypothesis suggested by Juan Gil Fernández[36] that Peisetaerus'
declaration in 670 (ὅσον δ' ἔχει τὸν χρυσόν), χρυσόν (by which the jewellery that
Procne was wearing is realistically described) may also contain a coarse pun on
κυσόν, a term that "in comedy was widely used to mean both cunt and anus (in
homosexual contexts)".[37] It is evident that, if we accept Gil Fernández's theory,
Procne would have had to first appear "probably naked or seminaked".[38] But
against the hypothesis that χρυσόν (670) contains a pun on κυσόν, it has also
been noted that κυσός, "not found in Ar. [...] seems to mean male *anus*", and
therefore that "perhaps the word expected was κύσθον, used by Ar. for the female organs".[39] We might thus find ourselves confronted by an example of the
punning games so dear to Aristophanes. Nonetheless, I posit that we can exclude this hypothesis, given the clear difference between the two sounds (χρυσόν / κύσθον). As mentioned, with χρυσόν Peisetaerus merely refers to the
jewellery Procne is wearing, and it is in any case unclear "perché Pisetero do-
vrebbe ricorrere a un gioco fonico tanto sottile, quando, un momento prima,
Evelpide non aveva usato giri di parole per esprimere la voglia di 'aprire le co-

---

35 It is useful to recall here that Wilamowitz 1927, 187, maintains that, of the two *mutae personae* active in *Peace*, only Theoria first appears nude.
36 Cf. Gil Fernández 1963, 135–136: the hypothesis has been noted by Zanetto (in Zanetto/Del
Corno 1987, 237) and Thiercy 1997, 1185.
37 Henderson 1991, 131. At Hsch. κ 4738 L.-C., κυσός is glossed ἡ πυγή. ἢ γυναικεῖον αἰδοῖον.
38 Henderson 1991, 131.
39 Dunbar 1995, 422–423.

sce' di Procne e, subito dopo, espliciterà il desiderio erotico di 'baciare' la fanciulla".[40]

Later, in 1706, a Herald announces the arrival of Peisetaerus and Βασίλεια ("Princess"), who are preparing to marry.[41] The hypothesis — which has not in fact enjoyed much favour — that Princess is nude, is not corroborated by any explicit reference to the erogenous parts of her body.[42] In 1713, the Herald limits himself to declaring that the girl is a "wife of beauty unspeakable to describe" (γυναικὸς κάλλος οὐ φατὸν λέγειν). Along with the majority of scholars, I would accordingly maintain that Princess, being about to join Peisetaerus in marriage, was wearing traditional bridal dress, similar to what is worn by Opora in the finale of *Peace* during the marriage procession.

(vi) At *Lysistrata* 1115, an attractive young woman, Διαλλαγή, "Reconciliation",[43] exits from the Acropolis (into which she returns at 1188). The fact that she is *nude* is shown by the explicit comments the Spartan Delegate makes upon seeing her in 1148 (ἀλλ' ὁ πρωκτὸς ἄφαντον ὡς καλός, "but that bum is unspeakably beautiful!"), as well as those offered by the First Athenian Delegate in 1158 (ἐγὼ δὲ κύσθον καλλίονα, "and I've never seen a prettier pussy").[44] This explains why, after the girl's appearance on stage, the First Athenian Delegate, in an evident state of sexual arousal, declares: ἐγὼ δ' ἀπόλλυμαί γ' ἀπεψωλημένος, "and my skinned cock is killing me!" (1136).

The possibility that Διαλλαγή is nude reveals itself in 1161 to 1170 through a dialogue between the two Delegates, who are attempting to create, thanks to Lysistrata's involvement, a truce between Athenians and Spartans:

Λυ.   τί δ' οὐ διηλλάγητε; φέρε, τί τοὐμποδών;
Λα.   ἁμές γα λῶμες, αἴ τις ἁμὶν τώγκυκλον
        λῇ τοῦτ' ἀποδόμεν.
Λυ.   ποῖον, ὦ τᾶν;
Λα.   τὰν Πύλον,
        τᾶσπερ πάλαι δεόμεθα καὶ βλιμάδδομες.

40 Totaro, in Mastromarco/Totaro 2006, 188 n. 143.
41 It is plausible that the two entered the scene in a nuptial carriage: cf. Bowie 1993, 165; Dunbar 1995, 751–752.
42 As far as I am aware, the hypothesis that Princess appears nude in the scene is proposed by Wilamowitz 1927, 187 n. 1, and Henderson 1987, 195. By contrast, it is treated as uncertain in Stone 1981, 149: "Basileia ... may or may not be represented as a naked female".
43 One cannot totally exclude, however, the possibility "that Reconciliation should exit in haste after line 1174, rather than wait to leave with Lysistrata and the Ambassadors after 1188" (Ewans 2008, 364).
44 The accusative κύσθον is supported by οὖπα ὄπωπα in the previous verse (1157).

Αθ.   μὰ τὸν Ποσειδῶ τοῦτο μέν γ' οὐ δράσετε.   1165
Λυ.   ἄφετ, ὦγάθ', αὐτοῖς.
Αθ.   κᾆτα τίνα κινήσομεν;
Λυ.   ἕτερόν γ' ἀπαιτεῖτ ἀντὶ τούτου χωρίον.
Αθ.   τὸ δεῖνα τοίνυν, παράδοθ' ἡμῖν τουτονὶ
        πρώτιστα τὸν Ἐχινοῦντα καὶ τὸν Μηλιᾶ
        κόλπον τὸν ὄπισθεν καὶ τὰ Μεγαρικὰ σκέλη.   1170

LY.   Why haven't you come to terms? Come on, what's standing in the way?
SP.   We for our part are willing, if they're prepared
       to give us back this Rotunda.
                          LY. What Rotunda, my man?
                                                SP. Pylos,
       which we've been longing for and probing around for a long time.
ATH.   By Poseidon, that you shan't get!
LY.   My good sir, let them have it.
ATH.   But then who will we be able to stir up?
LY.   Well, ask for another place in return for that one.
ATH.   Well then — um, ah — you first of all hand over to us this Hedgehog location
       here, and the Malian inlet behind it, and the Legs of Megara.

At 1162–1163, therefore, the Spartan Delegate asks that the Athenians return τὥγκυκλον / τοῦτ' to the Spartans. Yet the request leaves the First Athenian Delegate perplexed, since he does not understand what the substantive alludes to, and in 1163b he accordingly asks his interlocutor to clarify which ἔγκυκλον he is speaking of. From 1163c, the Spartan Delegate explains that by ἔγκυκλον, a substantive that usually indicates a women's 'mantle', "ampio, pesante, di forma arrotondata, bordato di rosso [...] inteso come "qualcosa che circonda", "qualcosa che sta intorno",[45] he is referring to the Peloponnesian city of Pylos (τὰν Πύλον), given that it is surrounded by walls. It should thus be evident that the toponym Πύλος, with its assonance with the substantive πύλη, "door",[46] lends itself to a sexual reading, as is confirmed by the following declaration by the Spartan Delegate in 1164: τὰν Πύλον, / τᾶσπερ πάλαι δεόμεθα καὶ βλιμάδδο-μες, in which τὰν Πύλον is "a *double entendre* referring to Reconciliation's anus" and the article τὰν serves as a "deictic".[47] The sexual interpretation of these verses is compounded by the verb βλιμάζειν, which "refers to the amatory

---

45 Perusino 2002, 131–132. On the ἔγκυκλον, see also Stone 1980, 164–165; Compton-Engle 2015, 57, 78.
46 This substantive is commonly used in comedy as a metaphor for the female sexual organ (cf. Henderson 1991, 137).
47 Henderson 1987, 204.

handling of women's erogenous zones".[48] We can understand, therefore, the way in which, in this context, ἔγκυκλον, with its round, smooth form, is a malicious reference to Reconcliation's behind, made by the Spartan Delegate.[49] Later, in 1168–1170a, the First Athenian Delegate asks that the Spartans concede two places to the Athenians, τὸν Ἐχινοῦντα and τὸν Μηλιᾶ κόλπον, toponyms that also lend themselves to sexual *double entendres*. (A) First, the name of the Thessalian city of Echinus recalls ἐχῖνος, "sea-urchin", which in the Greek sexual imaginary could be "used to denote the female pubic region with its prickly hair (cf. Ar. fr. 425 K.–A., Hipponax fr. 70.8)".[50] Thus, as the deictic τουτονί (1168) shows, when the First Athenian Delegate names Echinus, this describes Reconciliation's pubic hair. (B) Second, the mention of the Malian Gulf that follows is "geographically incorrect, since for anyone coming (whether by land or sea) from Attica or the Peloponnese the Malian Gulf lies *in front* of the coast on which Echinus stood. The speaker, however, is not thinking in terms of geography but of anatomy: the 'Malian inlet' (*Melieus kolpos*) that lies behind Reconciliation's pubic region is her vagina (for which *kolpos* was a standard medical term: see Pollux 2.222 and LSJ s.v. *kolpos* I 2), located as it is (from certain angles) between two *mela* (properly "apples" or "quinces", but applied to anything rounded and soft; here evidently buttocks)".[51]

(vii) In 1160 of *Thesmophoriazusae*, Euripides enters the scene;[52] he is dressed as an old woman and has a harp with him. A boy piper, Τερηδών (Woodworm), and a dancing-girl, Ἐλάφιον (Fawn), follow him, and he invites the girl to dance while performing, as the notes of the harp and pipes rise.[53]

---

48 Sommerstein 1990, 215; and see also Henderson 1991, 173–174; Dunbar 1995, 362. For the lexicographers that confirm the meaning of βλιμάζειν, cf. Beta 1992, 97 n. 15, and particularly Olson/Seaberg 2018, 99–101.

49 Cf. Willems 1919, II 446; and for the hypothesis that, with Πύλος, the Spartan alludes to Reconciliation's behind, that he was explicitly praising in 1148, cf. Henderson 1987, 204 (and Henderson 1991, 139 n. 160), as well as Perusino 2002, 130 n. 8; Perusino/Beta 2020, 304: the Spartans privilege the anal.

50 Sommerstein 1990, 216; and on Ar. fr. 425 K.–A., see in particular Pellegrino 2015, 251–252; Torchio 2021, 126–128.

51 Sommerstein 1990, 216; Perusino/Beta 2020, 305.

52 A recent analysis of the entire scene can be found in Totaro 2022.

53 Cf. δίελθε κἀνακάλπασον (1174): it has been rigorously argued that "ἀνακαλπάζειν è denominativo di κάλπη, 'corsa al trotto', che nella terminologia agonistica greca indicava un tipo di corsa, riservata alle giumente e disputata ad Olimpia dal 496 al 444 a.C., nel cui ultimo tratto il fantino smontava dalla cavalla per condurla al trotto sino al traguardo: *lato sensu*, nel presente passo, il verbo evoca l'incedere flessuoso e ancheggiante della danzatrice Elafione [...]. La metaforica associazione, evocata da ἀνακαλπάζειν, fra movimenti orchestici di Elafione e

Awoken by the sound of the musical instruments (cf. 1175 τί τὸ βόμβο τοῦτο; κῶμό τις ἀνεγεῖρί μοι;), the Scythian Archer, seeing the dancing Fawn, offers, in broken Attic, a comparison clearly intended to express his wholehearted admiration of the girl's beauty, but one that is, in accord with his *ethos* and the squalor of his lifestyle, remarkably coarse (1180 ὡς ἐλαπρός, ὥσπερ ψύλλο κατὰ τὸ κῴδιο, "'Ow nimble she is, like a flea on a blanget!"). His mode of expression is in polar opposition to the high literary comparison between the woman-*hetaira* and the mare Euripides made shortly before. The tragedian thus begins his strategic plan to liberate the Inlaw. In 1181 he orders the Fawn to undress herself (φέρε θοἰμάτιον ἄνωθεν, ὦ τέκνον, τοδί, "Come, child, let's have this mantle — over your head, so");[54] it follows that the girl is, at this point, nude.[55] In 1182, in order to plunge the Archer even deeper into the throes of excitement, Euripides invites Fawn to sit on the Scythian's knee (καθιζομένη δ' ἐπὶ τοῖσ‹ι› γόνασι τοῦ Σκύθου). Seized by irrepressible sexual desire, in 1185 he fondles her breasts while addressing her with another crude compliment (οἴμ' ὡς στέριπο τὸ τιττί, ὥσπερ γογγυλί, "My, my, 'ow firm dat diddy is, like a durnip!"). In 1187, after having exalted Elaphion's behind (καλό γε τὸ πυγή, "dat bum, 'e is gorgeous"), he directly addresses his (theatrical) phallus which, in a clear state of erection, repeatedly protrudes from his trousers (κλαῦσί γ', ἢν μὴ 'νδον μένῃς, "You for it if you don' stay inside"). Then the Archer and Fawn leave to have sex in a secluded place, out of sight from the spectators.[56] When they re-enter the scene, at 1214, the dancing-girl, most likely still nude, quickly distances herself via an *eisodos*, while the Scythian despairs that Inlaw has escaped.

On the basis of the above analysis of Aristophanic scenes in which sexy mutes are active, I find the following conclusions reasonable:

---

andatura equina si inserisce a pieno titolo nel tradizionale motivo letterario del confronto fra la donna-etera e la cavalla" (Di Bari 2009, 146; see also Di Bari 2013, 376–377).

54 We owe the correct interpretation of this verse to Willems 1919, who, followed by Austin 1987, 86, argues: ἱμάτιον "se dit aussi d'un vêtement quelconque; ici il désigne le chiton: preuve, le démonstratif τοδί, qui serait superflu s'il s'agissait du manteau [...] ἄνωθεν veut dire par en haut, c'est-à-dire en le passant par-dessus la tête, ce qui est, en effet, la manière la plus usitée d'ôter une tunique ou une chemise" (II 579).

55 As Sommerstein (1994, 133) notes in the stage directions in the margins of his translation of 1181, "*Fawn removes her mantle; she is wearing nothing underneath*"; Austin/Olson 2004, 342 are too cautious in their annotation: "Elaphion is now dressed only in a skimpy chiton — or perhaps in nothing at all": that the dancing-girl should be completely nude is clear from 1185 and 1187.

56 We can plausibly identify the place as Echo's cave; cf. Mastromarco 2019.

(a) explicit references to the erogenous zones of Dardanis (in *Wasps*), Theoria (in *Peace*), Reconciliation (in *Lysistrata*) and Fawn (in *Thesmophoriazusae*), supported by the use of deictics, demonstrate that these girls were *nude* in the scenes in question. It must be said that such references are particularly necessary for spectators in the back rows of Dionysus' theatre, who would have found it difficult to see the erotic body parts of the girls. In such cases, the text acts as 'stage directions', suggesting to the minds of the spectators what their eyes could not see, or could see only approximately: "the most precise indications often concern, somewhat paradoxically, what was invisible to the audience, or visible in so rudimentary a form that they needed help in interpreting what they saw. Here the text elucidates and supplements the spectacle".[57]

(b) It is unlikely that the two prostitutes in the final scene of *Acharnians* were completely nude: the references to their bodies regard only their breasts and mouths, and hence one cannot exclude the possibility (which I in fact incline to consider the most plausible) that they were dressed in skimpy clothing. The hypothesis that Procne is naked or semi-naked in *Birds* is subject to significant objections, since it is founded solely on a presumed and unlikely coarse pun on χρυσόν (670) and κυσόν, or rather κύσθον. Moreover, the absence of any explicit reference to the erogenous parts of Procne's body leads me to prefer the conclusion that she too was wearing a revealing outfit.

(c) Since explicit references to the sexual body parts of Thirty-Year-Truce (in *Knights*), Opora (in *Peace*) and Princess (in *Birds*) are absent from the text, it seems reasonable to conclude that none of them appears on stage nude. In particular, on the basis of the dramaturgical contexts, there is a strong foundation for maintaining that Opora and Princess put on wedding dresses in the finales of *Peace* and *Birds*, respectively. I am of course aware that the absence of explicit, precise references to the sexual organs of Thirty-Year-Truce, Opora and Princess is not in itself sufficient to prove that the *mutae personae* that played these roles *did not act nude* on the stage: since the Aristophanic text is intended primarily for theatrical performances, it does not necessarily present directions that allow a reader to reconstruct the scenic action. After all, the playwright composed his texts for an audience not of readers but of spectators, who could see what was happening on stage. Nonetheless, I believe it is improbable, if not impossible, that, in a theatre frequented by an audience composed for the most part if not entirely of male spectators, the spectacular stage presence of beautiful naked girls could pass uncommented.

---

57 Dale 1956, 96 (also in Dale 1969, 119).

Bibliography

Adams, James N. (1982), *The Latin Sexual Vocabulary*, London.

Austin, Colin (1987), "Textual Problems in Ar. *Thesm.*", in: *Dodone* 16, 61–92.

Austin, Colin/Olson, S. Douglas (2004) (eds.), *Aristophanes. Thesmophoriazusae*, Oxford.

Beta, Simone (1992), "Il linguaggio erotico di Cratino", in: *Quaderni Urbinati di Cultura Classica*, n. s. 40, 95–108.

Boggione, Valter/Casalegno, Giovanni (2000), *Dizionario letterario del lessico amoroso. Metafore, eufemismi, trivialismi*, Torino.

Bowie, Angus M. (1993), *Aristophanes. Myth, Ritual and Comedy*, Cambridge.

Biles, Zachary/Olson, S. Douglas (2015) (eds.), *Aristophanes Wasps*, Oxford.

Carey, Christopher (2017), "Staging Allegory", in: Fountoulakis, Andreas/Markantonatos, Andreas/Vasilaros, Georgios (eds.), *Theatre World. Critical Perspectives on Greek Tragedy and Comedy. Studies in Honour of Georgia Xanthakis-Karamanos*, Berlin/Boston, 49–64.

Compton-Engle, Gwendolyn (2015), *Costume in the Comedies of Aristophanes*, Cambridge.

Dale, Amy M. (1956), "Seen and Unseen on the Greek Stage: A Study in Scenic Conventions", in: *Wiener Studien* 69, 96–106 (repr. in: Ead. [1969], *Collected Papers*, Cambridge, 119–129).

Di Bari, Marta F. (2009), "Una Cerbiatta 'equina' (Ar. *Th.* 1174, 1210s.)", in: *Eikasmós* 20, 139–149.

Di Bari, Marta F. (2013), *Scene finali di Aristofane. Cavalieri Nuvole Tesmoforiazuse*, Lecce/Brescia.

Dover, Kenneth J. (1972), *Aristophanic Comedy*, London.

Droysen, Johann G. (1835), *Des Aristophanes Werke*, Berlin.

Dunbar, Nan (1995) (ed.), *Aristophanes Birds*, Oxford.

Ewans, Michael (2008), Rev. of Revermann, Martin (2006), *Comic Business. Theatricality, Dramatic Technique, and Performance Contexts of Aristophanic Comedy*, Oxford; in: *Classical Review* n. s. 58, 363–364.

Gil Fernández, Juan (1963), *Parerga II,2*, in: *Emerita* 31, 131–137.

Gil Fernández, Luis (1995) (ed.), *Aristófanes. Comedias*, I (*Los Acarnienses-Los Caballeros*), Madrid.

Henderson, Jeffrey (1987) (ed.), *Aristophanes. Lysistrata*, Oxford.

Henderson, Jeffrey (1991[2]), *The Maculate Muse. Obscene Language in Attic Comedy*, New York/Oxford.

Holzinger, Karl von (1928), *Erklärungen umstrittener Stellen des Aristophanes*, I, Vienna/Leipzig.

MacDowell, Douglas M. (1971) (ed.), *Aristophanes. Wasps*, Oxford.

MacDowell, Douglas M. (1995), *Aristophanes and Athens. An Introduction to the Plays*, Oxford.

Mastromarco, Giuseppe (1983) (ed.), *Aristofane Commedie*, vol. I, Torino.

Mastromarco, Giuseppe/Totaro, Piero (2006) (eds.), *Commedie di Aristofane,* vol. II, Torino.

Mastromarco, Giuseppe (2019), "Sulla scena delle *Tesmoforiazuse* di Aristofane (vv. 1001–1231)", in: *Seminari Romani di cultura greca* n.s. 8, 197–214.

Mastromarco, Giuseppe (2021), "Aristofane, *Ecclesiazuse* 1129–1153", in: Beta, Simone/Romani, Silvia (eds.), *Tirsi per Dioniso: a Giulio Guidorizzi*, Alessandria, 215–218.

Meineke, August (1860) (ed.), *Aristophanis Comoediae*, vol. I, Leipzig.

Meineke, August (1865), *Vindiciarum Aristophanearum liber*, Leipzig.

Newiger, Hans-Joachim (1957), *Metapher und Allegorie. Studien zu Aristophanes*, Munich.

Olson, S. Douglas (1998) (ed.), *Aristophanes. Peace*, Oxford (*Addenda* 2003).

Olson, S. Douglas (2002) (ed.), *Aristophanes. Acharnians*, Oxford.

Olson, S. Douglas/Seaberg, Ryan (2018) (eds.), *Kratinos frr. 299–514. Translation and Commentary* (Fragmenta Comica 3.6), Göttingen.

Pellegrino, Matteo (2015) (ed.), *Aristofane. Frammenti. Testo, traduzione e commento*, Lecce/Brescia.

Perusino, Franca (2002), "L'ἔγκυκλον, un mantello femminile nelle commedie di Aristofane", in: *Quaderni Urbinati di Cultura Classica* n. s. 72, 129–133.

Perusino, Franca/Beta, Simone (2020) (eds.), *Aristofane. Lisistrata*, Milan.

Pickard-Cambridge, Arthur (1968²), *The Dramatic Festivals of Athens*, Oxford (*Select Addenda* 1988, 359–65).

Pohlenz, Max (1952), "Aristophanes' *Ritter*", in: *Nachrichten der Akademie der Wissenschaften in Göttingen, Philol.-Hist. Klasse*, 95–128 (repr. in: Id. [1965], *Kleine Schriften*, ed. von Dörrie, Heinrich, II, Hildesheim, 511–544).

Revermann, Martin (2006), *Comic Business. Theatricality, Dramatic Technique, and Performance Contexts of Aristophanic Comedy*, Oxford.

Russo, Carlo F. (1994), *Aristophanes, an Author for the Stage*, revised and expanded English edition by Wren, Kevin, London/New York.

Seager, Robin (1981), "Notes on Aristophanes", in: *Classical Quarterly* n.s. 31, 244–251.

Sommerstein, Alan H. (1983) (ed.), *The Comedies of Aristophanes*, vol. 4: *Wasps*, Warminster.

Sommerstein, Alan H. (1985) (ed.), *The Comedies of Aristophanes*, vol. 5: *Peace*, Warminster.

Sommerstein, Alan H. (1990) (ed.), *The Comedies of Aristophanes*, vol. 7: *Lysistrata*, Warminster.

Sommerstein, Alan H. (1994) (ed.), *The Comedies of Aristophanes*, vol. 8: *Thesmophoriasusae*, Warminster.

Sommerstein, Alan H. (1996) (ed.), *The Comedies of Aristophanes*, vol. 9: *Frogs*, Warminster.

Sommerstein, Alan H. (1998) (ed.), *The Comedies of Aristophanes*, vol. 10: *Ecclesiazusae*, Warminster.

Sommerstein, Alan H. (2001) (ed.), *The Comedies of Aristophanes*, vol. 11: *Wealth*, Warminster.

Sommerstein, Alan H. (2009) (ed.), *Talking about Laughter and other Studies in Greek Comedy*, Oxford.

Sonnino, Maurizio (2012), "Le fornaie comiche e i pani di Periandro", in: *Prometheus* n.s. 1, 67–88.

Stone, Laura M. (1981), *Costume in Aristophanic Poetry*, New York.

Taillardat, Jean (1965²), *Les images d'Aristophane. Études de langue et de style*, Paris.

Taplin, Oliver (1993), *Comic Angels and Other Approaches to Greek Drama through Vase-Paintings*, Oxford.

Thiercy, Pascal (1997) (ed.), *Aristophane. Théâtre complet*. Textes présentés, établis et annotés, Paris.

Torchio, Maria Cristina (2021) (ed.), *Aristofane. Nephelai protai — Proagon (frr. 392–486). Traduzione e commento* (FrC 10.7), Göttingen.

Totaro, Piero (2022), "Note sceniche sulla *performance* orchestico-musicale del trio Euripide/Teredon/Elaphion nel finale delle *Tesmoforiazuse* di Aristofane", in: Gostoli, Antonietta/Zimmermann, Bernhard (eds.), *Nuove volute di versi. Poesia e musica nella commedia greca di V e IV sec. a.C.*, Göttingen, 49–68.

Van Herwerden, Heinrich (1897) (ed.), *ΑΡΙΣΤΟΦΑΝΟΥΣ ΕΙΡΗΝΗ*, I–II, Leiden.

Wilamowitz-Moellendorff, Ulrich von (1927) (ed.), *Aristophanes. Lysistrate*, Berlin.
Willems, Alphonse (1919) (ed.), *Aristophane*. Traduction avec notes et commentaires critiques, I–III, Paris/Bruxelles.
Wilson, Nigel G. (2007a) (ed.), *Aristophanis fabulae*, I–II, Oxonii.
Wilson, Nigel G. (2007b), *Aristophanea. Studies on the Text of Aristophanes*, Oxford.
Zanetto, Giuseppe/Del Corno, Dario (1987) (eds.), *Aristofane. Gli Uccelli*, Milano.
Zweig, Bella (1992), "The Mute Nude Female Characters in Aristophanes' Plays", in: Richlin, Amy (ed.), *Pornography and Representation in Greece and Rome*, New York/Oxford, 73–89.

Piero Totaro

Pseudartabas and the Persian Eunuchs in Aristophanes' *Acharnians*: Textual and Staging Problems

Abstract: Beginning with a detailed examination of Ar. *Ach.* 94–121, this article aims to offer a detailed, up-to-date overview of the staging problems of the passage, especially with regard to the representation of Pseudartabas and the two eunuchs who accompany him. Moreover, by means of a fresh analysis of the parodied hypotext at 120–121 (Archil. fr. 187 W.[2]), I argue that one of the eunuchs on stage (perhaps representing Cleisthenes) was probably beardless.

Keywords: Aristophanes, *Acharnians*, Persians, eunuchs, staging

In the prologue of Aristophanes' *Acharnians*, at the beginning of the popular assembly at which the old peasant Dicaeopolis (protagonist of the comedy) is eager to finally discuss peace with the Spartans, Athenian ambassadors return from the court of the Great King of Persia.[1] They are accompanied by Pseudartabas and two eunuchs.[2]

Pseudartabas, the Eye of the King

The first part of the compound name Pseudartabas, modelled on Greek ψευδής, communicates the idea of falsehood and cheating. The second part recalls the Persian word *artabe*, which denoted a measure (equivalent to one *medimnos* plus three Attic *choinikes*, according to Hdt. 1.192.3), or alternatively *arta*, which meant 'justice, cosmic order' and occurs as the initial element in several Persian proper names (*e.g.* Artaxerxes, Artaphernes, Artabazus).[3] The name might thus

---

1 Wearing Eastern dress: see Olson 2021.
2 On the embassy scene in the prologue of *Acharnians*, see recently Hutzfeldt 1999, 154–158, Buis 2008.
3 Cf. Olson 2002, 101 (*ad* Ar. *Ach.* 91–92). In some exhilarating verses from Plautus' *Persa*, the slave Sagaristion comically mocks the abnormal and exotic length of Persian names: DO. *Quid est tibi nomen?* [...] SA. *Ausculta ergo, ut scias:* / *Vaniloquidorus Virginisvendonides* / *Nugiepiloquides, Argentumexterebronides,* / *Tedigniloquides, Nugides, Palponides,* / *Quodsemelarripides*

https://doi.org/10.1515/9783111248028-008

be legitimately interpreted as 'Someone who gives false measures'[4] or 'False right'.[5] The character is officially introduced to the assembly in his role of Eye of the King, a title usually attributed to inspectors sent by the Great King of Persia to the various satrapies of the empire and charged with oversight functions.[6] At 94–97, Dicaeopolis describes his appearance:

> ὦναξ Ἡράκλεις.
> πρὸς τῶν θεῶν, ἄνθρωπε, ναύφαρκτον βλέπεις;   95
> ἢ περὶ ἄκραν κάμπτων νεώσοικον σκοπεῖς;
> ἄσκωμ' ἔχεις που περὶ τὸν ὀφθαλμὸν κάτω.

> Lord Heracles!
> Heavens, man, are you giving me a hostile nautical look,   95
> or, rounding a cape, are you looking out for a ship-shed?
> I guess that's an oarport leather you've got around your eye down there![7]

It is reasonable to assume that the character's mask included a large eye, i.e. a concrete visual manifestation of his role as Eye of the King.[8] The interpretation of the nautical metaphor in 97 is particularly problematic. Aligning with Taillardat (1965, 65–67), as Mastromarco (1983, 123) had previously, Pretagostini (1998, 49) comments as follows:

> "la maschera dell'attore che impersona Pseudartabano è costituita da un grande occhio, che richiama le cubie, cioè i fori sulle fiancate delle triremi, e, sotto di esso, da un lembo di cuoio, che vuole evocare una magnifica barba orientale; ma nel contesto della metafora il termine ἄσκωμα fa riferimento alle coperture di cuoio che, quando la nave solcava il mare, chiudevano le cubie (τὸν ὀφθαλμόν) da cui uscivano i remi".

Gil Fernández (1995, 112, n. 22), on the other hand, observes:

Numquameripides. Em tibi! / DO. *Eu hercle, nomen multimodis scriptumst tuum.* / SA. *Ita sunt Persarum mores; longa nomina / contortiplicata habemus* (699–708, printed here following Ernout 1961); see Faller 2001, 189ff. for an interesting comparison with the Pseudartabas scene in *Acharnians*.

4 Mastromarco 1983, 122–123, n. 27.

5 See Treu 2011.

6 See Olson 2002, 101–102 (*ad* Ar. *Ach.* 91–92).

7 My translation is based on the critical text established by Olson 2002, 22, who rejects the manuscript reading ναύφρακτον (95) in favour of Dindorf's ναύφαρκτον (conjectured on the basis of Phot. v 64 Theodoridis: see Olson 2002, 103 *ad loc.*).

8 Aveline 2000, 500, going perhaps too far with fantasy, conjectured that the entire costume consisted of a gigantic eye endowed with arms, legs and comic phallus.

"Normalmente se interpreta *áskōma* como una funda de cuero que cubría la parte superior del remo. Creo más probable que se trate del estrobo o correa con la que se ajustaba éste al tolete o escálamo. Si fuera la funda del remo, ¿cómo podría colgar por debajo del 'ojo', tronera o escobén por donde se introducía el remo?"

According to Olson (2002, 103–104), the Persian emissary's mask features a huge eye or pair of eyes resembling the ὀφθαλμοί painted on the prows of Greek ships in all periods. In the metaphor of 97, the 'lower eye' might thus perhaps be either his mouth (which would be surrounded by a huge, bushy beard) or his anus, assuming that Pseudartabas wore the traditional Persian trousers. In Aveline's view (2000, 500), "the actor's phallos, hanging just underneath this ludicrous eye, could humorously be described as an oar-flap (ἄσκωμα)".

As the Ambassador asks him to tell the Athenians the Great King's thoughts, Pseudartabas speaks a line that is variously transmitted by the manuscripts: Olson and Wilson, the two most recent editors, opt for aligning with part of the medieval paradosis and print ἰαρταμαν ἐξαρξαν ἀπισσονα σατρα (*Ach.* 100).[9] This passage, rightly described as "one of the most hotly debated lines of Greek literature" (Willi 2004, 657), has sparked considerable scholarly curiosity and produced an impressive critical bibliography. What follows is a selection of the most influential interpretations offered in the last two centuries, often radically divergent from one another:

–   Friedrich 1921, read ι αρταμανε Ξαρξας απιαονα σατρα (imitated shortly afterwards by Coulon 1923, 16), interpreted: "The wise Xerxes to the Athenian people...";[10]

–   West 1968, 5–7 proposed ῑ-αρτα-νᾱμε-ξαρξᾰνᾰπισσονᾱ σατρα, in a language he regarded as senseless although evocative of Persian words and sounds, such as personal names (*e.g.* Artaxerxes, Xerxes, Pissutnes satrap of Sardis) and the term 'satrap';[11]

–   Willi 2004, 657–681, attempts to restore an acceptable meaning for the line in light of linguistic evidence for ancient Persian. His 'approximate translation'

---

9 Thus Wilson 2007, I 11; Olson 2002, 11 and 105 *ad loc.* prefers not to split the *vox* into single words. A comprehensive list of the ancient variants is reported in Olson's critical apparatus *ad loc.* and by Negri/Ornaghi 2008.
10 This interpretation is recently endorsed by Negri/Ornaghi 2008 and Treu 2011 (who also provide a detailed report of the massive bibliography produced on the line). But see also the fine dissertation of Bravo 2009.
11 Remarkable consensus emerged about this interpretation as well: see e.g. Mastromarco, 1983, 123; Pretagostini 1998, 49; Colvin 1999, 289. Beginning from the analysis of this line, Kidd 2014, 5–7, wonders what 'nonsense' or 'gibberish' are actually supposed to mean in ancient comic texts.

is roughly ὁ εὐμενὴς Ξέρξης (κατ)έγραψε τάδε ἐνταῦθα, "the wise/pious Xerxes has written down these exact things" (implying that Pseudartabas brings a missive from the Great King with him and exhibits it on stage).

–   In the unpublished *Updates* to his edition of Aristophanes (which I had the opportunity to consult in their 2009 version through the kindness of the author), Sommerstein changes his mind on line 100, rejecting West's thesis (which he had previously embraced in his commentary on *Acharnians*: 1980, 162) and accepting Willi's. He also focuses on a detail which, in his opinion, had not previously been adequately investigated, i.e. the reason why the Great King mentioned in the text is Xerxes and not Artaxerxes (who reigned over the Persian empire at the time of *Acharnians*' première in 425 BCE). Sommerstein claims that the Persian form *Artaxšaçā* would not have been easy for the audience to recognize; the Greek transliteration would have been approximately Αρταξατρα. In addition, the name usually adopted in Greek would not fit into iambic trimeter, forcing Aristophanes to ask his Persian language consultant for a solution consisting of the name 'Xerxes' accompanied by an epithet containing the prefix *arta-*. Sommerstein in fact accepts Willi's conjecture that Aristophanes asked a local expert in Persian to help him produce the verse: evidence supporting the existence of such figures is provided by Thuc. 4.50, according to whom, in 425 BCE, a Persian headed for Sparta on behalf of the Great King was captured and the Athenians had the opportunity to have the letter he was carrying translated.[12]

In response to the reaction of Dicaeopolis, who confesses that he has failed to understand anything Pseudartabas said, the Ambassador interprets the remark in his own way and for his own benefit (102–104):

ΠΡ.   πέμψειν βασιλέα φησὶν ὑμῖν χρυσίον.
       λέγε δὴ σὺ μεῖζον καὶ σαφῶς τὸ χρυσίον.
ΨΕ.   οὐ λῆψι χρυσό, χαυνόπρωκτ' Ἰαοναῦ.

AM.   He claims the King will send you some gold.
       And you—say loud and clear "gold"!
PS.   You not vill get goldo, you open ass Iaonian.

12 Thuc. 4.50 καὶ αὐτοῦ κομισθέντος οἱ Ἀθηναῖοι τὰς μὲν ἐπιστολὰς μεταγραψάμενοι ἐκ τῶν Ἀσσυρίων γραμμάτων ἀνέγνωσαν.

In order to produce greater clarity (as well as to allow Aristophanes to employ one more expedient of linguistic humour), after this the Eye of the King speaks a language that is closer to Greek but still incorrect, like that used by the Scythian archer in *Thesmophoriazusae*.[13] He also addresses his Athenian interlocutor in a grossly offensive way, by calling him 'Ionian'. (Real Persians referred to Greeks as *Yauna*.)[14] This time Dicaeopolis — and certainly the audience as well — understands the remark correctly and begins to question the Persian personally.

Dicaeopolis first asks a precise question (113): "Will the Great King send us gold?" As he asks this, he threatens to strike Pseudartabas (cf. 112 ἵνα μή σε βάψω βάμμα Σαρδιανικόν).[15] But how is he supposed to do this? with a fist or a staff? The two options are carefully evaluated by Olson (2002, 107–108 *ad* 111–112), who is inclined to think that a fist (κόνδυλος, i.e. a masculine noun better matching the masculine pronoun πρὸς τουτονί transmitted by the manuscripts at 111; the Greek term for 'staff' is either feminine [βακτηρία, βακτηρίς] or neuter[16] [βάκτρον, βάκτρευμα, βακτήριον]) is in question; unless, following Dover (1963, 9), we opted for σκίπων (cf. Cratin. fr. 257.2 K.–A., Ar. *V.* 727) or assume the existence of another masculine noun signifying the same object. The latter option, however, risks attempting to explain "*obscurum per obscurius*" (Olson).[17]

Pseudartabas replies by shaking his head, as we can infer from the question he is asked shortly afterward — "So we're just being deceived by our ambassadors?" (114) — to which the Eye of the King and the two eunuchs offer an affirmative response, causing Dicaeopolis to remark: "Very Greek, the way these fellows nod. I'm quite sure they come from this very city" (115–116).

The two eunuchs

In Dicaeopolis' view, the eunuchs resemble two real contemporary Athenian citizens, Cleisthenes and Strato. The former is often mocked in Aristophanes'

---

13 On this, see Willi 2003, 223–224; Di Bari 2013, 384ff.

14 Cf. e.g. Atossa at Aesch. *Pers.* 178 Ἰαόνων γῆν.

15 With regard to the expression βάμμα Σαρδιανικόν, which indicates the vivid red color of blood, see Totaro 2000, 131.

16 Robertson's emendation πρὸς τουτογί would in fact perfectly suit a hypothetical neuter in the text.

17 Henderson (1998, 71) prints the masculine form πρὸς τουτονί in his text, and the stage direction accompanying his translation explicitly mentions a "walking stick" brandished by Dicaeopolis. However, he recently retracts this assumption by arguing that it would actually be "his fist, to judge by the pronoun's gender" (Henderson 2022, 97).

comedies for his effeminacy and is associated with Strato again at *Eq.* 1374 and probably in one of the preserved fragments from the lost *Merchant Ships* (fr. 422 K.–A.).[18] Interpretation of this passage from *Acharnians* thus confronts complex difficulties regarding the true identity of Pseudartabas and his eunuch *entourage*. Are they true or false Persians? Should the three men be regarded as Athenians dressed up like Persians? Is the Eye of the King alone to be understood as a genuine Persian (even if the first element of the compound 'Pseudartabas', as mentioned above, points towards the idea of falsehood), the two eunuchs impostors? Or perhaps the 'recognition' of the eunuchs by Dicaeopolis is mere speculation and simply represents further Aristophanic invective against Cleisthenes? These exegetical options are effectively summarised in brilliant monographs by Charalampos Orfanos (2006, 54–61) and Anne De Cremoux (2011, 53–57) both in the light of previous bibliography and in an attempt to define the current status of an intricate dramaturgical issue. In this case, the linguistic evidence, crucial as it is, can nonetheless be used in support of either thesis — as acutely noted by Roberto Pretagostini, who inclined to believe that Aristophanes represented on stage a badly designed scam, an actual 'masquerade' and its successful 'exposure':

> "In questa ottica anche le due brevi frasi pronunciate da Pseudartabano assumono un diverso rilievo: il suo presunto persiano come del resto il suo greco sgrammaticato non sono attestazione — come in realtà dovrebbero essere, se egli fosse veramente un suddito del Re di Persia — l'uno della conoscenza di una lingua diversa da quella parlata dagli Ateniesi, l'altro della scarsa conoscenza di quella che per lui è una lingua straniera; al contrario essi rappresentano il tentativo, messo in atto da un abile impostore, da una parte di riprodurre, attraverso un ridicolo *grammelot*, una lingua per lui completamente sconosciuta, dall'altra di nascondere la conoscenza di quella che è la sua propria lingua".[19]

---

18 In *Ach.* 118, Cleisthenes (*PA* 8525; *LGPN* II, s.v. nr. 2; *PAA* 575540 ~ 575545) is defined as "Sibyrtius' son". But it is reasonable to assume that this claim reflects comic purposes, ironically highlighting the contrast between a notoriously effeminate son and a father renowned for his virility: indeed, we know that Sibyrtius owned a gym (cf. Antipho fr. 66 Blass–Thalheim [*ap.* Plut. *Alc.* 3]). Recently, Olson (2002, 109–110 *ad loc.*) proposed identifying Cleisthenes with the son of Autocrates, who belonged to the tribe Erectheis (*PA* 8524; *LGPN* II, s.v. nr. 6; *PAA* 575550) and was choregus between 430 and 405 BCE (*IG* I³ 965.1); see Mastromarco/Totaro 2006, 488–489.

19 Pretagostini 1998, 54. Pretagostini himself (pp. 54–55) proposed a suggestive comparison with several scenes from one of Carlo Goldoni's comedies, *La famiglia dell'antiquario* (Venice, Teatro Sant'Angelo, Carnival 1750), in which Arlecchino, on Brighella's advice, shows up disguised as an Armenian antiquarian, with a false beard and in the proper clothing, speaking a broken dialect and a sort of 'Armenizing' *grammelot* that allows him to successfully cheat

As regards the exegetical difficulty of discerning the link between page and stage here, *Ach.* 119–121, in which Dicaeopolis addresses the eunuch-Cleisthenes, is particularly interesting:

ὦ θερμόβουλον πρωκτὸν ἐξυρημένε,[20]
τοιόνδε γ᾽, ὦ πίθηκε, τὸν πώγων᾽ ἔχων
εὐνοῦχος ἡμῖν ἦλθες ἐσκευασμένος;

O you who shave your hot-desiring ass,
do you, O monkey, with a beard like this,
come among us dressed up as a eunuch?

According to the scholia, this passage contains a double parody:

schol. **REΓLh** *Ach.* 119 Wilson ὦ θερμόβουλον: παρῳδίᾳ χρῆται. ἔστι γὰρ ἐν Τημενίδαις (Rutherford : ἐν τῇ Μηδείᾳ **REΓ** : ἐκ Μηδείας **Lh**) Εὐριπίδου "ὦ θερμόβουλον σπλάγχνον". οὗτος οὖν σκώπτων Εὐριπίδην προσέθηκε "πρωκτὸν" παρὰ προσδοκίαν.

O thermoboulon: (scil. the author) is using a parody. Because in Euripides' Temenids (?), there is in fact the expression "O hot desiring heart". In order to mock Euripides, he unexpectedly inserted "ass".

Count Anselmo. Indeed, he manages to convince the Count to buy an ordinary oil lantern at an exorbitant price, by depicting it as an eternal lamp found "in palamida de getto, in sepolcro Bartolomeo", "nelle piramidi d'Egitto, nel sepolcro de Tolomeo", as promptly translated by Brighella for Anselmo, who is completely uncapable of understanding any part of this strange Armenian idiom (Act I, Scene XVII). The cheating is eventually revealed, however, and the fraud unmasked, with Arlecchino offering a full confession before the Count: ARLECCHINO: "Siori, ve domando perdon …". / ANSELMO: "(Questi è l'armeno) (*da sé*). Siete voi l'armeno?" / ARLECCHINO: "Sior sì, son un armeno da Bergamo" (Act III, Scene IV [ed. Davico Bonino 1983]). Pretagostini's interpretation is not endorsed by Kloss 2001, according to whom «Pseudartabas kein Komplize des Gesandten sein kann, also auch kein Athener» (p. 38). While discussing the various scholarly positions on the prologue of *Acharnians*, Kloss (*ibid.*, pp. 34–42) is mainly interested in outlining the comic dynamic adopted in the employment of foreign idioms in Aristophanes' comedies (in the *Acharnians* as well as in *Birds*, where the barbarian god Triballus is active on stage). On the language of the 'barbarian' characters in the abovementioned scenes from *Acharnians* and *Birds*, see also Brixhe 1988; Morenilla-Talens 1989; de Fátima Sousa e Silva 1999; Lamagna 2000, 248–250; De Luna 2003, 245–264. On the 'barbarian' idiom spoken by a character depicted on a comic vase from Magna Graecia (saec. V^ex–IV^in BCE), see now Totaro 2017; *Id.* 2019, 309–314.
20 In light of the fact that this joke focusses on Cleisthenes' female habits (such as depilation), editors rightly prefer the *Suda*'s ἐξυρημένε to ἐξευρημένε transmitted by the manuscripts of Aristophanes.

The manuscripts that preserve the scholion assign the parodied hypotext ὦ θερμόβουλον σπλάγχνον to *Medea*. But the expression is not found in the extant version of the play, hence both Rutherford's emendation of the title (accepted by Wilson, perhaps too confidently) and (an editorial option which I am inclined to endorse) the more cautious inclusion of the words among Euripides' *incertarum fabularum fragmenta* (fr. 858 Nauck[2] = Kannicht = Collard–Cropp).[21]

> *schol.* **ELh** *Ach.* 120 Wilson τοιόνδε δ᾽, ὦ πίθηκε: καὶ τοῦτο παρῴδηκεν ἐκ τῶν Ἀρχιλόχου ἐπῳδῶν (Huschke : ἐπῶν codd.)· τοιάνδε δ᾽, ὦ πίθηκε, τὴν πυγὴν ἔχεις (**E** : ἔχων **Lh**).
>
> *toiond'o pitheke*: (*scil.* the author) also forged this expression by parodying Archilochus' epods: "*O monkey, you have such a butt*".

The quotation of Archilochus (fr. 187, printed by West[2] and Swift as τοιήνδε δ᾽ ὦ πίθηκε τὴν πυγὴν ἔχων — according to Triclinius' [**Lh**] textual assessment) stems from a fable in which a fox and a monkey acted as protagonists (see also Archil. frr. 185–186 W.[2]).[22] Many scholars believe that the contents of the fragment resemble those attested in *fab.* 83 Hausrath–Hunger (= 38 Chambry) from the Aesopic *corpus*:[23] this focuses on the story of a monkey (whose choreutic abilities were so admired by an assembly of animals that it ended up with being elected as their king) and an envious fox (which escorted the monkey somewhere by persuading it that a marvelous treasure awaited it there). The treasure actually consisted of a piece of flesh put in a trap; the unsuspecting monkey ended up with being trapped, and accused the fox of having cheated it, leading to a sardonic comment from the fox. The moral of the story is that the sole reward for reckless actions is failure (and sometimes mockery). The final apostrophe of the fox to the monkey, variously transmitted in the multiple Aesopic versions of the fable,[24] is approximately: "O Monkey, you that have such a fate" (or "such a foolish fate", or "such a foolish attitude" or "such stupidity"), "de-

---

21 Fr. *incertae fabulae* 852 in Nauck's first edition (1856, 502). Jouan/Van Looy (1993, 13; *Id.* 2003, 8), by contrast, assign it to *Aegeus* (fr. ****18**). A detailed report of the wide range of attributions conjectured by modern scholars can be found in Kannicht's (2004, 890) critical apparatus.

22 See Kugelmeier 1996, 172–174; Schirru 2009, 82–88.

23 Against this thesis, scholars have observed that the fox and the monkey are protagonists in another fable in the Aesopic *corpus* (14 Hausrath–Hunger = 39 Chambry), in which they discuss nobility of birth. But they could be protagonists in other fables as well. See now Mosconi 2005, 279–280 and Tosi 2022, 359–360, n. 67.

24 See the critical apparatus of Chantry 1925, 95–97 (*ad* Aesop. *fab.* 38) and Hausrath/Hunger 1970, 109–111 (*ad* Aesop. *fab.* 83, I–III).

sire to reign over the animals?" I thus find it reasonable to claim that the Aesopic version of the sentence ultimately stems from Archilochus' phrase (fr. 187 W.²) through a process of 'de-sexualization', which converted the anatomical πυγή of the iambic model into a more 'moralised' diction, adopting terms such as τύχη, "fate", ψυχή, "attitude", or μωρία, "foolishness".²⁵ In Aristophanes, the mechanism of the parody consists in both cases in replacing a key-term in the hypotext with another word that is highly functional for comic mockery: Euripides' σπλάγχνον ("bowel, soul, heart") becomes πρωκτόν ("ass"), while Archilochus' πυγήν ("buttocks") is converted into πώγων(α) ("beard").

The final question we need to answer is thus the following: in the prologue of *Acharnians*, was the eunuch (or the false eunuch, the Athenian Cleisthenes) bearded? Even here there is wide disagreement among Aristophanic scholars, and a wide variety of scenarios are conjectured. In addition to eunuchs castrated before puberty (and thus inevitably beardless), Mueller (1863, 27) conjectured the existence of an older type, which one or both eunuchs on stage (thought of as real bearded Persians) belong to. One can easily imagine how harshly this fanciful theory was criticized later on. But we cannot help but notice that a strong scholarly tradition recognizes Cleisthenes as an actual bearded character:

"ad hominem, qui propter faciem glabram corpusque depilatum inter omnes notus erat, ridicule referens Dicaeopolis *tunc igitur,* ait, *quem tali barba cernamus ornatum* – et manu fictam illam barbam indicat – *eunuchum agis?* (van Leeuwen 1901, 30);

"If the attendants are indeed Persian, however, the point of 120–21 may be ridicule of a distinctively Oriental style of beard – quite plausibly, I think, the kind of beard worn by Persian royalty in Achaemenid reliefs, especially those at Persepolis, which celebrate the reigns of Darius I and Xerxes and are dated between the late sixth and mid-fifth centuries. Persian rulers depicted in these reliefs wear a beard that is long and square-tipped, and the sight of such a beard (assuming that it is not merely artistic convention) must have amused an Athenian audience no less than the spectacle of native Persian dress. Of course, the beard is funnier still because worn by a eunuch, whom Dicaeopolis obviously expects to find smooth-cheeked or lightly bearded [...] the lowly attendant unveiled by Dicaeopolis bears a striking similarity to the Great King himself. Thus, there are perhaps two implications underlying Dicaeopolis incredulous question: not only 'You're too heavily bearded to be a eunuch' but also 'With a beard like that you should be a king!' [...] Pseudartabas, "Shambyses" is accompanied, appropriately, by a sham eunuch" (Chiasson 1984, 135–136);

---

25 Nøjgaard 1964, 524; Swift 2019, 350 (*ad* Archil. fr. 187 W.²).

"l'Occhio del Re e i due eunuchi sono degli impostori travestiti da Persiani; in sostanza si tratta di una mascherata che in un particolare, la falsa barba di Clistene, viene svelata da Diceopoli con un sottile gioco di parole [...] in Aristofane la sarcastica osservazione di Diceopoli nei confronti del barbuto, ma effeminato Clistene non ha altra funzione se non quella di svelare l'inganno della barba posticcia" (Pretagostini 1998, 53).

In the opinion of some scholars, Dicaeopolis unveils Cleisthenes by ripping off his beard (e.g. Olson 2002, 108 *ad* 117–122: "Dik. rips a false beard off first one [118] and then the other [122]"; but see also p. 109 *ad* 117–118 and p. 111 *ad* 122) or even his entire mask: "Possibly, Dicaeopolis literally unmasks the eunuch by taking away the latter's bearded mask, thus — with typical Aristophanic rupture of the dramatic illusion — revealing the actor's 'real' face" (Van Dijk 1997, 202). A complete 'unmasking' was also conjectured by Starkie (1909, 37), who, after criticizing the staging reconstruction offered by Müller-Strübing 1873, 691–692 (according to whom the term πώγων refers to Cleisthenes' phallus), argued the following:

'Clisthenes' had provided himself with a mask, so as entirely to cover his features. Dic. tears this aside and discloses the beardless face of Clisthenes, and the meaning is 'with such a beard as this (viz., no beard) was it necessary to disguise yourself as a eunuch?'.

His interpretation was coherent, however, with a radically different exegetical position that can be summarized under the label 'no beard', ranging from Ribbeck (1864, 205) and Paley (1876, 18) to Long (1986, 102–103), with some significant interpretative steps taken by Rennie (1909, 108: "I think it probable that the eunuch wears a beardless mask") and Dover (1963, 10–11). The latter in fact argues that after Dicaeopolis uncovers the lower part of the eunuch's face (cloaked in the Persian fashion) and makes it clear that his mask is beardless, he pinches his hairless cheek and ironically exclaims "It's because you have the kind of beard you have [i.e. 'no beard'] that you've come dressed up as a eunuch".[26]

As I hope I made clear, a secure reconstruction of the Aristophanic staging is once again impossible to obtain by relying exclusively on textual evidence. It is thus legitimate to prefer one thesis or the other, even if we need to be aware that all these conjectures are far from unquestionable and perfectly clear. I too have a preference, which is mainly founded on two pieces of anthropological and textual evidence:

---

26 Dover's reconstruction and the undeniable irony of the joke at 120–121 are strongly endorsed by Stone 1981, 51.

a) In the Greeks' view, Persian eunuchs were traditionally effeminate and beardless;[27]
b) In Archilochus' fable (fr. 187 W.²), alluded to in Ar. *Ach.* 120, the joke plausibly contained an ironic *pointe* consisting in the fox's merciless remark on the ridiculously small size of the monkey's πυγή ― a narrative element broadly attested in archaic Greek literature, as Semonides' *Poem on Women* demonstrates by giving the 'monkey-woman' the attribute ἄπυγος, "without buttocks" (fr. 7.76 W.² = Pellizer–Tedeschi).[28]

If Archilochus' expression "you, that have such buttocks" actually meant, with injurious irony, "you, that *do not* have buttocks", we may thus legitimately infer that the same comic mechanism aptly suits Aristophanes' parody: "you, that have such a beard" was meant to signify the exact opposite and as a consequence to mercilessly underline the notorious effeminacy of the Athenian Cleisthenes (the 'man' *par exellence* ἀγένειος),[29] who could adequately impersonate a eunuch on stage. This assumption may also find some support in the scholiastic explanation *ad loc.*: "This Cleisthenes always shaved his chin in order to appear always young. For this reason, (*scil.* the author) compares him to a eunuch" (*schol.* **REΓLh** *Ach.* 118 Wilson οὗτος δὲ ὁ Κλεισθένης ἀεὶ τὸ γένειον ἐξυρᾶτο πρὸς τὸ ἀεὶ φαίνεσθαι νέος. διὰ τοῦτο εὐνούχῳ αὐτὸν εἰκάζει)[30] ― although, as

---

27 See Hall 1989, 157; Miller 2006–2007 (esp. p. 120: "to Greek eyes the beardless eunuch of the royal imagery probably looked female"). Greek sources documenting eunuchs' traditional occupations are reported in detail by Miller 1997, 213–215 and Olson 2002, 109 (*ad* Ar. *Ach.* 117–118). On eunuchs at the Achaemenid court, see Llewellyn-Jones 2002. A good discussion on how eunuchs were represented in Attic tragedy can be found in Lenfant 2013.
28 See McDermott 1935, 171; Lilja 1980, 31 n. 2. Ugly, cheating, imitative, false and ridiculous are some of the unflattering qualities that Greeks attributed to monkeys (and to persons injuriously assimilated to monkeys). On the profile of monkeys in antiquity, see McDermott 1938, and more recently Connor 2004, Steiner 2016, Vespa 2022. On representation of monkeys in Greek choroplasty, see Mackowiak 2012–2013. Further evidence testifying the connection between the size of a πυγή and the related moral inclinations of its owner can be found in Ar. *Nu.* 1014, in which the Just Argument characterizes "good people" as having "a tiny penis, a big ass" (πυγὴν μεγάλην, πόσθην μικράν). Dover (1968, 222 *ad l.*) effectively points out that in contemporary vase-painting, having a physically large ass seems to be a mark of masculinity/strength. I owe this last point to S. Douglas Olson.
29 Cf. especially Ar. *Eq.* 1373–1374; *Nu.* 355; *Th.* 235, 574–575.
30 Alternatively, Swift (2019, 351) thought that Cleisthenes' lack of beard may make his face look as absurd as a monkey's hairless rear end. This interpretation had already been proposed by Schirru (2009, 88), who reconstructed the Aristophanic staging thus: "Diceopoli si dirigeva deciso verso l'eunuco e, anziché le terga, ne scopriva... la faccia, glabra come le natiche di un πίθηκος". Apart from being skinny, monkeys' buttocks could safely be assumed to be glabrous;

previously noted, the problem of whether Cleisthenes' presence on stage was a fact or merely an assumption by Dicaeopolis is far from resolved.

What can be taken for certain is that *Ach.* 91–122, "one of the most puzzling scenes in Aristophanic comedy",[31] is an excellent case study, an arduous and challenging testing ground for numerous staging questions the dramatic text leaves unanswered for modern readers who, unlike the Athenian theatrical audience in 425 BCE, lack the privilege of watching the *première* of the comedy and enjoying at first hand the spectacular entrance of the Eye of the King and his pair of eunuch attendants.[32]

Bibliography

Aveline, John (2000), "Aristophanes' *Acharnians* 95–97 and 100: Persians in the Athenian Assembly", in: *Hermes* 128, 500–501.

Brixhe, Claude (1988), "La langue de l'étranger non-Grec chez Aristophane", in: Lonis, Raoul (dir.), *L'Etranger dans le monde grec*, Nancy, 113–138

Buis, Emiliano J. (2008), "Diplomáticos y farsantes (Ar. *Ach.* 61–174): estretegias para una desarticulación cómica de la política exterior ateniense", in: *Cuadernos de Filología Clásica. Estudios griegos e indoeuropeos* 18, 249–266.

Bravo, Christopher Delante (2009), *Chirping Like the Swallows: Aristophanes' Portrayals of the Barbarian "Other"*, Diss. University of Arizona.

Chambry, Émile (1925) (ed.), *Aesopi Fabulae*, Pars prior, Paris.

Chiasson, Charles C. (1984), "Pseudartabas and his Eunuchs: *Acharnians* 91–122", in: *Classical Philology* 79, 131–136.

Collard, Christopher/Cropp, Martin, (eds.) (2008), *Euripides. Fragments, Oedipus – Chrysippus Other Fragments*, Cambridge, Mass./London.

Colvin, Stephen (1999), *Dialect in Aristophanes and the Politics of Language in Ancient Greek Literature*, Oxford.

Connor, Catherine (2004), "Monkey Business: Imitation, Authenticity, and Identity from Pithekoussai to Plautus", in: *Classical Antiquity* 23, 179–207.

Coulon, Victor (1923) (ed.), *Aristophane*, Texte établi par V. C. et traduit par Hilaire van Daele, I, Paris.

---

this is why I fail to understand the interpretation recently proposed by Edith Hall (2013, 285): "The physical image of a monkey with a hairy bottom is somehow connected, through mask or costume, with the appearance of Pseudartabas' attendant, who is likely to have worn an imposing beard".

31 Chiasson 1984, 131.

32 They are not mentioned again by Dicaeopolis, except for the contemptuous comment he makes about the Herald's official request (on behalf of the Boulé) for the Eye of the King to go to the Prytaneum, where he will be hosted at state expense (*Ach.* 123–127).

Davico Bonino, Guido (1983), *Carlo Goldoni. La famiglia dell'antiquario*, Torino.
De Cremoux, Anne (2011), *La cité parodique. Études sur les* Acharniens *d'Aristophane*, Amsterdam.
De Fátima Sousa e Silva, Maria (1999), "O estrangeiro na comédia grega antiga", in: *Humanitas* 51, 23–48 (= de Fátima Sousa e Silva, Maria [2007], *Ensaios sobre Aristófanes*, Lisbon, 229–256).
De Luna, Maria Elena (2003), *La comunicazione linguistica fra alloglotti nel mondo greco. Da Omero a Senofonte*, Pisa.
Di Bari, Marta F. (2013), *Scene finali di Aristofane. Cavalieri. Nuvole. Tesmoforiazuse*, Lecce/Brescia.
Dover, Kenneth J. (1963), "Notes on Aristophanes' *Acharnians*", in: *Maia* 15, 6–25 (= Dover, Kenneth J. [1987], *Greek and the Greeks. Collected Papers*, vol. I: *Language, Poetry, Drama*, Oxford/New York, 288–306).
Dover, Kenneth J. (1968) (ed.), *Aristophanes. Clouds*, Oxford.
Ernout, Alfred (1961) (ed.), *Plaute*, T. V: *Mostellaria, Persa, Poenulus*, Paris.
Faller, Stefan (2001), "Persisches im *Persa*", in: Faller, Stefan (ed.), *Studien zu Plautus' Persa*, Tübingen, 177–207.
Friedrich, Johannes (1921), "Die altpersische Stelle in Aristophanes 'Acharnern' (v. 100)", in: *Indogermanische Forschungen* 39, 93–102, 231.
Gil Fernández, Luis (1995) (ed.), *Aristófanes. Comedias, I: Los acarnenses – Los caballeros*, Madrid.
Hall, Edith (1989), *Inventing the Barbarian. Greek Self-Definition through Tragedy*, Oxford.
Hall, Edith (2013), "The Aesopic in Aristophanes", in: Bakola, Emmanuela/Prauscello, Lucia/Telò, Mario (eds.), *Greek Comedy and the Discourse of Genres*, Cambridge, 277–297.
Hausrath, August/Hunger, Herbert, eds. (1970), *Corpus Fabularum Aesopicarum*, Vol. I Fasc. 1, editionem alteram, Leipzig.
Henderson, Jeffrey (1998) (ed.), *Aristophanes, I: Acharnians – Knights*, Cambridge, Mass./London.
Henderson, Jeffrey (2022), *Three More Plays by Aristophanes. Staging Politics*, Oxon/New York.
Hutzfeldt, Birger (1999), *Das Bild der Perser in der griechischen Dichtung des 5. vorchristlichen Jahrhunderts*, Wiesbaden.
Kannicht, Richard (2004) (ed.), *Tragicorum Graecorum Fragmenta*, vol. 5: *Euripides*, Göttingen.
Kidd, Stephen E. (2014), *Nonsense and Meaning in Ancient Greek Comedy*, Cambridge.
Kloss, Gerrit (2001), *Erscheinungsformen komischen Sprechens bei Aristophanes*, Berlin/New York.
Kugelmeier, Christoph (1996), *Reflexe früher und zeitgenössischer Lyrik in der Alten attischen Komödie*, Stuttgart/Leipzig.
Jouan, François/Van Looy, Herman (eds.) (1998), *Euripide. Fragments*, 1re partie: *Aigeus – Autolykos*, Paris.
Jouan, François/Van Looy, Herman (eds.) (2003), *Euripide. Tragédies*, 4e partie: *Fragments de drames non identifiés*, Paris.
Lamagna, Mario (2000), "Lingue straniere nel teatro greco e romano", in: Garzya, Antonio (a cura di), *Idee e forme nel teatro greco*, Naples, 237–256.
Lenfant, Dominique (2013), "Des eunuques dans la tragédie greque. L'orientalisme antique à l'épreuve des textes", in: *Erga-Logoi* 2, 7–30.
Lilja, Saara (1980), "The Ape in Ancient Comedy", in: *Arctos* 14, 31–38.

Llewellyn-Jones, Lloyd (2002), "Eunuchs and the royal harem in Achaemenid Persia (559–331 BC)", in: Tougher, Shaun (ed.), *Eunuchs in Antiquity and Beyond*, Swansea/London/ Oakville.

Long, Timothy (1986), *Barbarians in Greek Comedy*, Carbondale/Edwardsville.

Mackowiak, Karin (2012–2013), "Le singe dans la coroplastie grecque: enquête et questions sur un type de réprésentation figurée", in: *Bulletin de Correspondance Hellénique* 136– 137, 421–482.

Mastromarco, Giuseppe (1983) (ed.), *Aristofane. Commedie*, vol. I, Torino.

Mastromarco, Giuseppe/Totaro, Piero (2006) (eds.), *Commedie di Aristofane*, vol. II, Torino.

McDermott, William Coffman (1935), "The Ape in Greek Literature", in: *Transactions and Proceedings of the American Philological Association* 66, 165–176.

McDermott, William Coffman (1938), *The Ape in Antiquity*, Baltimore.

Miller, Margaret C. (1997), *Athens and Persia in the Fifth Century B.C. A Study in Cultural Receptivity*, Cambridge.

Miller, Margaret (2006-2007), "Persians in the Greek Imagination", in: *Mediterranean Archaeology* 19–20, 109–123.

Morenilla-Talens, Carmen (1989), "Die Charakterisierung der Ausländer durch lautliche Ausdrucksmittel in den *Persern* des Aischylos sowie den *Acharnern* und *Vögeln* des Aristophanes", in: *Indogermanische Forschungen* 94, 158–176.

Mosconi, Gianfranco (2005), "Musica e potere: tracce di una polemica ateniese in due favole del *corpus* esopico", in: *Seminari Romani di cultura greca* 8.2, 273–289.

Mueller, Albert (1863) (ed.), *Aristophanis Acharnenses*, Hannover.

Müller-Strübing, Hermann (1873), *Aristophanes und die historische Kritik. Polemische Studien zur Geschichte von Athen im fünften Jahrhundert vor Ch.g.*, Leipzig.

Nauck, August (1856) (ed.), *Tragicorum Graecorum Fragmenta*, Lipsiae.

Nauck, August (1889) (ed.), *Tragicorum Graecorum Fragmenta*, Editio secunda, Lipsiae.

Negri, Mario/Ornaghi, Massimiliano (2008), "Pseudartabas e gli Ioni. Appunti per l'esegesi linguistica e drammat(urg)ica di Ar. *Ach.* 100 (-106)", in: *Ἀλεξάνδρεια, Alessandria. Rivista di glottologia* 2, 81–126.

Nøjgaard, Morten (1964), *La fable antique*, Tome Premier: *La fable grecque avant Phèdre*, Copenhagen.

Olson, S. Douglas (2002) (ed.), *Aristophanes. Acharnians*, Oxford.

Olson, S. Douglas (2021), "Dressing like the Great King: Amerindian Perspectives on Persian Fashion in Classical Athens", in: *Polis* 38.1, 9–20.

Orfanos, Charalampos (2006), *Les sauvageons d'Athènes ou la didactique du rire chez Aristophane*, Paris.

Paley, Frederick A. (1876) (ed.), *The Acharnians of Aristophanes*, Cambridge.

Pretagostini, Roberto (1998), "Aristofane 'etnologo': il mondo persiano nella falsa ambasceria del prologo degli *Acarnesi*", in: *Seminari Romani di cultura greca* 1, 41–56.

Rennie, William (1909) (ed.), *The Acharnians of Aristophanes*, London.

Ribbeck, Woldemar (1864), *Die Acharner des Aristophanes*, griechisch und deutsch mit kritischen und erklärenden Anmerkungen und einem Anhang über die dramatischen Parodien bei den attischen Komikern, Leipzig.

Rutherford, William G. (1896) (ed.), *Scholia Aristophanica*, vol. II, London.

Schirru, Silvio (2009), *La Favola in Aristofane*, Berlin.

Sommerstein, Alan H. (1980) (ed.), *The Comedies of Aristophanes*, I: *Acharnians*, Warminster.

Sommerstein, Alan H., *Updates to A.H. Sommerstein's Aris & Phillips Editions of Aristophanes* (*Additional to those printed in Aristophanes:* Wealth [Warminster, 2001, pp. 219–321]): unpublished.

Starkie, William Joseph Myles (1909) (ed.), *The Acharnians of Aristophanes*, London.

Steiner, Deborah (2016), "Making Monkeys: Archilochus frr. 185–187 W. in Performance", in: Cazzato, Vanessa/Lardinois, André (eds.), *The Look of Lyric: Greek Song and Visual. Studies in Archaic and Classical Greek Song*, vol. 1, Leiden/Boston, 108–145.

Stone, Laura M. (1981), *Costume in Aristophanic Comedy*, New York.

Swift, Laura (2019) (ed.), *Archilochus: The Poems*, Oxford.

Taillardat, Jean (1965), *Les images d'Aristophane. Études de langue et de style*, deuxième tirage revu et corrigé, Paris.

Tosi, Renzo (2022) (ed.), *Esopo. Favole*, Santarcangelo di Romagna.

Totaro, Piero (2000), *Le seconde parabasi di Aristofane*, 2nd ed., Stuttgart/Weimar.

Totaro, Piero (2017), "Maschera e alterità su un vaso magnogreco: il 'New York Goose Play'", in: Sisto, Pietro/Totaro, Piero (eds.), *Maschera e alterità*, Bari, 31–40.

Totaro, Piero (2019), "Maschere e lingue 'barbare' nell'iconografia e nei testi della commedia attica antica", in: *Seminari Romani di cultura greca*, n.s. 8, 309–329.

Treu, Martina (2011), "Diceopoli e il 'Falso-Giusto'. Gli *Acarnesi* di Aristofane tra verità e finzione, in *Dionysus ex Machina* 2, 357–371.

Van Dijk, Gert-Jan (1997), *ΑΙΝΟΙ, ΛΟΓΟΙ, ΜΥΘΟΙ. Fables in Archaic, Classical, and Hellenistic Greek Literature*, With a Study of the Theory and Terminology of the Genre, Leiden/New York/Cologne.

Van Leeuwen, Jan, ed. (1901), *Aristophanis Acharnenses*, Leiden.

Vespa, Marco (2022), *Geloion mimēma. Studi sulla rappresentazione culturale della scimmia nei testi greci e greco-romani*, Turnhout.

West, Martin L. (1968), "Two Passages of Aristophanes", in: *Classical Review* 18, 5–8.

West, Martin L. (1989) (ed.), *Iambi et elegi Graeci ante Alexandrum cantati*, vol. I: *Archilochus Hipponax Theognidea*, Editio altera aucta atque emendata, Oxford.

Willi, Andreas (2003), *The Languages of Aristophanes. Aspects of Linguistic Variation in Classical Attic Greek*, Oxford.

Willi, Andreas (2004), "Old Persian in Athens Revisited (Ar. *Ach.* 100)", in: *Mnemosyne* 57, 657–681.

Wilson, Nigel G. (1975) (ed.), *Scholia in Aristophanem*, Pars I, Fasc. Ib: *Scholia in Aristophanis Acharnenses*, Groningen.

Wilson, Nigel G. (2007) (ed.), *Aristophanis fabulae*, I–II, Oxford.

Bernhard Zimmermann
Poetics of Props: On Aristophanes, *Acharnians* 393–489

Abstract: Props, like other elements of Greek drama dealing with staging, have so far attracted little attention in research. This changed fundamentally with Oliver Taplin's *The stagecraft of Aeschylus* (Oxford 1977). The analysis of Aristophanes, *Acharnians* 393–498 — a metapoetics of the props — shows the importance of props in the staging of a drama in the 5th century BC.

Keywords: props, Aristophanes, Euripides, metapoetics

Today it is taken for granted in the scholarly world that Greek drama of the 5th century BCE was a multi-media event. Language, song, music and dance, as well as the venue and the physical space of the Theatre, all played key and complementary roles. This understanding comes after a hundred-year period in which ὄψις and μελοποιία, the staging and setting of a tragedy, were often ignored or left on the sidelines, not only because of the scanty materials available to us but also, perhaps largely, because of Aristotle's judgement that the optical and acoustic aspects of a drama do not belong to the art of the poet (*Poetics* 1450b.15–20). In response to Oliver Taplin's groundbreaking study *The Stagecraft of Aeschylus: The Dramatic Use of Exits and Entrances in Greek Tragedy* (Oxford 1977), however, many studies have emerged since the 1980s on the performative aspects of tragedy. Taplin had as a forerunner K. Reinhardt, who wrote a small book *Aischylos als Regisseur und Theologe* (Bern 1949), elucidating how the poet, serving as his own director, can add meaningful dimensions to his play.[1] Reinhardt primarily demonstrated the function of the semantic significance of props in the actions and sense structure of a play. A particularly impressive example is Aeschylus' *Agamemnon*. The purple or red carpet, which the servant girls (908) roll out for Agamemnon at the behest of Clytemnestra as he returns home, is endowed with numerous meanings.[2] Purple is the color of kings and victors. The purple-dyed, embroidered (923, 936 ποικίλος) blankets

I wish to thank Rachel Bruzzone (Bilkent University, Ankara) for kindly agreeing to produce the English translation of this paper.

1 Cf. also Taplin 1985.
2 Cf. Taplin 1977, 78–81.

https://doi.org/10.1515/9783111248028-009

and carpets are considerable indicators of wealth (962); spreading them before the ruler likewise indicates a type of tyranny on a Persian scale (919f.).[3] Additionally, purple is the color of blood (827f.). Agamemnon, giving in to Clytemnestra's seductive words, steps on the purple spread before him (910),[4] although he had sworn shortly beforehand that he did not want to call down the anger of the gods upon himself in the triumph of victory (921f., 947). Thus, the victor of Troy is defeated in the fight against his wife (917, 940) and his own arrogance, only superficially suppressed. By walking into the palace on the blood-red carpet, stained with the atrocities of the "human slaughter" of Atreus (1092), he thus walks into his own death. Agamemnon's only apparently triumphant return home stands in strong contrast to Odysseus' sly return, which the viewer is nudged to consider through Agamemnon's words (841–844): the wife of Odysseus prepares no such colorful web for his return home, but rather works on a shroud in order to hold off the troublesome suitors, in the hope of her husband's return, while Clytemnestra catches her husband in a fishing net (1116, 1126, 1382f.) and thus kills him.[5] The wealth the purple suggests becomes the "terrible wealth of the death trap" (1383),[6] which in the mirroring scene in *Choephori* (980ff.) Orestes shows as proof of the correctness of his murderous actions and spreads over the bodies of Clytemnestra and Aegisthus in order to take vengeance for his dead father.[7] This example from the Aeschylean *Agamemnon* shows that props, as part of the synthetic fabric of the work of art, are deeply meaningful, in that they often have a close relationship to the metaphors and, through speech and music, call to mind the evocative world of images in a tragedy.

It is the case, however, that — except for instances in which the use of props is clearly indicated by "internal didaskalia" — it is difficult to make any statements about their use and implementation, or indeed their dramatic function in tragedy. As is so often the case, 5th-century comedy — which always encourages comparison with its sister-genre — can offer a view into the meaning not only of

---

3 Cf. Fraenkel 1950, II 416f. *ad l.*

4 πατεῖν, "to step on" (957, 963), can also mean "to trample": when Agamemnon walks on the carpet, he also tramples his own power and life. This motif appears constantly in the trilogy (*Ag.* 369ff., 381ff.; *Ch.* 369ff.; *Eum.* 538ff.).

5 "Netting" in the tragedy serves as a symbol of female guile in any case — although in contrast to Penelope's deviously constructed shroud. Here it brings death (Eur. *Med.* 1159; see also Nessus' poisoned garments in Sophocles' *Trachiniae*).

6 On the motif of wealth, see *Ag.* 374ff., 776ff., 1088ff. Another web, the clothes made by Electra for her brother, become an identifying token for Orestes in the second part of the trilogy (*Ch.* 251).

7 Cf. Reinhardt 1949, 137f.; Newiger 1996, 176.

the props in a staging but also on a semantic level, as a meaningful element that supports, clarifies or resists the text.

A key example which can illuminate the function of tragic props (σκευάρια) takes place in the parody of Euripides in Aristophanes' *Acharnians* (393–489). The comic hero Dicaeopolis forces the charcoal-burners of Acharnae to listen to him by taking hostage a charcoal-basket, their most beloved object. He intends to deliver his speech "about and for the Spartans" (356, cf. 316, 369, 482)[8] with his head on a chopping block. In order to appear as pitiful as possible (384 οἶον ἀθλιώτατον), he would like to be outfitted by the tragedian Euripides (384, 436 ἐνσκευάσασθαι, cf. Phryn. Com. fr. 39.1 K.-A.). The tragic complexion of the scene — in which the parody of Telephus is unmistakeable[9] — is reinforced by the chorus' use of dochmiacs (358–365 = 385–392), as well as by the use of a tragic theatre machine, the *ekkyklema* (407f.). There follows, in modern terms, an act of reception of the Euripidean "rag-heroes," i.e. the comic handling also functions on a second level, and by breaking the illusion, facilitates discussion of what function costume and props can have. The dirty rags and scraps (412, 418, 423, 426, 423) the Euripidean heroes wear, and the other fitting props such as the Mysian felt hat (438f.), immediately show that the production concerns a beggar (439f.), as do the basket with a hole burnt through it (453), an oil pot (462), a cup with a broken handle (459), a beggar's staff (448) and a beggar's basket (469). Even more important than these visual signals is the pity that the costume and the various dingy objects ought to arouse in the audience (413–416). Dikaiopolis distinguishes — theoretically on the highest level — between two types of spectators: on the one hand the comic chorus, before whom he must, in his guise of a pitiable beggar, deliver a long *rhesis* (416), and on the other hand the public audience in the Theatre, which knows very well that he is not a beggar (442–444). He thus distinguishes between a conversation that is internal to the drama, a part of the play, and one that is external. The double identity the comic hero takes on points to a typical comic game of confused identities (A playing B), which appears in many titles, for example, Cratinus' *Dionysalexandros*,[10] Aristophanes' *Aiolosikon* and Timocles' *Orestautokleides*.[11]

---

8 Cf. Olson 2002, 169.

9 On this point, see Preiser 2000, 71–97; Olson 2002, liv–lxi.

10 Cf. Luppe 2006, 61f.; Bianchi 2016, 198–301.

11 Cf. Sommerstein 1996, 201. On Timocles, cf. *PCG* VII 774. Cf. also Ar. *Ra.* 499 *Herakleioxan-thias*: Dionysus in the costume of Heracles requires his slave Xanthias to pretend to be Heracles. Presumably Menekrates' *Manektor* (the slave Manes as Hector) belongs to this category of play, along with Eubulus' *Sphingokarion*, and Lucian's *Ikaromenippos* belongs to the same tradition. Strattis' *Anthroporestes* and Pherecrates' *Anthropherakles* also appear to involve role-

Euripides reacts with irritation and anger (456) to the plundering of his prop chest with the desperate cries "This guy is trying to steal my tragic poetry!" (464)[12] and "You are ruining me! Go ahead, take it! My plays are finished!" (470). The mocking criticism is unmistakable: the power of Euripidean tragedy is based on the staging, namely the costuming and props, rather than on the conception of the pieces, as the master himself admits. In this Aristophanes meets Aristotle, given that the latter emphasizes in his *Poetics* that the influence and power (δύναμις) of a tragedy, and most importantly its *telos,* namely arousing fear and pity, must be independent of the elements of directing and actors (1450[b]18f.).

That the props in comedies perhaps deserve more attention than we can know on the basis of fragments is clear in a piece by Plato Comicus with the title *Skeuai,* or *Props* (frr. 136–142 K.–A.).[13] The fragments suggest literary-critical contents. Somewhere in the course of the action, the tragedians Sthenelos, Morsimos and Melanthios were mocked (frr. 136; 140). Fr. 142 probably pertains to the Euripidean *Electra.* Perhaps a perceived injury to the decorum of tragic art was denounced: the tendency of Euripidean tragedy to make heroic content have a middle- or even lower-class appearance. Fr. 138 revives the old artistry of dance, which may have been a sight for sore eyes in comparison with the new, static art. It is possible that the title hints at the comic chorus; one could even imagine that the chorus members embodied individual "props" in the form of an individualized chorus.[14]

Bibliography

Bakola, Emmanuela (2010), *Cratinus and the Art of Comedy*, Oxford.

Bianchi, Francesco Paolo (2016), *Cratino, Archilochoi – Empipramenoi (frr. 1–68). Introduzione, traduzione, commento*, Heidelberg.

Fraenkel, Eduard (1950) (ed.), *Aeschylus. Agamemnon*, I–III, Oxford.

---

switching, probably with Orestes and Heracles taking up the identity of an average Athenian and therefore encountering situations not in keeping with their heroic natures. Pacuvius' *Dulorestes* ("Orestes as slave") employs the same comic trope.

12 Cf. Olson 2002, 194.

13 Cf. Pirrotta 2009, 272–283.

14 A comparable "metatheatrical" comedy could be Ekphantides' *Rehearsals* (Πεῖραι), along with Cratinus' *Didaskaliai* (on this, cf. Bakola 2010, 48f.), and Aristophanes' *Proagon* — pieces that offer insight from a comic perspective into the Theatre and its practices. Plato's *Staff Bearers* (Ῥαβδοῦχοι) might be another example; cf. Pirrotta 2009, 270f.

Luppe, Wolfgang (2006), "Kratinos 1984–2004", in: *Lustrum* 48, 45–72.

Newiger, Hans-Joachim (1996), *Drama und Theater. Ausgewählte Schriften zum griechischen Drama*, Stuttgart.

Olson, S. Douglas (2002) (ed.), *Aristophanes. Acharnians*, Oxford.

Pirrotta, Serena (2009) (ed.), *Plato Comicus: Die fragmentarischen Komödien*, Berlin.

Preiser, Claudia (2000) (ed.), *Euripides. Telephos. Introduction, Text, Commentary*, Zurich/New York.

Reinhardt, Karl (1949), *Aischylos als Regisseur und Theologe*, Bern.

Sommerstein, Alan H. (1996) (ed.), *The Comedies of Aristophanes*, Vol. 9: *Frogs*, Warminster.

Taplin, Oliver (1977), *The Stagecraft of Aeschylus: The Dramatic Use of Exits and Entrances in Greek Tragedy*, Oxford.

Taplin, Oliver (1985²), *Greek Tragedy in Action*, Cambridge.

Christian Orth
Comic Fragments and Lost Dramatic Scenes: Some Considerations

Abstract: The comic fragments are incomplete on both a textual and a performative level. Discussing examples from four fragmentary plays of Aristophanes (*Aeolosicon*, *Amphiaraus*, *Anagyrus* and *Babylonians*), I argue that for understanding comic fragments it is always essential to try to recover as much of the original performative context as possible. This approach may offer a corrective to more speculative attempts to reconstruct lost plays by combining several pieces of evidence.

Keywords: Aristophanes, fragments, performance, recontextualization, reconstruction

In recent years, there has been an increasingly strong conviction among scholars of Greek comedy that a true understanding of the genre is only possible if one takes into account that the pieces were written for performance on stage and found their actual completion in performance. In the end, this means that even the completely or almost completely preserved comedies of Aristophanes and Menander are incomplete and fragmentary, if they are considered as the remains of a lost theatrical performance. Essential aspects such as music, dance, the actors' movements and their voices and gestures, as well as the visual design of the stage and the props used, can only be inferred roughly and imperfectly from the texts themselves. If even the complete plays are fragmentary, the fragmentary ones, i.e. the comedies preserved only in a few quotations from an indirect tradition, are twice fragmentary, and on both a textual and a performative level: we do not know the words that were spoken before or after our fragment, and we do not know what the audience could see while they were spoken. Each kind of incompleteness makes study of the other more complicated. A detailed knowledge of what happens on stage would immediately enable us to exclude some otherwise possible reconstructions of an incomplete text, and the most important information for the performative context of a single verse is often not found in that verse itself but somewhere in the preceding or following (and therefore in the case of fragments usually lost) context.

If one tries to look beyond the text of a fragment to (re)contextualize it, the two types of context mentioned here require different kinds of evidence in the preserved text itself. For the "textual" context, particularly interesting are

https://doi.org/10.1515/9783111248028-010

incomplete syntax, which may allow one to speculate on what the complete sentence looked like, and single elements like connecting particles and anaphoric or cataphoric pronouns. For the "performative" context, on the other hand, one must look for verbs in the first or second person, imperatives, direct address and deictic elements that make direct reference to something present and/or visible on stage. Thus in a verse like Ar. fr. 7 δοῖδυξ, θύεια, τυρόκνηστις, ἐσχάρα ("pestle, mortar, cheese-grater, brazier"),[1] on the textual level the incomplete syntax allows at least some speculation as to why all the objects are in the nominative case, but the complete lack of any element that can elucidate the performative context makes it impossible to say anything about what was going on on stage in that moment (and without further evidence, there is no reason to suppose that the objects mentioned were present on stage as props). So too a participial phrase such Ar. fr. 48 ἐν τῷ στόματι τριημιωβέλιον ἔχων ("holding a three-half-obol my/your/his mouth") may at least tell us that the superordinate verb had a male subject (cf. ἔχων), but without the superordinate verb, it remains unclear whether the speaker is talking about himself,[2] the interlocutor, or another male person present or not present, and whether he or she is referring to something that has happened before, is happening at the moment, will happen at some time in the future, or might or might not happen.

But although, as a rule, much less can be said about the performative context of a fragment than about that of a single verse from a complete text, our inability to answer a question in an approximately complete manner does not mean that we should not ask it at all. That the comic fragments had a scenic context is no less certain than that they had a textual context, and ignoring these contexts would easily lead to problematic interpretations of the preserved words themselves. I would like to discuss here in more detail some of the most frequent types of references to performative context in the comic fragments. Examples can be found everywhere in the fragments, but for convenience I limit myself here to the first 100 of Aristophanes in the *Poetae Comici Graeci* by Rudolf Kassel and Colin Austin, on which I have worked in detail for vol. 10.3 of the *Fragmenta Comica* series. My paper is therefore a kind of methodological reflection accompanying my commentary on these fragments, to which the reader is referred for further details.

Comic fragments often contain references to the interaction of different characters on stage, and in particular to a dialogue that is going on between two

---

1 This and the following translations are taken from Henderson 2007 (some of them modified).
2 Henderson translates ἐν τῷ στόματι by "in my mouth", which is plausible, but only one of several possibilities.

or more persons. This is the case not only in fragments where we still can discern a change of speaker,[3] but also in fragments with no change of speaker but that contain clear hints that one character is speaking to another. We can distinguish two speakers, for instance, in Ar. fr. 17 (from *Amphiaraus*), which contains a question from a first speaker, an answer from a second, and a reaction to this answer, probably again by the first speaker: (A.) γύναι, τί τὸ ψοφῆσάν ἐσθ'; (B.) ἡ ἀλεκτρυὼν / τὴν κύλικα καταβέβληκεν. (A.) οἰμώζουσά γε ("(A.) Woman, what was it made that noise? (B.) The hen / knocked over the wine-cup. (A.) She'll be sorry for that!"). We also learn that a noise was heard earlier, to which speaker A reacts, that speaker B is a woman, and that (at least in the dramatic fiction, but not necessarily in the actual stage situation) there is a hen nearby, which could be responsible for the noise (note the article in ἡ ἀλεκτρυών). This last piece of information also provides clues as to the whereabouts of the speakers: the simplest explanation would be that the hen was kept in a part of a house belonging to one (or both) speakers, while another, somewhat more complicated explanation that incorporates the title of the play (and is therefore usually preferred by scholars) would be that it was brought as an offering to the sanctuary of Amphiaraus. Speaker A's question and in particular the exclamation at the end seem to indicate concern or even nervousness. On the other hand, only with great caution can we draw conclusions from the answer of speaker B, since we cannot know whether she is telling the truth or trying to hide the real origin of the noise.

In fr. 2 from *Aeolosicon*, ἀλλ' ἄνυσον, οὐ μέλλειν ἐχρῆν, ὡς ἀγοράσω / ἀπαξάπανθ' ὅσ' ἂν κελεύῃς, ὦ γύναι ("But hurry up: no more delay, so I can shop / for everything you'll want, woman!"), even if there is no change of speaker, we can recover several elements of the performative context: On stage are at least two characters, the speaker (male of female) and a female character he addresses. The speaker is in a hurry and asks the woman to tell him what he (or she) should buy and promises to buy it all. If one is familiar with the scenic conventions of Athenian theatre, one can also conclude that, if the speaker keeps his promise, he (or she) will leave the stage from the one of the two side-entrances that represents the way to the city, and so also to the market. A study of the use of ὦ γύναι in Greek comedy based on the occurrences of this appellation could provide us with further information (or at least statistical probabilities) about

---

3 It goes without saying that the changes of speaker can only be inferred from the text with varying degrees of probability, and that — as even in complete texts — in the fragments there are often cases where the position or existence of a change of speaker is disputed.

the speaker and his relations with the woman he addresses here (it is well possible, but not certain, that the speaker here addresses his own wife).

Indications about the spatial setting of the scene and the props can be obtained from fr. 18 from *Amphiaraus*, καὶ νὴ Δί᾽ ἐκ τοῦ δωματίου γε νῷν φέρε / κνέφαλλον ἅμα καὶ προσκεφάλαιον τῶν λινῶν ("by Zeus, fetch us out of the bedroom / a cushion and a pillow, the linen ones"). The person speaking asks another character to bring a mattress and a pillow from a δωμάτιον. In particular, the mention of a δωμάτιον (probably a bedroom) suggests that the action takes place in front of the speaker's house, although it has repeatedly been suggested that the setting is instead the sanctuary of Amphiaraus. Another important clue is provided by the dual νῷν, which shows that objects are requested for two people (perhaps a couple); whether one of them is the person who is being asked to bring them, or whether the speaker is addressing a third person, perhaps a slave, remains uncertain.

In fragments with a verb in the first person, the speaker sometimes describes quite precisely what he is doing in the moment of the fragment, or what he has done immediately before it. This is the case in fr. 1 from *Aeolosicon*, ἥκω Θεαρίωνος ἀρτοπώλιον / λιπών, ἵν᾽ ἐστὶ κριβάνων ἐδώλια ("Back from Thearion's bakery I come / where lie the abodes of ovens"), a parody of the beginning of Euripides' *Hecuba* (1–3 ἥκω νεκρῶν κευθμῶνα καὶ σκότου πύλας / λιπών, ἵν᾽ Ἅιδης χωρὶς ᾤκισται θεῶν, / Πολύδωρος).[4] In the tragic model, the ghost of Polydorus perhaps spoke these words, as Donald Mastronarde suggested, from the *theologeion* on the roof of the stage building.[5] But even if this is the case in Euripides' play, it does not necessarily follow that Aristophanes' speaker did the same, just as it is uncertain whether Aristophanes' play too began with these lines. What can be said with some confidence is that the speaker has just appeared on stage (ἥκω), and since he comes from a place in Athens that was probably well-known to the audience, the simplest assumption is that he has just entered from a side-entrance (the one that leads to the city). He may be a slave or a cook who has just purchased some bread from Thearion, and it is possible (but far from certain) that the speaker is the title-hero of the play himself, who combines the identities of Sikon (perhaps a slave, but more likely a

---

4 It is curious that the words of Euripides' first verse that are omitted here appear in another Aristophanic play, *Gerytades* (fr. 156.1–2 καὶ τίς νεκρῶν κευθμῶνα καὶ σκότου πύλας / ἔτλη κατελθεῖν;).

5 Mastronarde 1990, 276–277 (who shows that the words contain indications of an elevated position and argues against the view that Polydorus' ghost spoke from the normal level of the stage), and cf. Battezzato 2018, 71 (who notes that a use of the μηχανή would be without parallel at the beginning of a play).

cook) and the mythical (and Euripidean) Aeolus.[6] We also can only speculate on whether the paratragic language was also underlined by a paratragic manner of acting or speaking.

Another example, where in addition to a first-person verb there is a deictic pronoun referring to an object brought by the speaker, is fr. 25 from *Amphiaraus*, ταυτὶ τὰ κρέ᾽ αὐτῷ παρὰ γυναικός του φέρω ("I'm bringing him this meat from someone's wife").[7] Here the person speaking obviously comes to the house of a male character (or to another place where he is expecting to find him) to bring him pieces of meat that are being offered to him (as he says) by a woman. He does not, however, address the man himself but another person (who might be, for instance, a slave who opens the door). It seems reasonable to assume that the person to whom the meat is offered is the hero of the play, probably near the end of the play when he has succeeded in his great plan (whatever that was). But it remains unclear whether (to name just two possibilities) the woman who sends the meat sees him as a potential lover or is grateful for some benefit he has done her husband.

In cases such as these, the elements that help us most in recovering something of the performative context were probably the least interesting, because most obvious, to the original audience, and are only justified by other less obvious elements contained in the same verses, such as the origin of the meat the speaker of fr. 25 is carrying or the place from where the speaker of fr. 1 enters the scene. But while the identification of such elements of the stage action is among the most important tasks in the interpretation of comic fragments, we are often confronted with another, even more elementary question, namely whether or not a fragment refers at all to what is happening on stage. We can have doubts about this not only in fragments in a metre other than iambic trimeter, which might, for instance, be part of an extradramatic section such as the parabasis, but also in fragments that might be part of a narrative. Particularly difficult problems are created by the possibility of quotations in *oratio recta* in a narrative. For instance, whenever I read fr. 42 from *Anagyrus*, μὴ κλᾶ᾽· ἐγώ σοι βουκέφαλον ὠνήσομαι ("Don't cry! I'll buy you an ox-head horse"), I cannot help thinking that this may be the words of a father quoted in a narration rather than words actually spoken at this moment to a child present on stage. The line might then come from a monologue similar that of Strepsiades at the beginning of *Clouds* and refer to the past behaviour of the speaker himself towards his son when the latter was a little boy, or it may be cited as an (exaggerated) example

---

6 Cf. (with further bibliography) Orth 2017, 15, 17–18, 40–41.

7 So Henderson. But παρὰ γυναικός του may simply mean "from some woman".

of behaviour a father should avoid, if he does not want to be ruined by the expensive wishes of his son.[8]

Both the importance and the difficulty of distinguishing between fragments with and without direct reference to what is happening on stage can be well illustrated by a few fragments from *Babylonians*, all of which have to do with ships, and probably in particular with the fleet of the Athenians or that of their allies.[9] These are frr. 80, 82, 85, 86, and 87, and it has been suggested that the mention of the Athenian general Phormio in fr. 88 and the adjective ἁλυκός ("briny") refer to the same nautical theme. One could conclude from these fragments that this was a generally important motive in *Babylonians*, which would be unsurprising in a play that dealt with the relationship between Athens and its allies from the islands. One might also be tempted, however, to assign all these fragments to the same part of the play, in which the arrival of a ship was represented.

A closer look at the individual fragments reveals that matters are not so simple. Even leaving aside the one-word fragments (of which, fr. 93 might simply refer to salty food), a first glance at the metres used in these fragments already shows that they can hardly be attributed to the same scene: fr. 80 ναυλόχιον ἐν τῷ μέσῳ ("anchorage in the middle") is probably part, perhaps the end, of a iambic trimeter, fr. 82 εὖ γ' ἐξεκολύμβησ' οὑπιβάτης ὡς ἐξοίσων ἐπίγυον ("the marine made a good dive to bring the stern-cable ashore") an anapaestic tetrameter, fr. 85 κατάγου ῥοθιάζων ("dash the ship onwards") the end of an anapaestic tetrameter (less likely part of an iambic trimeter), fr. 86 ναῦς ὅταν ἐκ πιτύλων ῥοθιάζῃ σώφρονι κόσμῳ ("when a ship by sweep of oars dashes in sound order") a hexameter or (perhaps more likely) the end of an anapaestic tetrameter,[10] while fr. 87 ἐς τὸν λιμένα ("shoreward") could belong to either an iambic or an anapaestic context. We seem to be dealing here with at least two different scenes, one in iambic trimeter and one in anapaestic tetrameter. But everything becomes even more complicated when we consider the content of the fragments: fr. 87 is a variation of a proverb, and the harbour it mentions could also be understood metaphorically. Fr. 80 is too short to decide where the

---

8 On this and other interesting parallels between fragments of *Anagyrus* (ca. 417 BCE) and the roughly contemporary second version of *Clouds*, see Orth 2017, 229–230.

9 On these fragments, cf. in particular Starkey 2013.

10 For the opposite view, see now Marcucci 2020, 22–23. There seems to be no example in hexameter of ὅτ' ἄν postponed after the subject of the subordinate clause, or of ὅτ' ἄν preceded by a noun of one syllable in enjambment. If the fragment is interpreted as part of an anapaestic tetrameter, with a supplement like ⟨ἀλλ' ὥσπερ⟩ at the beginning (see below), the word order would be more straightforward.

anchorage it mentions is located. Fr. 82 seems to be an exclamation of a character who is at that moment observing the arrival of a ship (cf. the emotional εὖ
γ'), while fr. 85 is an exhortation to row ashore. In fr. 86, however, reference is
made to the movement of the rowers of a ship only in general terms, in a subordinate clause beginning with ὅταν. One could easily complete an anapestic
tetrameter with ἀλλ' ὥσπερ added at the beginning: ⟨ἀλλ' ὥσπερ⟩ ναῦς ὅταν ἐκ
πιτύλων ῥοθιάζῃ σώφρονι κόσμῳ, "but like a ship when it dashes by sweep of
oars in sound order" (cf. Menecrates fr. 1 ἀλλ' ὥσπερ παῖς ὅταν ἀστραγάλους
ἐκκόψας ἀνταποπαίζῃ, "but like a child when it has won with knucklebones and
then loses again"), which would mean that the rowing ship is only mentioned
here in a comparison, which might refer, for instance, to a polis that functions
well, i.e. is not ruled by demagogues like Cleon.

This leaves only two fragments that seem to refer directly to what is happening on stage, frr. 82 and 85, which in metrical terms could belong to the same
anapaestic tetrameter scene. But while in both fragments a ship seems to be
arriving, the perspective of the speaker is different: whereas in fr. 82 he addresses an oarsman (or perhaps a chorus of oarsmen)[11] directly, in fr. 85 his role
seems to be that of an observer enthusiastically commenting on what is going
on. The question of whether the two fragments belong to an arrival of a ship
somehow represented on stage is further complicated by more general considerations on the content of *Babylonians*. One possibility is that near the beginning of the play the chorus of Babylonians arrived with a ship, and that both
fragments therefore belong to the parodos. But this would mean that the Babylonians cannot have been represented from the beginning as slaves of the Athenians in a mill (a plausible scenario for a picturesque prologue scene),[12] and
nothing in these fragments indicates that the persons who are on the ship are
Babylonians. One could think instead of rowers in the Athenian fleet, and both
fragments could belong to a race between ships which is somehow commented
on by an obviously not impartial observer. But where would such a scene fit in
the *Babylonians*, and how could it have been staged? There is no easy answer to
that question, but one possibility that perhaps should not be excluded is that we
have here part of an epirrhematic agon which is — at least on a metaphorical
level — represented as a race between two ships. But this would also mean that

---

11 Cf. Starkey 2013, 507 with n. 26, and on addresses to the Chorus in the singular in general
Kaimio 1970, 127–131.
12 Cf. Orth 2017, 353–355. If the Babylonians were from the beginning represented as slaves in
a mill, and Dionysus as the comic hero of the play tries to liberate them, the constellation
would be very similar to that in many satyr plays.

we cannot really trust the indications here that seem to suggest a direct reference to something visible on stage, and further reflection would be necessary on how to decide between literal and metaphorical language in the passage.

While the fragments discussed so far contain indications of the stage action they presuppose, only rarely in the comic fragments is there a more direct allusion to technical elements of a theatrical performance. Interesting examples in this respect are the direct allusions to the μηχανή, the crane used for both divine and human flying characters, in Aristophanes fr. 160 and in two fragments of Strattis (frr. 4 and 46). Another, albeit less obvious and more uncertain, example is found in fr. 76 of *Babylonians*, μέσην ἔρειδε πρὸς τὸ σιμόν ("Push on by the middle way toward the snub!"), where the speaker urges another character to ascend to a higher place, and where we may wonder what this place corresponded to on the stage of a theatre in Aristophanes' time. A possible (and simple) explanation would be that it is here the difference between the orchestra and the modestly elevated stage,[13] and in this case we might ask whether (despite the singular) the exhortation is addressed to the chorus. (Metrically, the fragment can be interpreted both as the beginning of an iambic trimeter and the end of an iambic tetrameter; the latter would fit a choral scene well.) Such an interpretation has been proposed by Peter Arnott, who discusses the fragment together with two other passages with the word τὸ σιμόν, Ar. *Lys.* 286–288 ἀλλ' αὐτὸ γάρ μοι τῆς ὁδοῦ / λοιπόν ἐστι χωρίον / τὸ πρὸς πόλιν τὸ σιμὸν οἷ σπουδὴν ἔχω ("But before I reach the citadel where I am hurrying, I have the rest of the road, the hill, to cover", transl. P. Arnott) and Plat. com. fr. 84 τουτὶ προσαναβῆναι τὸ σιμὸν δεῖ ("there's still this slope to climb", transl. P. Arnott). Together with some other comic passages like Ar. *Ach.* 732 (ἄμβατε) and *V.* 1341 (ἀνάβαινε δεῦρο), 1514 (ἀτὰρ καταβατέον γ' ἐπ' αὐτούς μοι), these fragments offer some of the best textual evidence for an elevated stage in the 5th century.[14]

The attempt to recover elements of performative context from individual fragments becomes particularly interesting and important when it conflicts with another (very common) way of interpreting fragments, explaining a fragment with the help of the title of the play and/or other fragments from the same play. Thus, in the already discussed fr. 18 of *Amphiaraus*, the text of the fragment itself points to a setting (at least for this scene) in front of the speaker's house rather than in front of Amphiaraus' sanctuary, as has been repeatedly supposed

---

13 On the controversial discussion of the existence of an elevated stage in Aristophanes' time, see e.g. Arnott 1962, 1–41; Olson 2002, 260 *ad* Ar. *Ach.* 732; Csapo 2010, 25–26; Biles/Olson 2015, 509 *ad* Ar. *V.* 1514–1515; and, for a more sceptical view, Maduit/Moretti 2019.
14 For pictorial evidence, see Csapo 2010, 25–26.

from the play's title. In such cases, it generally seems reasonable to follow the clues in the fragments themselves rather than a hypothetical connection to the title, and it is often precisely these elements that can be used to evaluate more tentative hypotheses that are sometimes made without careful examination of such details.

A similar tension between the clues provided by the fragment itself and attempts to explain it from other available information about the play can be observed in fr. 68 from *Babylonians*, (A.) δεῖ διακοσίων δραχμῶν. / (B.) πόθεν οὖν γένοιντ' ἄν; (A.) τὸν κότυλον τοῦτον φέρε ("(A.) Two hundred drachmas are needed. / (B.) So where will they come from? / (A.) Give this cup!"). Since we know from fr. 75 that Dionysus at one point in the play recounted how, when he himself was on trial, the Athenian demagogues attempted to blackmail him and demanded two *oxybapha*, i.e. small drinking vessels, the dialogue in fr. 68 is often interpreted as just such blackmail attempted by a demagogue, who would then be the first speaker.[15] Although it is certainly suggestive that in both fragments vessels used for wine are mentioned, this interpretation of fr. 68 is problematic on more than one level. First, fr. 75 seems to testify that Dionysus in *Babylonians* only reported about an attempt at blackmail, not that this attempt was carried out on stage in the play, and it might even be argued from ἐπὶ τὴν δίκην ἀπελθόντα that the reported event happened after Dionysus left the stage.[16] In addition, blackmail is not the simplest and most obvious interpretation when one looks at fr. 68 alone and tries to imagine its underlying situation. Rather, the words of the dialogue indicate that speaker A urgently needs a certain amount of money, and together with speaker B he tries to find a solution for this problem. He accordingly asks speaker B to bring a *kotylos*, which is somewhere at hand, perhaps to pawn it.[17] This does not mean that blackmail can be excluded, but it is doubtful whether, without fr. 75, anyone would have thought that fr. 68 was a dialogue between a blackmailer and his victim.

These are just a few examples from the rich inventory of comic fragments in *Poetae Comici Graeci*, and similar points could be made in regard to many others. But I hope that the few cases discussed here have already lent some support to the two main points of my argument: (1) a careful examination not only of the

---

15 For a list of scholars who interpret the fragment in this way, see Orth 2017, 420–421.

16 Orth 2017, 421 with n. 188, and cf. for a more detailed interpretation of fr. 75 *ibid.* 459–460, where it is argued that Dionysus may have left the stage for taking part in the Court case before the parabasis and then returned (and reported about it) after the parabasis (in a similar way as the Sausage Seller leaves for the Council before the parabasis of *Knights*, and afterwards reports about his Dispute with Cleon there).

17 Cf. Ar. *Ec.* 755, Hermipp. fr. 29, and the discussion in Orth 2017, 423–424.

textual but also of the performative context is essential for understanding comic fragments, and (2) this examination should always precede any attempt to combine different pieces of evidence in order to reconstruct part of the content of a lost play, and may serve also as a corrective by which more speculative attempts to connect fragments to each other or to the title of the play may be evaluated. In this way, this discussion may also be read as a plea for a form of philological commentary that first tries to do justice to every fragment and to recontextualize it as far as possible from its own words, and only then, in a second step, reflects on how the single items of evidence (play titles, fragments and testimonia) may interact and help us to arrive at a reasonable, although necessarily more or less uncertain and approximate idea of what happened in the action of a lost comedy.

Bibliography

Arnott, Peter D. (1962), *Greek Scenic Conventions in the Fifth Century B.C.*, Oxford.

Battezzato, Luigi (2018), *Euripides. Hecuba*, Cambridge.

Biles, Zachary P./Olson, S. Douglas (eds.) (2015), *Aristophanes. Wasps*, Oxford.

Csapo, Eric (2010), *Actors and Icons of the Ancient Theatre*, Chichester.

Kaimio, Maarit (1970), *The Chorus of Greek Drama within the Light of the Person and Number Used*, Helsinki.

Maduit, Christine/Moretti, Jean-Charles (2019), "stage, elevated", in: Alan H. Sommerstein (ed.), *The Encyclopedia of Greek Comedy*, III, Hoboken, 900–901.

Marcucci, Andrea (2020), *I frammenti esametrici dell'Archaia. Traduzione e commento*, Rome.

Mastronarde, Donald (1990), "Actors on High: The Skene Roof, the Crane, and the Gods in Attic Drama", in: *Classical Antiquity* 9, 247–294.

Olson, S. Douglas (ed.) (2002), *Aristophanes. Acharnians*, Oxford.

Orth, Christian (2017), *Aristophanes. Aiolosikon—Babylonioi (fr. 1–100). Übersetzung und Kommentar* (FrC 10.3), Heidelberg.

Starkey, J. (2013), "Soldiers and Sailors in Aristophanes' *Babylonians*", in: *Classical Quarterly* 63, 501–510.

Fausto Montana

Dramaturgical Memory and Virtual Theatre in the Scholia to Aristophanes' *Frogs*

Abstract: The close examination of a sample of *scholia vetera* to Aristophanes' *Frogs*, concerning aspects of theatrical staging inherent to the prologue and the parodos of that comedy, reveals a general sensitivity of some ancient commentators to these issues but, at the same time, displays the complex and multilayer character of this testimony. The Alexandrian grammarians seem to have drawn on sources possibly rooted in the performative culture of the previous centuries, though with an interest which appears predominantly diorthotic. The same dramaturgical notions were refunctionalised by exegetes of the subsequent eras and the compiler(s) of the scholiastic corpus to construct a virtual theatre, that is a stage practice explained in words to an audience of readers and students of written texts.

Keywords: Aristophanes, *Frogs*, scholia, ancient scholarly tradition, theatrical staging

The *testimonia*: a theatre for reading

Anytime we wonder about the nature of an ancient Greek literary text, we should go back and leaf through the medieval codices that have transmitted it. We need only open manuscripts of the comedies of Aristophanes, such as Ravennas 429 of the 10th century, or Venetus Graecus 474 of the 11th, to be reminded that these works have come to us through textual editions intended for consumption by educated readers of the middle Byzantine period. We know that the codices represent the end result of a long process of cultural history: works and genres of poetic communication in the ancient world responding to the logic of a performance culture have ultimately been channelled into and recast for a very different communicative system, which used solely writing. The process of reception of the 'classics' during the Graeco-Roman era and into the Byzantine period was fed by interests such as training in language, advances in

This research benefited from the resources of the University of Pavia (Blue Sky Research 2017-2019). English translation by Orla Mulholland.

https://doi.org/10.1515/9783111248028-011

expressive and rhetorical skills, the acquisition of an intellectual *koine*, the assimilation of models charged with an ideological standing and, all in all, the definition of a deep cultural identity. Readers of the middle Byzantine era encountered ancient drama in books furnished with explanatory paratexts written alongside the poetic text on the margins of the page. In the medieval tradition of ancient literature, text and paratext exist and interact in close symbiosis, since they cooperate to guarantee comprehension of works that originated within a profoundly different cultural code.[1]

In this light, the extent to which memory of the dramaturgical dimension survived in Byzantine editions of Aristophanes and their commentaries turns out to be a complex problem which splits into a wide range of separate questions. Were Byzantine readers interested in the actual staging? In that case, which particular aspects of ancient staging interested them? What sources did they have, which did they favour and how did they select among them?

The scholiastic heritage preserves traces of distant exegetical sources, some of them professional (philological) and putatively based on direct documentation, such as inscriptions, archaeological fieldwork, actor's scripts and scribal copies derived from such scripts. The colometry of the dramas represented in the textual layout of the comedies of Aristophanes and the layers of exegesis in the scholiastic *corpora* of the medieval codices have their roots in the attempts at reconstruction begun in Ptolemaic Alexandria: Lycophron, Eratosthenes, Aristophanes of Byzantium and Aristarchus are the pioneers of an activity that had its big bang in the discovery of just how much textual damage had been done in the centuries of anarchy during which the works were copied and transmitted.[2] *Diorthosis*, the discussion of textual problems and construction of a nuanced exegetical discourse, would proliferate throughout the Hellenistic period and would continue in subsequent eras and changing cultural contexts, encountering varied processes of reception and digestion. Ultimately these processes would inspire projects of epitomisation and abbreviated compilation, at first in the form of continuous commentaries separate from the text of the plays (which is how we imagine the writings of Didymus, Symmachus and Phaeinus) and then as anonymous marginal paratext (the scholia of the Byzantine manuscripts). The pragmatic nature of scholiography ensured its malleability and adaptation to contexts of transmission, releasing copyists and scholars from the inhibitions and complexes they had understandably cultivated when

---

1 Specifically, on "drama" and "theatre" in Byzantium, see Puchner 2002.
2 For an up-to-date overview: Montana 2020.

faced with literary works.[3] Only the arrival of printing in the West, at a time that fatefully coincided with the years in which Constantinople became Ottoman, contrasted with and cooled the metamorphic morphology of exegesis, setting underway the practices that led to the hardening of the text and, finally, the need for critical editions.

Anyone familiar with the scholia to the comedies of Aristophanes knows that their most common feature by far is an attempt to explain linguistic forms and literary contents, i.e. to understand the plays as works of literature at the cost of features linked to the performative aspect and those that are extra-verbal in character. This very disproportion gives a special importance to the minority of comments related to staging. The fact that such exist at all demonstrates that the Byzantine editions with commentaries presupposed readers aware that they held in their hands the text of plays that had been composed to go on stage, in which movement, music, and the other extra-verbal components of both visual and aural types, played an essential role that could not be entirely overlooked. This theatre for reading preserved traces of the texts' original performative nature, in a descriptive form and of a kind that permitted virtual reconstruction of the staged dimension mediated by the paratextual exegesis offered on the page alongside the work.

Today we find ourselves in a position not much different from that of the Byzantine reader and, for that reason, scholars have examined and exploited the dramaturgical *testimonia* present in the exegeses. But the anonymous character of the scholia and the difficulty or impossibility of dating their strata often causes present-day interpreters to be discouraged and hesitant. It is easy to yield to a sense of powerlessness when faced with desultory notices presented in apodictic form and without attribution to an author, or at times distorted by epitomisation or corruption. Added to this is the justifiable fear that isolated *testimonia* that are both uncertain and obscure will lead to mistaken interpretations. All this does not excuse us, however, from the painstaking work of dissecting and scrutinising the magmatic layers of scholia. This is what I propose to undertake here, by retracing as a case study a selection of scholia on the prologue and parodos of Aristophanes' *Frogs*. This material has already been widely noted and studied.[4] Here, however, I will address it from a less common perspective,

---

3 Montana 2011 and 2019; Montana/Porro 2014.
4 To cite one example, the scholia to the *Frogs* with dramaturgical content have been selected, arranged in a thematic typology, translated and given a partial commentary in the MA Thesis of Caterina Denora, *Scolî scenici alla Rane di Aristofane* (Università di Bari, a.a. 2005–2006, supervisor: Giuseppe Mastromarco). Among the thematic types that would merit further study, I

documenting the processes by which the most ancient memory of staging, of Hellenistic origin at least, is re-used in scholiastic exegesis for the sake of readers rather than spectators, and investigating whether annotations with dramaturgical contents offer indications of an organic and coherent vision that can be situated in time and cultural space. At a minimum, I hope to advance our knowledge of the history of reception of the play and to identify specific, homogeneous clusters of *testimonia* concerning ancient theatrical performance.[5]

Theatrical memory in the scholia to the prologue and parodos of *Frogs*

In the scholia to the prologue and parodos of *Frogs* (1–459), three interrelated strands emerge concerning dramaturgical themes: the composition and positioning on stage of the chorus of frogs; the composition and movements of the chorus of Initiates into the Mysteries; and the satiric metatheatrical gains achieved by Aristophanes via the logistics of the action. I will examine the main examples of such comments in the order in which the Byzantine reader would have encountered them when reading the play in a good manuscript of the time.[6]

Dionysus and Xanthias on the Acherousian Lake

A first series of explanations concerns the arrival of Dionysus and Xanthias at the Acherusian Lake, the god's crossing of the lake and the encounter with the chorus of frogs. Xanthias informs Dionysus that they have arrived beside the

---

note the dramaturgical interpretation of the relationship between speech and silence on the theatrical stage documented by a group of scholia to the second part of the play, the agon between Aeschylus and Euripides. As well as having interest as Aristophanes' poetic reading of the theatre of Aeschylus in particular, the theme may have a connection to ritual silence (εὐφημεῖν), a motive in the first part of *Frogs* in connection with the rite of initiation (silence as meaningful).

5 Although the approach to tragic scholia undertaken by Falkner 2002 is inspired by a similar perspective, I shall pay more attention here to the differences and interaction between Hellenistic and mid-Byzantine receptions.

6 The scholia are cited according to the edition of Chantry 1999. Chantry 2009 offers a useful thematic guide to the scholia with dramaturgical content.

lake that gives access to Hades, and the scholium comments as follows (*schol. Ar. Ra.* 181b):

(1) τοῦτο; λίμνη, νὴ Δία: ἐνταῦθα τοῦ πλοίου ὀφθέντος, ἠλλοιῶσθαι χρὴ τὴν σκηνήν, καὶ εἶναι τὸν τόπον κατὰ τὴν Ἀχερουσίαν λίμνην, ἐπὶ τοῦ λογείου ἢ ἐπὶ τῆς ὀρχήστρας, μη- δέπω δὲ ἐν Ἅιδου. **VMEΘBarbV**[57]**(Ald)**

(Xanthias) This? The lake, by Zeus!: at this point, when the boat is visible, the scene must have been changed, and the location is near the Acherousian Lake, on the stage-platform or in the orchestra, not yet in Hades.

The point of view of this comment is focused on the visual dimension of the theatrical experience (ὀφθέντος). The terminology (σκηνή, λογεῖον, ὀρχήστρα) suggests technical competence in regard to the stage spaces. The localisation of the dramatic fiction in the Acherousian Lake suggests that σκηνή is used in the figurative sense 'fictional context of the action' rather than the concrete sense 'scenography'. The note on the setting (εἶναι τὸν τόπον κατὰ τὴν Ἀχερουσίαν λίμνην ..., μηδέπω δὲ ἐν Ἅιδου) functions both as erudite information about the staging of *Frogs* and as a recreation in virtual form of its performative dimension for the sake of those engaging with the play as a book;[7] the anticipation "*not yet* in Hades" in fact presupposes that the reader has a prior awareness of the play's settings (and thus is understood to be educated and well informed about Aristophanic theatre; at a minimum, the reader would already know the *hypothesis* to *Frogs*, in which the various settings of the action are set out). The logistical alternatives ἐπὶ τοῦ λογείου ἢ ἐπὶ τῆς ὀρχήστρας show that secure information

---

7 The important aspects of the problem are missed by Del Corno 1985, 166: "Ma quando inizia il viaggio, si leva il canto delle rane: se nascoste o alla vista del pubblico, è un vacuo problema della pseudoerudizione, come lo è chiedersi come fosse o si muovesse la barca di Caronte" ("But when the voyage begins, the song of the frogs starts up: whether they are hidden or in view of the audience is a pointless problem of pseudo-erudition, as is the question of what Charon's boat was like and whether it moved"). Voices in favour of the invisibility of the chorus include Allison 1983; Stanford 1958, xxxi and 92; Russo 1962, 329, and 1994, 212; Zimmermann 1985, 166. More doubtfully Sommerstein 1996, 175–176, is inclined to accept the thesis of Marshall 1996, according to whom the chorus of frogs was invisible to Dionysus but visible to the audience. For the visibility of the chorus: Sifakis 1971, 94–95; MacDowell 1972 and 1995, 280; Dover 1993, 57. Totaro in Mastromarco-Totaro 2006, 587, observes: "Chi crede alla visibilità del coro (...) può inoltre facilmente spiegare che i coreuti-Rane hanno tutto il tempo (circa 50 versi, coperti dalla scena con Empusa) per cambiare abito e rientrare come Iniziati (al v. 323)" ("Anyone who believes in the visibility of the chorus ... can, further, easily explain that the choreutai-frogs have plenty of time (ca. 50 lines, covered by the scene with Empusa) to change costume and re-enter as Initiates (at line 323)").

was lacking and the problem is being posed conjecturally, but that this is done within the framework of a clear awareness of the possible spaces and dynamics for the action.

Schol. Ar. Ra. 209b accompanies the beginning of the choral song of the frogs:

(2) *(βρεκεκὲξ)*: ταῦτα καλεῖται παραχορηγήματα, ἐπειδὴ οὐχ ὁρῶνται ἐν τῷ θεάτρῳ οἱ βάτραχοι, οὐδὲ ὁ χορός, ἀλλ᾽ ἔσωθεν μιμοῦνται τοὺς βατράχους. **VMEΘBarb(Ald)**
α. ὁ δὲ χορὸς ἐκ τῶν εὐσεβῶν. | β. ὁ δὲ ἀληθῶς χορὸς ἐκ τῶν εὐσεβῶν
MEΘBarb(Ald) | νεκρῶν συνέστηκεν. **V**

(brekekèx): These parts are called "supplementary interventions" (παραχορηγήματα),[8] since the frogs are not visible in the theatre, nor (is) the chorus (visible),[9] but rather (the choreutai) offstage imitate the frogs.
α. The chorus (is composed) of believers. | β. The true chorus is composed of dead believers

The commentator once again assumes the perspective of a spectator, in this case stressing the function of 'seeing' in the theatre, underlined by its contrary (οὐχ ὁρῶνται ἐν τῷ θεάτρῳ). The use of the present tense of the verb describes the scenic situation with the abstract atemporality of a literary work, but would function equally well in a description of the performative event or of a *parepigraphē* (stage direction). The adverb ἔσωθεν indicates the backstage area. The word παραχορηγήματα is introduced as a technical term and apparently with sensitivity for nomenclature (καλεῖται): the word and the function it expresses were therefore unfamiliar to the implicit reader, or at least were expected to be. The exegete has grasped the dialectic between reality and fiction, both by observing that the βάτραχοι and the χορός are invisible to the public, and by using μιμεῖσθαι to describe a vocal role with strikingly mimetic and onomatopoeic features. At the conclusion of the scholium, the question of the play's two choruses emerges and is resolved, it seems, by distinguishing two roles interpreted by the same choral group. Only in the group of the Initiates does the commentator acknowledge the costume of the dramatic chorus in a strict sense, since the

---

8 Cf. Poll. 4.110, said of a fourth actor, perhaps in the sense of a chorus-member who acts as fourth actor if necessary; and *schol. Ar. Pax* 114d (**RVLh**) ὦ πάτερ ὦ πάτερ: τὰ τοιαῦτα παραχορηγήματα καλοῦσιν, οἷα νῦν τὰ παιδία ποιεῖ καλοῦντα τὸν πατέρα, εἶτα πρὸς οὐδὲν ἔτι τούτοις χρήσεται, "*Oh daddy, oh daddy!*: Such actor's lines are called *parachoregemata*, as, for instance, now (Aristophanes) introduces the children who invoke their father, then he will not use them (i.e. the children) anymore at all" (*scil.* in this drama after the present scene, ll. 114–149).
9 Differently Denora 2005–2006, 327: (the frogs) "non (sono) il coro" ('are not the chorus').

chorus of frogs occupies an offstage position and plays only a limited part in the prologue.

This interpretation is picked up again in *schol. Ar. Ra.* 258:

(3) ἀλλὰ μὴν **VBarb** κεκραξόμεσθα **V**: δεῖ νοεῖν ὡς οἱ βάτραχοι ὑπὸ σκηνήν εἰσιν ἀλλ᾽ οὐκ ἐν τῷ φανερῷ. ἡ μέντοι φωνὴ αὐτῶν ἐξακούεται, ὥσπερ καὶ αὐτοὶ κατὰ τὴν λίμνην ἠχοῦσιν. **RVEΘBarb(Ald)**

well then we'll roar: it is necessary to suppose that the frogs are hidden behind the scene and not in view. However, their voice is heard from a distance, just as real frogs echo in the lake.

The expression δεῖ νοεῖν ὡς … marks the reconstructive tenor of the explanation (δεῖ), addressed to readers who are understood as virtual spectators who must rely on their imagination (νοεῖν, "to envisage through thought"). As with the signalling of the change of setting in scholium 181b (ἠλλοιῶσθαι χρὴ τὴν σκηνήν), the dramaturgical information seems to be extrapolated from the text. The chorus of frogs declared that it would croak as loud as it could, since it was not located in the orchestra but ὑπὸ σκηνήν, behind the scenes, and hence its voice reached the spectators from a distance and was muffled. οὐκ ἐν τῷ φανερῷ once again invokes the visual faculty by a negative, and by default signifies that the performance of the frogs had only an aural dimension. The situation is described from the point of view of the spectator, as an imitation of the real experience of the invisibility and distance of frogs croaking in a swamp. The Aristophanic frogs were likewise acting outside of the spectators' vision and hence ὑπὸ σκηνήν, behind the scenes. Here σκηνή unequivocally designates the *scaenae frons*.

The two choruses

A second block of explanations concerns the alternation of the chorus of frogs with the chorus of Initiates: whereas the former is linked to the setting of the lake, the latter chorus greets Dionysus when he lands in Hades. The comments in the scholia concern the relationship between the fictitious setting (the lake, Hades) and the real logistics (the backstage area, the proscenium, the orchestra), but also deal with the composition of the two choruses and the dynamics between them.

At 268 Dionysus boasts with satisfaction that he has beaten the frogs: "Sooner or later I'd have made this *koax* of yours shut up!" The scholium on the line (*schol. Ar. Ra.* 268b) observes:

(4) ἔμελλον ἄρα **RVE** παύσειν **V**: σιωπῶσιν οἱ βάτραχοι καὶ ἕτερος χορὸς εἰσέρχεται, ὡς προείπομεν, ὁ τῶν μυστῶν, ὅς ἐστιν ἀναγκαῖος. **RVMEΘBarb(Ald)**

I would finally have made it stop: the frogs are silent and a different chorus enters, as we said before, that of the Initiates, which is necessary.[10]

A little further on, another annotation remarks on the change of chorus, associating it with the change of setting (*schol*. Ar. *Ra*. 273):

(5) σκότος] μεταβέβληται ἡ σκηνὴ καὶ γέγονεν ὑπόγειος. μεταβέβληται δὲ καὶ ὁ χορὸς τῶν βατράχων εἰς τοὺς μύστας. **V**

darkness] The scene has been changed and now it is underground. The chorus of frogs has also been changed into that of the Initiates.

The change of chorus and scene is noted also in the scholium to line 316:

(6) μετεβλήθη ὁ χορὸς εἰς μύστας. **RVV**[57]

The chorus was changed into that of the Initiates.

as well in the first argument to the play (*Argum*. Ar. *Ra*. I 7–11):

(7) ὁ δὲ Διόνυσος δύο ὀβολῶν περαιοῦται, προσπαίζων ἅμα τοῖς κατὰ τὸν πόρον ᾄδουσι βατράχοις καὶ γελωτοποιῶν. μετὰ ταῦτα ἐν Ἅιδου τῶν πραγμάτων ἤδη χειριζομένων, οἵ τε μύσται χορεύοντες ἐν τῷ προφανεῖ καὶ τὸν Ἴακχον ᾄδοντες ἐν χοροῦ σχήματι καθορῶνται, ὅ τε Διόνυσος μετὰ τοῦ θεράποντος εἰς ταὐτὸν ἔρχεται τούτοις. **RVMEMatrBarb(Pa, Ald)**

Dionysus makes the crossing for two obols, kidding and joking together with the chanting frogs during the trip. Then, when things are being settled in the Hades, the Initiates become visible in the form of a chorus dancing in the view and singing Iacchus, and Dionysus comes to the same place together with his servant.

The entrance of the Initiates will occur only at 323, but the commentator notices the usefulness of making a close connection between the change of chorus and the change of scene, which takes place at this point. The presence in *Frogs* of what appears to be a double chorus invited two questions from readers: what is the location of each of the two choruses in the scenic fiction and in the performative space, and are the two choruses played by the same group of performers? The answers to these *aporiai* seem to derive from a coherent vision (or imagining) of the theatrical dynamics, which encompasses both this block

---

10 Denora 2005–2006, 329: "… che è quello regolamentare". ('… which is the regular one').

of explanations and the previous one. The chorus of frogs, which intervenes before the chorus of Initiates (and so before the parodos), sings from the backstage area while Dionysus is crossing the Acherousian Lake (text 7 and see above, text 1); the frogs fall silent, and after a short interval (50 lines) the chorus of Initiates enters the orchestra dancing and singing the parodos song (text 4 εἰσέρχεται; text 7 ἐν τῷ προφανεῖ ... καθορῶνται); this is the "necessary" chorus (text 4) in the sense that it is the "real chorus" of the drama (cf. above, text 2), the canonical one, which now performs the parodos and then the following choral sections of the play, which take place in the orchestra. The two related notices on the (final) silencing of the frogs and the need for the chorus of Initiates imply that the groups are distinct in the dramatic fiction, but that the actual performers are the same persons, a single body of choreutai. The two choruses thus do not alternate with each other, but instead one changes into the other (text 5 μεταβέβληται ... ὁ χορὸς τῶν βατράχων εἰς τοὺς μύστας).[11] By the same logic, in scholium 268b (text 4) ἕτερος χορός must mean not just "the other chorus"[12] but "a different chorus" — different, that is, from the one the public might have expected after the entirely vocal backstage performance of the frogs. The reconstruction of the reciprocal dynamics of the two choruses casts light on the *aprosdoketon* achieved by Aristophanes, who after leading the spectators to expect a dramatic chorus in animal form, of the typical skoptic and farcical type, has instead staged a chaste and pious procession of deceased initiates. The commentary underlines the double *metabolē* (texts 5 and 6): the transformation of the chorus brings with it the change in setting — from now on, we are in Hades (text 5 γέγονεν ὑπόγειος; text 7 ἐν Ἄιδου τῶν πραγμάτων ἤδη χειριζομένων). The terminology is both technical and exhaustive: εἰσέρχεσθαι, σκηνή, μεταβεβλῆσθαι, χορεύοντες ... καὶ ... ᾄδοντες ἐν χοροῦ σχήματι. The homogeneity and coherence of the explanations are given an anonymous *sphragis* in scholium 268b (text 4), where the internal cross-reference ὡς προείπομεν connects to what was anticipated in 209b (text 2).

---

11 Defenders of the invisibility of the chorus of frogs also tend to maintain that a single group of choreutai performs both parts (e.g. Stanford 1958, xxx–xxxi; Russo 1962, 329): the latter theory is not even considered by Dover 1993, 55–57. Sommerstein 1996, 12 speaks of a "subsidiary chorus". See above, n. 7.

12 As maintained *e.g.* by Denora 2005–2006, 329.

Metatheatre

A third group of comments dwells on the metatheatrical effects set in motion by Aristophanes by placing the Hades scene in the orchestra, in direct contact with the *prohedria*. This choice reduces to nothing the conventional wall that separates fiction and reality, and it is remarkable that the commentator recognises in it the essential key to understanding the textual jokes in the gags set up by Dionysus with the audience and in particular with the priest of his own cult, who was sitting in the first row of the Theatre. The following are the relevant explanations:

(8) *schol. Ar. Ra.* 276a καὶ νυνί γ᾽ ὁρῶ **M(Ald)**: τοὺς ἐν τῷ θεάτρῳ ἐπιόρκους ὁρᾶν φησιν. **RVMEV[57](Ald)**

even now I am seeing: he says that he is seeing the perjurers sitting in the Theatre.

(9) *schol. Ar. Ra.* 276b ὁρῶ] ἵνα κωμῳδήσῃ τοὺς Ἀθηναίους ὡς τοιούτους, σκώπτει τοὺς ἐν τῷ θεάτρῳ, λέγων ὅτι "καὶ νῦν ὁρῶ ἐνταῦθα τοὺς πατραλοίας". **V**

I am seeing: in order to making fun of the Athenians as such, he lampoons those in the Theatre, saying that "even now I am seeing the parricides here".

(10) *schol. Ar. Ra.* 297a Ἱερεῦ, διαφύλαξόν μ᾽ **VMEBarb**:

α. παρὰ ταῖς θέαις προεδρίᾳ ἐτετίμητο ὁ ἱερεὺς τοῦ Διονύσου. **VMEΘBarb**	**β.** ἐν προεδρίᾳ κάθηται ὁ τοῦ Διονύσου ἱερεύς. **V**

Oh my priest, protect me!:

α. during the shows, the priest of Dionysus had the honor of the first row.	**β.** the priest of Dionysus used to sit in the first row.

(11) *schol. Ar. Ra.* 297 πρὸς βοήθειαν καλεῖ ὁ Διόνυσος τὸν ἱερέα. **VMEBarb(Ald)**

Dionysus calls the priest to the rescue.

(12) *schol. Ar. Ra.* 297c ἀποροῦσί τινες πῶς ἀπὸ τοῦ λογείου παρελθὼν καὶ κρυφθεὶς ὄπισθε τοῦ ἱερέως τοῦτο λέγει. φαίνονται δὲ οὐκ εἶναι ἐπὶ τοῦ λογείου ἀλλ᾽ ἐπὶ τῆς ὀρχήστρας, ἐν ᾗ ὁ Διόνυσος ἐνέβη καὶ ὁ πλοῦς ἐτελεῖτο, ὥστε μηκέτι ὁμοίως ἄλογον εἶναι, ἀλλὰ μὴν οὐ διὰ παντὸς ὄπισθε δεῖ γενέσθαι αὐτόν. **V**

Some wonder how it can be that he says these words while (i) coming from the stage-platform and (ii) hiding behind the priest. It is evident that they (sc. the characters) are not on the stage-platform, but in the orchestra, where Dionysus embarked and the sailing was completed, so that (i) this movement is not illogical anyway, and furthermore (ii) it is not necessary for him (i.e. Dionysus) to stay behind (the priest) the whole time.

As soon as they arrive in Hades, Dionysus and Xanthias experience the infernal apparitions Heracles told them about: perjurers and parricides, whom they mistake for the audience surrounding them in the *cavea*, and a monstrous metamorphic being, recognised as Empusa. In terror, Dionysus seeks refuge in the arms of the priest of his cult, who is sitting in the *prohedria*. The comment on Dionysus' skoptic jokes at the expense of the audience highlights the paradoxical relationship, set up by the line of sight, between subjects that belong to disparate, alien spaces, namely fiction and reality. Texts 8 and 9 underline that Dionysus uses the verb 'to see' in reference to the spectators sitting in the hemicycle of the Theatre and that the joke is against τοὺς Ἀθηναίους ὡς τοιούτους, "the Athenians as such, as they really are". In texts 10 and 11, the help sought by the god from his priest is interpreted as a physical breach of the boundary between fiction and reality made possible by the position of the characters in the orchestra and the neighbouring positions of the orchestra and the *prohedria*. Scholium 297c (text 12), transmitted only in the codex Venetus, preserves the memory of an exegetical *aporia* (ἀποροῦσί τινες) about Dionysus' movements. The commentator rejects the idea that the god goes from the *logeion* to the *prohedria* across the orchestra in order to hide behind the priest; this is because Dionysus appears to already be in the orchestra, where he boarded and where his boat-journey ended. Furthermore, nothing requires one to suppose that Dionysus remained hidden behind the priest for as long as he uttered these lines. Note again the verb δεῖ, probably a mark of an exegetical inference based on the text. The technical terminology of these scholia and the discussion of movements on stage are an indication of the commentator's competence regarding the spaces available for the action. On the other hand, the course of the action is the topic of an *aporia*, that is a critical discussion of a problem of literary interpretation, and the solution envisaged is the product not of direct experience of a performance but of reasoning based on plausibility taking its start from the text — φαίνονται, the characters "prove to be", in the orchestra.

The parodos

Dionysus has had no time to recover from the fright Empusa caused him when he hears a melody played by *auloi*: this is the prelude to the procession of the Initiates, who shortly make their entrance into the orchestra and begin the parodos at 323. The section occupies less than 140 lines, but is quite complex. It begins with a pair of choral odes separated by an *a parte* by Dionysus and Xanthias (323–353), then proceeds with a section of 18 anapaestic tetrameters recited by the chorus-leader (354–371), and finally develops into a series of lyric strophes partly in responsion and interspersed with interventions by the god and his servant (372–459).[13] A number of scholia show attention to the developments in the staging of this part. For the sake of brevity, I will concentrate on two groups, the first connected in the manuscripts to line 354, the start of the anapaestic section, and the second to line 372, where the following strophic series begins.

Scholium 354a (text 13) has suffered serious textual corruption. I give the text and the corresponding translation according to the correction proposed by J. van Leeuwen:[14]

(13) *schol.* Ar. *Ra.* 354a *εὐφημεῖν χρή* **VMEBarb**: Ἀρίσταρχος ἐπὶ τούτων λέγει τὸν χορὸν μεμερίσθαι **RVMEΘBarb(Ald)** εἰς μέρη β′ <καὶ τὸν κορυφαῖον λέγειν τ>ὰ ἀνάπαιστα, ἄλλα δὲ ἀμείβεσθαι τὸν χορόν. **VMEΘBarb(Ald)**

1 ἐπὶ τούτων: ἀπὸ τούτων Fritzsche, Rutherford, i.e. ab v. 372   2 εἰς—ἀνάπαιστα: corr. et suppl. van Leeuwen: εἰς μερικὰ ἀνάπαιστα codd.

it is necessary to be silent: Aristarchus says that at this point the chorus is divided in two parts <and the chorus-leader speaks the> anapaests, but the rest is executed by the chorus in amoebaic form.

The same manuscripts continue with scholium 354b, clearly a reply to the idea of Aristarchus that has just been reported, though unfortunately it too has not escaped textual damage:[15]

(14) *schol.* Ar. *Ra.* 354b καὶ τί ἄρα σύνοιδεν ὁ Ἀρίσταρχος; δύναται δὲ καὶ ἐνσύζυγον εἶναι τὸ λεγόμενον, πολλαχοῦ δὲ μεμερίσθαι καὶ εἰς διχορείαν τὸ λοιπὸν ὥστε εἰς ιβ′ καὶ ιβ′ διαμεμερίσθαι. **VMEΘBarb(Ald)**

1 ἐνσύζυγον: ἐν συζυγίᾳ Schuringa   2 πολλαχοῦ: ἀλλαχοῦ? Chantry

And what does Aristarchus know? It is also possible that these words are a single song, and that often (or, with Chantry's ἀλλαχοῦ, "elsewhere") the rest is divided into two hemichoruses in such a way as to form two groups of twelve (sc. choreutai).

---

13 Dover 1993, 63–68.
14 Leeuwen 1896, 354–355.
15 Note that, in the manuscript tradition, scholia 354a and 354b Chantry form an exegetical unit, offering Aristarchus' opinion and its refutation, both most likely found and excerpted as a whole from an ancient commentary by the compiler of the scholiastic corpus. As such, they should have been edited as a single scholium. For similar cases and the related methodological issues, see Montana 2017 and 2021.

Despite the uncertainty, the sense of the objection becomes clearer in light of the explanations accompanying the beginning of the choral series following the anapaests, at 372. Here we read attributions of the text which match Aristarchus' thesis:

(15) *schol.* Ar. *Ra.* 372a ἡμιχόριόν **RVEΘBarbRs** ἐστιν. **V**

(This) is a hemichorus.

(16) *schol.* Ar. *Ra.* 372b ἔστι ὁ χορὸς τὸ ἄλλο μέρος τοῦ χοροῦ. **VEV**[57]

The chorus (here is) the other part of the (whole) chorus.

The next three scholia pick up the two opposed theses reported above at 354a and 354b. The first specifies that Aristarchus based his idea of the doubling of the chorus on this line, in which the choreutai exhort themselves to proceed "like men":[16]

(17) *schol.* Ar. *Ra.* 372c χώρει δὴ νῦν πᾶς **VM** ἀνδρείως **V**: ἐντεῦθεν Ἀρίσταρχος ὑπενόησε μὴ ὅλου τοῦ χοροῦ εἶναι τὸ πρόσωπον. **RVMEΘBarb(Ald)**

so let each (of us) proceed courageously now!: It is from this line that Aristarchus argued that the speaking character is not the chorus in its entirety.

The verb ὑπενόησε marks the Aristarchean observation as a speculative supposition. The next two scholia maintain the objection that requests addressed by choreutai to themselves do not necessarily imply a division into hemichoruses:[17]

(18) *Schol.* Ar. *Ra.* 372d τοῦτο οὐκ ἀξιόπιστον· πολλάκις γὰρ ἀλλήλοις οὕτω παρακελεύο-νται **RVMEΘBarb(Ald)** οἱ περὶ τὸν χορόν. **VMEΘBarb(Ald)**

This (i.e. Aristarchus' inference) is not credible. In fact, the choreutai often address their words in this way to each other.

(19) *Schol.* Ar. *Ra.* 372e οἱ τοῦ χοροῦ μύσται ἀλλήλοις παρακελεύονται. **RVEV**[57] | χορὸς πρὸς ἀλλήλους. **M**

---

16 J. van Leeuwen held that the scholium actually refers to the chorus-leader's apostrophe to the chorus, understood as one part of the chorus (370 ὑμεῖς).
17 The scholia 372c and 372d Chantry form again a single excerpt in the manuscripts (372d begins τοῦτο δὲ οὐκ ἀξιόπιστον, 'normalized' by Chantry into τοῦτο οὐκ ἀξιόπιστον): see above, n. 15.

> The Initiates of the chorus address their words to each other. | The chorus, to each other.

This is not the place to enter into the modern discussions that have dissected these passages, but it is worth noting that the correction proposed by J. van Leeuwen in scholium 354a (text 13) was rejected by Dover, who found it unnecessary.[18] To my mind, however, it has a double value: it explains the possible origin of the textual error as a *saut du même au même* (from λέγει to λέγειν), and it lends sense to Aristarchus' view of a division of the chorus after the anapaests, no matter whether that is correct or mistaken.[19]

"No matter whether that is correct or mistaken" is also my conclusion on this point. Aristarchus had in his hands the *ekdosis* of Aristophanes of Byzantium and other, unknown tools and resources regarding the performance history of *Frogs* and ancient theatrical practice generally. It will suffice to cite the deep investigations carried out by Lycophron and Eratosthenes. Beginning with those resources, and on the basis of the text of the comedy, he found it plausible that the chorus recited the second part of the parodos subdivided into two formations. This was an inference, and its anonymous detractor censured it as such, with personal vehemence: καὶ τί ἄρα σύνοιδεν ὁ Ἀρίσταρχος; (354b), τοῦτο δὲ οὐκ ἀξιόπιστον (372d).

The Alexandrian sources

Taken as a whole, the comments examined here display a fair degree of coherence. The terminological precision about theatrical spaces and functions, the consistency of the reconstructions, and the recognition of the boundaries and dialectic between artistic fiction and real performance context indicate that the compiler of the scholia was following one or more commentaries that collected notices and research findings which were in their turn informed by and founded upon dramaturgical material. A positive indication of their homogeneity is the

---

18 Dover 1993, 67.

19 The textual corruption in scholium 354a is an error common to all the medieval manuscripts and therefore derives from their archetype. The explanation as a *saut du même au même* implies that the model from which the scholium was excerpted had a line of 41 letters (the number contained, in the correction of van Leeuwen, between λέγει and λέγειν): this is compatible with a column of writing in a book-roll, which would push back the date of the error to the phase of transition from roll to codex, that is to the transition from a *hypomnēma* to a continuous commentary in a codex, whether in the form of marginal or full-page comment.

internal cross-reference ὡς προείπομεν in scholium 268b about the alternation of the chorus of frogs and the chorus of Initiates. It is hard to decide whether this linkage was an initiative taken by the compiler of the scholia or by his ancient source.

It is no less difficult to form an opinion about the identity and cultural setting of the compiler's 'philo-dramaturgical' source or sources.[20] The most important clue is the criticism of the opinion of Aristarchus on the division of the chorus of Initiates (scholia 354a+b and 372c+d). This is, first of all, testimony to Aristarchus' interest in an aspect linked to the actual staging of the comedy, probably for the sake of constituting the text.[21] Second, the direct personal criticism leads one to think that whoever formulated it was not too distant in time from Aristarchus himself.

At least one other testimony mentioned in the scholia points towards the heyday of Alexandrian philology, and although it is not strictly related to our sample of scholia here, it is nonetheless worth highlighting. A note to 1414 shows that Apollonius, a commentator on Aristophanes who is perhaps to be identified as of Aristarchus' pupils,[22] observed the presence of four speaking characters in the staging of *Frogs*:

(20) *schol. Ar. Ra.* 1414a οὐδὲν ἄρα πράξεις **RVE**: Ἀπολλώνιος τοῦ Πλούτωνος εἶναί φησι τοῦτο, **RVEΘ(Ald)** καὶ γίνεται πρόσωπα ἐν τῇ σκηνῇ **VEΘ(Ald)** δ΄ **VE(Ald)**.

So you won't do anything: Apollonius states that this part belongs to Pluto, and the characters on stage become four.

The comic context is as follows: after the weighing of the lines of Aeschylus and Euripides, Dionysus declares himself unable to choose which of the two he should bring back to life (1411–1416): "Those people are friends of mine and I don't know how to judge them. I don't want to quarrel with either of them: in my view, one is a great poet; I like the other one." At this point, a voice intervenes to converse with Dionysus: "In that case it will have been pointless for you to come here". Dionysus: "And if I express my preference?" The other char-

---

20 Among the ancient scholia to the plays of Aristophanes, those to the *Frogs* form one of the corpora that have preserved the greatest amount of explicitly cited Hellenistic exegesis: cf. the index of *Auctores citati* in Chantry 1999; and further, e.g., Denora 2005–2006; Muzzolon 2005; Perrone 2005.

21 Other interventions by Aristarchus documented in the corpus of scholia to the *Frogs* attest his interest in attribution of lines to characters: Muzzolon 2005; Denora 2005–2006, 104–109.

22 Schmidt 1854, 285–286; Blau 1883, 50–55; Boudreaux 1919, 77; Montanari 1996a and 1996b; Perrone 2022.

acter: "Take the one you have chosen and carry him away: that way you will not have come here for no reason." The authoritativeness and content of the two interventions in reply to Dionysus must have persuaded Apollonius that they belong to Pluto, god of Hades. The alternative attribution to the chorus, that is, to the chorus-leader,

> (21) *schol. Ar. Ra.* 1414b τινὲς <εἶναί φασι> τοῦ χοροῦ **RVEΘ(Ald)**

> some say that (it) belongs to the chorus.

sounds like an attempt to avoid having to admit the presence of four actors onstage. Claiming that the character speaking is Pluto brings with it the admission of the presence of a fourth actor, and it is therefore natural to assign both observations, or rather the two complementary parts of a single observation, to the *grammatikos* Apollonius.[23]

A comment analogous to the one formulated by Apollonius on 1414 is found in scholium 549b, this time anonymously:

> (22) *schol. Ar. Ra.* 549b παρατηρητέον ὅτι τέσσαρες ἐπὶ σκηνῆς διαλέγονται. **RVMΘBarbV**[57]

> It should be noted that four persons are in dialogue on stage.

The line occurs at the point in the play where Dionysus, dressed as Heracles, and Xanthias are encountered in Hades by the two inn-ladies whose stores were cleaned out by Heracles, when he descended to the underworld to capture Cerberus. The first landlady, believing she is looking at Heracles, at once calls her colleague Plathane, who runs in. In quickfire exchanges the two confirm for each other that the person before them is indeed the same charmer as last time, and they recount his misdeeds, including his refusal to pay his bill. Dionysus and Xanthias, in terror, perform an amusing *controcanto*, and so the two pairs of characters converse with each other onstage.[24] The annotation forms a matching pair with that to 1414, and it is tempting to attribute this too to Apollonius.

About this commentator we have few objective facts. The name Apollonius, without further specification, is mentioned frequently in the scholia to the plays of Aristophanes, including at least a dozen times in those to *Frogs*, in interventions that reveal an approach tied to decoding points of detail or to the

---

23 On the scholium, see Denora 2005–2006, 112–116.

24 Although the manuscripts record the scholium around line 570 (perhaps by attraction from scholium 570c, which is formulated in a similar way but concerns a different subject), it must refer to the start of the scene, i.e. to 549: see Chantry 1999, 83.

constitution of the text, sometimes in association with the name of Aristarchus.[25] The observation about the simultaneous presence of four speaking characters should be ascribed to the philological task of attributing the lines and thus ultimately concerns textual criticism. But it is clear that this type of intervention presupposes research questions and observations that are typically dramaturgical.

In conclusion: materials twice re-used

Clues like the one just highlighted show that at least part of the observations on staging transmitted in the scholia to the *Frogs* derive from philological/scholarly investigations conducted in the Hellenistic era by Alexandrian grammarians.[26] On the other hand, whoever put together the scholiastic compilation seems to have made himself a conduit for information that he did not verify and was perhaps not in a position to verify, and his exegetical point of view reveals that he belongs to a cultural context where the performative practice was no longer knowable at first hand. The mingling of a lexicon and concepts appropriate to theatrical staging, on the one hand, and a lack of direct experience of staged action, on the other, suggests a Byzantine compiler who drew on ancient, well-informed sources, but who had in mind a readership, not an audience, and whose own environment was a book culture. For whoever it was who transmitted these comments to us, Attic theatre had definitively turned into literature. Through an unknown number of steps and mediations in transmission and culture, the compiler discovered in his sources the remains of a memory still rooted in theatrical performance. And seeing a use in them — that is, the use of re-deploying them himself — he re-transmitted them in turn in the service of an entirely different context and purposes. The dramaturgical notions were able to take on a new value and meaning by being refunctionalised to construct a virtual theatre, that is a stage practice explained in words to readers of written texts.

Ultimately, the scholia to *Frogs* with dramaturgical content represent the result of a double re-use. The first stage is the reception of Attic theatre by Hel-

---

25 Cf. Rutherford 1905, 432 n. 11.

26 Whether the philologists of the Museum also made use of actor's scripts (*Bühnenexemplare*) in their work of textual *diorthosis*, in particular in order to glean information of a metrical (and musical?) kind, has been a matter of intense critical debate: for a summary, see Montana 2020, 137–138. Falkner 2002, especially 346–348, maintains that some tragic scholia offer testimony to the influence of contemporary performances on Alexandrian scholarship.

lenistic philologists. The *grammatikoi*, who also had access to direct, first-hand sources, bore in mind and investigated the traces of comic performance, though this was done primarily in the service of textual *diorthosis* and literary history. The second stage is the century-long process of filtering and recycling the Hellenistic sources by the Alexandrians' heirs and followers, all the way down to the compiler of the scholia, who were always most interested in a contextualising, reconstructive explanation for the benefit of pure readers. The task now falls to us of deciphering this double palimpsest without being naïve about the problems it poses, but also without sceptically prejudging them.

Bibliography

Allison, Richard H. (1983), "Amphibian ambiguities. Aristophanes and his *Frogs*", in: *Greece and Rome* 30, 8–20.

Blau, August (1883), *De Aristarchi discipulis*, Diss. Jena.

Boudreaux, Pierre (1919), *Le texte d'Aristophane et ses commentateurs*, Paris.

Chantry, Marcel (1999) (ed.), *Scholia in Aristophanem*, Pars III: *Scholia in Thesmophoriazusas, Ranas, Ecclesiazusas et Plutum*, Fasc. Iᵃ continens *Scholia vetera in Aristophanis Ranas*, Groningen.

Chantry, Marcel (2009) (ed.), *Scholies anciennes aux Grenouilles et au Ploutos d'Aristophanes*, Paris.

Del Corno, Dario (1985) (ed.), *Aristofane. Le rane*, Milan.

Denora, Caterina (2005–2006), *Scolî scenici alla Rane di Aristofane*, tesi di laurea, Università di Bari.

Dover, Kenneth J. (1993) (ed.), *Aristophanes. Frogs*, Oxford.

Falkner, Thomas M. (2002), "Scholars versus Actors: Text and Performance in the Greek Tragic Scholia", in: Easterling, Pat/Hall, Edith (eds.), *Greek and Roman Actors: Aspects of an Ancient Profession*, Cambridge, 342–361.

Leeuwen, Jan van (1896) (ed.), *Aristophanis Ranae*, Leiden.

MacDowell, Douglas M. (1972), "The *Frogs*' chorus", in: *Classical Review* 22, 3–5.

MacDowell, Douglas M. (1995), *Aristophanes and Athens. An Introduction to the Plays*, Oxford.

Marshall, Christopher W. (1996), "Amphibian ambiguities answered", in: *Échos du Monde Classique* 40, 251–265.

Mastromarco, Giuseppe/Totaro, Piero (2006) (eds.), *Commedie di Aristofane*, vol. II, Torino.

Montana, Fausto (2011), "The making of Greek scholiastic *corpora*", in: Montanari, Franco/Pagani, Lara (eds.), *From Scholars to Scholia. Chapters in the History of Ancient Greek Scholarship*, Berlin/New York, 105–161.

Montana, Fausto (2017), "Zetemata alessandrini negli scoli alle *Rane* di Aristofane. Riflessioni ecdotiche", in: Mastromarco, Giuseppe/Totaro, Piero/Zimmermann, Bernhard (eds.), *La commedia attica antica. Forme e contenuti*, Lecce, 195–229.

Montana, Fausto (2019), „Editing anonymous voices: the *scholia uetera* to the *Iliad*", in: Schorn, Stefan/Boodts, Shari/De Leemans, Pieter (eds.), *Sicut dicit. Editing Ancient and Medieval Commentaries on Authoritative Texts*, Turnhout, 97–125.

Montana, Fausto (2020), "Hellenistic scholarship", in: Montanari, Franco (ed.), *History of Ancient Greek Scholarship from the Beginnings to the End of the Hellenistic Age*, Leiden/ Boston, 132–259.

Montana, Fausto (2021), "Antichi filologi in ballo. Testo e interpretazione di *schol.* Ar. *Th.* 1175", in: *Eikasmós* 32, 231–241.

Montana, Fausto/Porro, Antonietta (2014) (eds.), *The Birth of Scholiography. From Types to Texts*, thematic issue of *Trends in Classics* 6, Berlin/Boston.

Montanari, Franco (1996a), *Apollonios* [n. 7], in: *DNP* 1, 880.

Montanari, Franco (1996b), *Apollonios* [n. 8], in: *DNP* 1, 880.

Muzzolon, M. Lorenza (2005), „Aristarco negli scolii ad Aristofane", in: Montana, Fausto (ed.), *Interpretazioni antiche di Aristofane*, La Spezia 2005 (repr. Rome 2006), 55–109.

Perrone, Serena (2005), "Aristofane e la religione negli *scholia vetera* alle *Rane*", in: Montana, Fausto (ed.), *Interpretazioni antiche di Aristofane*, La Spezia 2005 (repr. Rome 2006), 111–129.

Perrone, Serena (2022), "Apollonius [1]", in: *Brill's Lexicon of Greek Grammarians of Antiquity*, <http://dx.doi.org/10.1163/2451-9278_Apollonius_1_it>.

Puchner, Walter (2002), "Acting in Byzantine theatre: evidence and problems", in: Easterling, Pat/Hall, Edith (eds.), *Greek and Roman Actors: Aspects of an Ancient Profession*, Cambridge, 304–324.

Russo, Carlo F. (1962), *Aristofane, autore di teatro*, Florence.

Russo, Carlo F. (1994), *Aristophanes, an Author for the Stage*, London.

Rutherford, William G. (1905), *A Chapter in the History of Annotation, being Scholia Aristophanica*, III, London.

Schmidt, Moritz (1854) (ed.), *Didymi Chalcenteri grammatici Alexandrini fragmenta quae supersunt omnia*, Leipzig.

Sifakis, Gregoris M. (1971), *Parabasis and Animal Choruses: A Contribution to the History of Attic Comedy*, London.

Sommerstein, Alan H. (1996) (ed.), *Aristophanes. Frogs*, Warminster.

Stanford, William B. (1958) (ed.), *Aristophanes. The Frogs*, London (2nd ed. 1963).

Zimmermann, Bernhard (1985[2]), *Untersuchungen zur Form und dramatischen Technik der Aristophanischen Komödien*, I: *Parodos und Amoibaion*, Königstein.

Alan H. Sommerstein
No, They Didn't Write Stage Instructions, but...

Abstract: While most in-text *parepigraphai* in dramatic scripts must be regarded as insertions or annotations by readers or commentators, those in Aeschylus' *Eumenides* and *Diktyoulkoi* which denote inarticulate vocalizations cannot be thus accounted for and should be treated as part of the author's script. Sophocles and Euripides did not follow Aeschylus' practice in this respect.

Keywords: stage-directions, interpolation, Aeschylus, annotation, vocalizations

It is well known that scattered through the texts of Greek dramatic poetry are found a small number of short notes — none is more than four words long, and there are less than a score of them all told[1] — which if they occurred in a modern play-script would be called stage directions. Many similar, and sometimes more elaborate, annotations are presented by, or directly inferable from, the dramatic scholia, especially those on Aristophanes, which often use in this connection the term παρεπιγραφή, whose literal meaning is approximately 'something incidental to a text, written adjacent to it'. These latter are now generally and rightly regarded as the work of ancient readers and commentators,[2] and the same view is mostly taken of what I will call the 'in-text annotations'. Thus Oliver Taplin, after reviewing all the tragic passages on which in-text annotations exist or have been alleged to exist, concluded that none of them were of authorial origin but that it had later become the practice for "keen readers ... [to] write in their own *parepigraphai* indicating any noises [or other non-verbal actions] they thought they could infer from the text" (Taplin 1977, 127); and Martin Revermann, after a review of the comic evidence (Revermann 2006, 320–325; cf. Taplin 1977, 128–129), came to a similar conclusion, basing it mainly on the paucity and random distribution of surviving in-text annotations.

---

1 Excluding those sometimes identified at Aesch. *Sept.* 84, 89; Soph. *Ph.* 787, fr. 314.107–108 R.²; Eur. *Or.* 1384, *IA* 1132–1133, 1416; [Eur.] *Rh.* 17 (on all of which, see Taplin 1977) and also Ar. *Th.* 1187b (ἀνακύπτι καὶ παρακύπτι ἀπεψωλημένος) which, like Revermann 2006, 322–323 and Hartwig 2008, I regard as part — though it must very early have become a corrupt part — of the main text.

2 Though some of those on tragedy and Menander may reflect performance practice in the annotator's time.

https://doi.org/10.1515/9783111248028-012

Both authors were aware that some of these annotations present more problems than others. Taplin identified four passages in tragedy and satyr-drama whose form, content and relationship to other texts suggested that they "might ... go back to the dramatist himself" (Taplin 1977, 127–128). One of these, *P.Oxy.* 2746 (= *trag. adesp.* 649), where the word ᾠδή 'song' is inserted six times, may well not come from "the text of a proper tragedy" at all (Taplin 1977, 127); and another, at Eur. *Cyc.* 487 (ᾠδή ἔνδοθεν 'song <heard> from within') is easily inferable from the poetic text and could therefore have been inserted by a reader at any time. This leaves just two sets of in-text annotations in the tragic corpus that are more difficult to account for on Taplin's hypothesis, both of them in plays of Aeschylus: *Eum.* 117–130 (especially 129 μυγμὸς διπλοῦς ὀξύς 'two high-pitched moans') and Aesch. fr. 47*a*.802 R. (and probably also 793) ποππυσμός 'a clucking noise'. In his case-by-case survey Taplin leaves open the possibility that these two annotations "might go back to Aeschylus" (Taplin 1977, 123), though by the end of his article he treats it as established that they too are the work of readers (*ibid.* 129).

As for comedy, both Taplin and Revermann focus on two annotations in Ar. *Thesm.*, on 129 ὀλολύζει ὁ γέρων (Suda: ὀλολύζεις γέρων **R**) 'the old man [i.e. Euripides' kinsman] utters a feminine cry of joy' and on 276–277 ὀλολύζουσι· τὸ (Ellebodius: -ζουσί τε **R**) ἱερὸν ὠθεῖται 'they [the women] ululate; the sanctuary is thrust [forward]'.[3] Both argue cogently that the note on 276–277 is unlikely to be authentic (because neither of the two directions of which it is composed is appropriate at that particular point), but both are tenderer towards the note on 129. Taplin (1977, 129) calls it "a nice touch [which] Aristophanes might have liked", while Revermann (2006, 324) says that in the Kinsman's mouth it "makes good sense as a funny response to Agathon's composition". It also, however, prematurely turns the hitherto very masculine Kinsman[4] into a quasi-woman, feminizing himself of his own volition — whereas later (209–276) he has to be all but forced, and certainly bullied, into making the same transition. Seeing that Agathon has just been impersonating a female chorus, has already been repeatedly spoken of in terms appropriate to a woman,[5] and will be so spoken of several times more,[6] it is arguably he rather than the Kinsman who should crown his lyric for a chorus of Trojan women with an *ololygmos*. Accord-

---

3 Apparently referring to the use of the ἐκκύκλημα.
4 Cf. 35 (he has fucked Agathon), 50, 57, 59–62 (he is ready to rape both Agathon and his servant), 98.
5 Cf. the passages cited in the previous note.
6 Cf. 130–145 *passim*, 157–158, 191–192, 204–205, 250–251.

ingly Sommerstein 1994, still believing the annotation to have originated with the dramatist himself, adopted Fritzsche's deletion of ὁ γέρων, perhaps without taking sufficient note of the questions this begs, especially the question whether it is at all plausible that a reader or commentator, faced with a script in which a typically feminine cry is uttered by a man whose extreme effeminacy has already been established, would deliberately transfer the cry to a man who is not effeminate at all.

It is thus likely that both the annotations just discussed are erroneous, and therefore that neither is authorial.[7] In that case, there remain only the above-noted Aeschylean passages from *Eumenides* and *Diktyoulkoi*.

Neither Taplin nor Revermann makes any serious attempt to suggest how a reader or commentator could have come up, *ex nihilo*, with μυγμὸς διπλοῦς ὀξύς or with ποππυσμός. I propose to re-examine the hypothesis that the in-text annotations in *Eumenides* and *Diktyoulkoi*, unlike all the other in-text annotations that survive, were inserted by the dramatist himself. Taplin brings forward several objections to this hypothesis.[8]

1. "Interjections and non-verbal utterances when they are supplied at all ... are normally written out phonetically", not represented, as in these annotations, by abstract nouns (Taplin 1977, 122, cf. 123). This is to lump together two very different kinds of vocalization. Interjections such as ὀτοτοτοῖ or παπαῖ were part of the language competence of those who uttered them; they were not merely interjections but *ancient Greek* interjections, and one would not expect to find an identical set in any other language. They are composed of Greek phonemes, and obey that language's constraints on syllable and word structure. They can even enter into syntactic relations as constituents of sentences.[9] Non-verbal (or, as they are better termed, non-linguistic) utterances need not satisfy these conditions and might, for example, in the mouth of a Greek speaker, include a syllable without a vowel (e.g. Soph. fr. 314.176 R.[2]) or a sound like a

---

7 That both include an *ololygmos* may suggest that they originated with the same person. It is curious, incidentally, that this cry, which would presumably be represented phonetically by ὀλολῦ or the like, never appears anywhere in any tragic or comic text (or indeed in any text of any kind known to *TLG* or to the PHI corpus of inscriptions), though we do find other phonetically similar cries that do not have the same ritual significance, such as ἐλελελεῦ (Ar. *Av.* 364) or ἀλαλαλαί (*ibid.* 1763). Was there a taboo against uttering the cry outside its proper ritual context, as there was against any theatrical enactment or even simulation of a sacrificial slaughter?

8 Revermann, whose focus is on comedy, does not attempt to present any arguments directed specifically against the authenticity of the annotations in the two Aeschylean passages.

9 Cf. Aesch. *Pers.* 1031–1032 (Χο.) παπαῖ παπαῖ. (Ξε.) καὶ πλέον ἢ παπαῖ μὲν οὖν.

ποππυσμός which is completely outside the Greek phonological system. The annotations with which we are concerned — seven of them in all, five in *Eumenides* and two in *Diktyoulkoi* — are all directions for non-linguistic vocalizations; moreover, these, so far as we can tell, are the *only* non-linguistic vocalizations in the surviving Aeschylean corpus. It is perfectly possible, therefore, that in this respect (as in so many others) Sophocles and Euripides did not follow Aeschylus' practice.

2. Taplin (*ibid.*) also notes that at *Eum.* 130 "Aeschylus has actually supplied the words of the dreaming chorus" and asks whether the "two high-pitched whines" are "meant to come before these words, or at the same time,[10] or to be a substitute for them". The manuscript tradition plainly indicates 'before', and this makes good dramatic sense as part of a gradual, step-by-step awakening of the Erinyes from the sleep cast upon them by Apollo or Hermes: they pass from silence and deep sleep for which they are upbraided by the ghost of Clytaemestra (94–116) to moaning (117–122) to a louder, lower-pitched sound (123–128) to an urgent, high-pitched shriek (129) to articulate words which still, however, sound like the breathing and barking of hounds on the trail (130; see Sommerstein 1989, 106) and then, after further rebukes by the ghost, to the actual waking first of the leader (140), then of two more (140–142) and finally of the whole band (143–148). There is no reason, except a blanket suspicion of in-text *parepigraphai*, to strike out any of these stages.

3. Taplin (1977, 127) correctly points out that we cannot say that the dramatists (or even, we may add, Aeschylus alone), while not writing stage directions of other kinds, "did [regularly] indicate noises", since "there are many places where noises which are clearly inferable from the text are *not* indicated explicitly" (citing as an example the sounding of the trumpet at Eum. 573). But the generalization thus rightly rejected is not the only one available: as has been shown above, what we can say is that Aeschylus (and, so far as our evidence goes, only Aeschylus) regularly indicated *non-linguistic vocalizations* by means of *parepigraphai*.

I conclude that this is probably what Aeschylus in fact did. Revermann (2006, 325) was quite right to ask "if authorial stage directions had been a regular feature of the texts, why do we have so extremely few of them?". A perfectly fair question, but not an unanswerable one; the answer is "because they were only used in one set of circumstances, and then only by one of the major dramatists."

Aeschylus regarded interjections within the Greek language system simply as part of the language, and as part of his play-script. Almost all other stage directions would be given orally to whichever member(s) of the performance/

---

10 I do not understand how this would be possible.

production team would be responsible for implementing them. But non-linguistic vocalizations formed a special category. They were a part of what the actor or chorus had to utter, just like their articulate words, yet they were not articulate, and some of them, such as a ποππυσμός, could not be represented by any letter or combination of letters that the Greek alphabet had to offer. Aeschylus' solution, apparently, was to represent such vocalizations by the nouns commonly used to denote them — some of which, including μυγμός and ὠγμός, incorporate a phonetic approximation to the sound referred to. Sophocles at least, and probably Euripides also, preferred to follow the principle that anything that *can* be phonetically represented *should* be phonetically represented. What they did with ποππυσμοί and the like we cannot tell. Perhaps, even in their satyr-plays, they just avoided them.

Bibliography

Hartwig, Andrew (2008), "Interpretive Notes on Aristophanes' *Thesmophoriazousae*", in: *Philologus* 152, 49–64.

Revermann, Martin (2006), *Comic Business: Theatricality, Dramatic Technique, and Performance Contexts of Aristophanic Comedy*, Oxford.

Sommerstein, Alan H. (1989), *Aeschylus. Eumenides*, Cambridge.

Sommerstein, Alan H. (1994), *The Comedies of Aristophanes*, Vol. 8: *Thesmophoriazusae*, Warminster.

Taplin, Oliver P. (1977), "Did Greek Dramatists Write Stage Instructions?", in: *Proceedings of the Cambridge Philological Society* 23, 121–132.

List of Contributors

Eric Csapo is British Academy Global Professor in Classics and Ancient History at Warwick University and an Honorary Professor in Classics and Ancient History at the University of Sydney. He has special interests in myth, dramatic literature and the history of the ancient theatre. His publications include *Theatre and Autocracy in the Ancient World* (de Gruyter 2022, co-edited with H.R. Goette, J.R. Green, B. Le Guen, E. Paillard, J. Stoop and P. Wilson); *Actors and Icons of the Ancient Theater* (Malden and Oxford 2010); *Theories of Mythology* (Oxford 2005); and *The Context of Ancient Drama* (Ann Arbor 1995, co-authored with W.J. Slater). Together with Peter Wilson he is currently writing a three-volume *Social and Economic History of the Theatre to 300 BC,* the second volume of which, *Theatre Beyond Athens*, was published in 2020.

Giuseppe Mastromarco is Emeritus Professor of Greek Language and Literature at the University of Bari "Aldo Moro". His scholarly interest mainly focussed on Homer, Attic tragedy and comedy, Demosthenes, literary mime, and epigrammatic production. He has published numerous articles in both Italian and foreign journals. Among his monographs: *Storia di una commedia di Atene*, Firenze, La Nuova Italia, 1974; *Il pubblico di Eronda*, Padova, Antenore, 1979 (Eng. transl.: *The Public of Herondas*, Amsterdam, Gieben, 1984); *Introduzione a Aristofane*, Roma-Bari, Laterza, 1994; *Aristofane. Le Commedie*, voll. I–II, Torino, UTET, 1983, 2006 (the latter in collaboration with Piero Totaro); and the handbook *Storia del teatro Greco*, Milano, Mondadori, 2008 (in collaboration with Piero Totaro). He is member of the Scientific Committee of numerous journals and editorial collections; with Piero Totaro, he is Co-Director of "Prosopa. Teatro Greco: studi e commenti". He is now preparing an edition, with translation and commentary, of Aristophanes' *Ecclesiazusae*.

Enrico Medda is Full Professor of Greek Literature in the Department of Philology, Literature and Linguistics at the University of Pisa and Member of the Accademia Nazionale dei Lincei in Rome. A former pupil of the Scuola Normale Superiore in Pisa, he was a Researcher at the Scuola, where he also taught as an Adjunct Professor. He has been 'Professeur invité' at the École Normale Supérieure de Paris, and is a member of the Conseil Scientifique International 'Lettres et Sciences Sociales' of the École Normale Supérieure de Paris/PSL. He is co-editor of the journal *Lexis. Poetics, Rhetoric and Communication in the Classical Tradition* and of the series *Supplements of Lexis. Studies in Greek and Latin Literature*. His research interests focus on ancient theatre, Attic oratory, metrics and history of classical philology. He has published annotated editions of Euripides' *Orestes* (2001) and *Phoenician Women* (2006), a critical edition with commentary of Aeschylus' *Agamemnon* (2017), and several monographs, including *La forma monologica. Studi su Omero e Sofocle* (1983), *La tragedia sulla scena. La tragedia greca in quanto spettacolo teatrale* (1997, with Vincenzo Di Benedetto), *Sed nullus editorum vidit. Gottfried Hermann e l'Agamennone di Eschilo* (2006) and the collection of essays *La saggezza dell'illusione. Studi sul teatro greco* (2013).

Fausto Montana is Full Professor of Ancient Greek Literature at the University of Pavia. He is a member of the *FIEC* board and the *SIBC*. He is General Co-Editor of the *Brill's Lexicon of Greek Grammarians of Antiquity*, of the series *Supplementum Grammaticum Graecum* (Brill), and of the *Commentaria et Lexica Graeca in Papyris Reperta* (De Gruyter), where he edited and commented on the papyrus fragments of exegesis to Aristophanes and Herodotus. With Antonietta Porro, he edited the volume *The Birth of Scholiography. From Types to Texts* (2014), and the chapter *Hellenistic Scholarship* in the *Brill's Companion to Ancient Greek Scholarship* (2015), updated in *History of Ancient Greek Scholarship from the Beginnings to the End of the Byzantine Age* edited by F. Montanari (2020).

S. Douglas Olson is Distinguished McKnight University Professor of Classical and Near Eastern Religions and Cultures at the University of Minnesota. The author or co-author of over 30 books on Greek literature, he is best known for his critical editions and commentaries on individual Aristophanic comedies (*Peace* (1998), *Acharnians* (2002), *Thesmophoriazusae* (2004, with Colin Austin), *Wasps* (2015, with Zachary Biles), and *Knights* (forthcoming 2024, with Zachary Biles) and on the fragments of Eupolis (3 vols., 2014–2017) and Antiphanes (3 vols., 2021–2023) for the *Fragmenta Comica* series. He has also produced both a bilingual Loeb edition (8 vols., 2006–2012) and a full-scale Teubner critical text (5 vols. in 9 fascicles, 2019–2024) of Athenaeus of Naucratis. In addition, he has produced a book-length study of the epigraphical evidence for the history of Athenian comedy (2012, with Benjamin Millis), and commentaries on the fragments of Matro of Pitane (1999, with Alex Sens) and Archestratus of Gela (2000, with Alex Sens), and on the *Homeric Hymn to Aphrodite* (2012), and is the General Editor of the Basel Homer Commentary English Edition. His current major research project is a critical text and translation of Eustathius of Thessalonica's *Commentary on the Odyssey* (projected 7 vols., 2022–, with Eric Cullhed).

Christian Orth is Titular Professor at the Albert-Ludwigs-Universität Freiburg and Research Associate of the Heidelberger Akademie der Wissenschaften in the project *Kommentierung der Fragmente der griechischen Komödie*. He has written commentaries on the fragments of Aristophanes' *Aiolosikon, Amphiaraos, Anagyros* and *Babylonians* (2017) and on many other Old and Middle Comic poets, including Strattis (2009), Alcaeus and Ameipsias (2013), Aristomenes, Cephisodorus and Metagenes (2014), Nicochares, Philyllius, Polyzelus and Sannyrion (2015), and Aristophon, Axionicus and Dionysius (2020). He is now preparing a commentary on 19 fragmentary plays of Menander.

Martin Revermann is Professor of Classics and Theatre Studies at the University of Toronto. He is the author of *Comic Business. Theatricality, Dramatic Technique and Performance Contexts of Aristophanic Comedy* (Oxford 2006). He has edited or co-edited five other books: *Performance, Iconography, Reception. Studies in Honour of Oliver Taplin* (Oxford 2008), *Beyond the Fifth Century: Interactions with Greek Tragedy from the Fourth Century BCE to the Middle Ages* (Berlin/New York 2010), *The Cambridge Companion to Greek Comedy* (Cambridge 2014), *A Cultural History of Theatre (Vol. 1: Antiquity)* (London 2017) and *Semiotics in Action* (Brno 2020). His latest monograph is *Brecht and Tragedy: Radicalism, Traditionalism, Eristics* (Cambridge 2022).

Alan H. Sommerstein is Emeritus Professor of Greek at the University of Nottingham. He is the author or editor of more than 40 books on ancient Greek drama, language and society, including *Aeschylean Tragedy* (2nd edn. 2010), *Talking about Laughter* (2009), *The Tangled Ways of Zeus* (2010), an edition with translation of the plays and fragments of Aeschylus (2008), and editions with commentary of Aeschylus' *Eumenides* (1989) and *Suppliants* (2019), of all the plays of Aristophanes (1980–2003), of Menander's *Samia* (2013), and (with others) of selected fragmentary plays of Sophocles (2006–12). He led a team of 187 scholars as editor of the Wiley-Blackwell *Encyclopaedia of Greek Comedy* (2019), and is now preparing an introduction to Aristophanes for the *Fragmenta Comica* series.

Oliver Taplin is Emeritus Professor of Classics at Oxford University and an Emeritus Fellow of Magdalen College. His first book was *The Stagecraft of Aeschylus* (OUP, 1977), and his publications since then include *Homeric Soundings* (OUP, 1991) and *Pots and Plays* (Getty Publications, 2007). He is (2022) nearing completion of a book on the practicalities and materialities of the early theatre, provisionally entitled *TRAGEDY – the first 50 years*. In recent years he has also been translating tragedies with the aim of capturing the kind of dynamic and colour which will be effective in live performance with verse and music. The leading recurrent theme of his work has been the reception of poetry and drama through performance and material culture, in both ancient and modern times.

Piero Totaro is Full Professor of Ancient Greek Language and Literature and History of Greek Drama at the University of Bari "Aldo Moro", where he was also Head of the Department of 'Scienze dell'Antichità e del Tardoantico'; currently, he is Head of the 'Centro Internazionale di Ricerca e Studi su Carnevale, Maschera e Satira' (CMS). His scholarly interests are mostly concerned with Greek comedy and tragedy. Among his publications: *Le seconde parabasi di Aristofane* (Metzler Verlag, Stuttgart/Weimar 2000²), various entries in the *Encyclopedia of Greek Comedy* edited by Alan H. Sommerstein (Wiley-Blackwell 2019); in collaboration with Giuseppe Mastromarco, *Commedie di Aristofane* (vol. II, UTET, Turin 2006) and *Storia del teatro greco* (Mondadori, Milan 2008). He is currently working on new critical editions with commentary of Aristophanes' *Wealth*, of Aeschylus' fragmentary plays (under the patronage of the 'Accademia Nazionale dei Lincei', with the collaboration of a multidisciplinary scholarly team), of Euripides' *Alcestis* (under the patronage of 'Fondazione Lorenzo Valla', in collaboration with Maria Pia Pattoni), and of *Adespota Comica* book-fragments in the frame of the international research project *Kommentierung der Fragmente der griechischen Komödie* (Heidelberg–Freiburg i.B.) led by Bernhard Zimmermann.

Bernhard Zimmermann (MA Classics and Ancient History in Konstanz and London, Promotion 1983, Habilitation 1988, Professor of Classical Philology in Zurich [1990–1992], Dusseldorf [1992–1997]), is Professor of Classical Philology in Freiburg since 1997. He is a member of the Heidelberger Akademie der Wissenschaften, the Academia Europaea, the Accademia Roveretana degli Agiati and the Academy of Athens, and the former President of the Deutscher Altphilologenverband (2011–2015). He has produced numerous works on ancient drama and the ancient novel, Greek metrics and the reception of Ancient Literature. Among his publications: *Untersuchungen zur Form und dramatischen Technik der Aristophanischen Komödien* (3 vols.), Königstein-Frankfurt 1984–1987; *Die griechische Komödie*, Düsseldorf-Zürich 1998; *Handbuch der griechischen Literatur der Antike* (3 vols.), München 2011–2022 (in collaboration with Antonios Rengakos).

Index Locorum

Aeschylus
Agamemnon

https://doi.org/10.1515/9783111248028-014

Index Rerum

https://doi.org/10.1515/9783111248028-015